DECADES

DECADES

DECADES

MEMOIRS OF A PROUD IRISH AMERICAN

BERNARD P. O'PREY

To my parents Kitty and Dick, my wife Evelyn,

and my daughters Kathleen, Elizabeth, and Noreen.

CONTENTS

PREFACE

"The longest journey begins with a first step."

Given a life-long penchant for procrastination, this ancient Chinese aphorism and the strong encouragement of each of my daughters, particularly Kathleen Truman, causes me to finally break this chain of unconscionable delay and set out to record my personal memoirs. Initially, this does not appear too daunting a task; just jot down facts, dates, anecdotes and maybe even a few opinions. As I have a veritable multitude of the latter though, how would I ever know when to stop? The more serious or more critical deterrent to writing for me personally is how much of the unvarnished truth can I or any of my family tolerate? There are limits to the nasty little secrets, open confessions and rueful regrets for actions or conduct either on my part or of others that are best taken to the grave or shared privately, face-to-face with the respectful or applicable family member.

There is a high risk too of creating resentment and anger; the giving of unintended offense or possibly omitting a commendable act of a family member, relative or friend. It's most helpful to recall that I am human, fallible and limited in my thought and memory by my own frailty and life experience. I am consoled greatly by the fact that my father must have weighed these risks too. With a remarkable lack of rancor and prolific objectivity, he left my family a veritable masterpiece of narrative in his journal, which outlined the events of his and my mother's all too short lives.

With characteristic grandiosity and over-reaching hope, I had originally conceived this story as an unbroken chronicle extending straight back over five generations to my great-grandparents. A brief reflection on this broad scope brought the humbling and sober reflection of how little I knew of people born five or six generations prior to my arrival on December 2, 1937. On my father's side they rest in the St. Malachy's Parish cemetery in Kilcoo, County Down; My mother's family, the Duggans and the Lynns, repose in the beautiful environs of Rathfran graveyard near Killala, County Mayo. We had the privilege of visiting Mayo in 1994 on the last Sunday in June, a day dedicated to the cleanup of family gravesites in Mayo, during which an outdoor Mass is celebrated in memory of all the families buried there. This was an edifying, spiritual and historical experience uniting us with the past immediate and long gone by. One meditates on such an occasion on the brevity of life as well as the sustenance of the precious Faith that these forebears left as their legacy. How presumptuous, speculative and arrogant it would be for me to speculate on the views, beliefs, practices or foibles of my forebears!

Nevertheless, getting in touch with the past is a natural and intellectually rewarding impulse, as well as a spiritual acknowledgment. In the early summer of 1997, we drove to Salt Lake City, Utah and for a small fee, obtained a copy of the birth certificate of my grandfather, Patrick O'Prey, from Liverpool, England. In Park City, Utah and in Butte, Montana, I felt as if I were retracing steps that he must have trod between 1912 and 1922. He and his brother Jack worked the copper mines of Butte-a harsh, life-limiting, frontier-type existence. It was fascinating to tour the reconstructed Irish Saloon, the International Workers of the World's (IWW) union hall, and the Ancient Order of Hibernian Meeting Hall, next to each other on one street with what must have been a lively brothel directly across the unpaved street.

Although I never met the man as he died of miner's lung disease in 1931, I could visualize a short, lonely, hard-working and hard-drinking Irishman, who with thousands of their own countrymen and other European immigrants, fueled U.S. prosperity prior to and during World War I. I remarked to the Butte Archive custodian during my taped interview, that it was an eloquent testimony to America's upward social mobility that a miner's son could become a New York City police officer, and his grandsons in turn, a U.S. Air Force officer, a professional educator and a New York police officer.

However, this rosy version of the "American Dream" was

not something totally shared by my grandmother, Lizzie O'Prey. She commented to me at one time that despite all its "Troubles," she never really wanted to leave Ireland. In her opinion, America was a "gangster" country of too much whiskey and too many loose women! As a teenager, I recall asking my father how he got along with his father. His laconic response was "He was no bargain!" He did go on to describe him however as a good man, unfortunately "taken to drinking too much." Yet, in that day and age, it was not at all uncommon for a man to leave his family for an extended period to earn a living or to seek employment opportunities.

To judge a previous age by mores and standards that didn't exist at the time is historically unconscionable and a blatant injustice. In the absence of written or oral evidence, it is preferable and more honorable to let the dead and their memory rest in peace. Additionally, the problem arises that for me to sit in judgment of either my father or grandfather can generate unfounded criticism and unparalleled opportunities for consummate hypocrisy. Like Frank McCourt's ambivalent love-hate relationship with his father in *Angela's Ashes*, my father Richard's words will speak for himself in Appendix I. So too will the letter of poetic love and principle entitled *"If I Could Speak One Last Time,"* written by my brother Richie in June 1984. His monograph captures more succinctly, powerfully, imaginatively, and lovingly, the proud heritage of our family. It is accordingly included as Appendix II. Finally, I have included Richie's recollections of my life in his recently penned collection of essays entitled *"Fraternal Witness"* in Appendix III. I humbly acknowledge my debt to my father and to my brother for their legacies of family history, tradition, continuity and love. I encourage the reader to peruse these prior to reading this memoir. In a manner I could never hope to replicate, these provide the *"Roots"* of the O'Prey Family and the religious, social, political, psychological and temperamental background from which we derive our unique heritage and perspective.

To the loving memory of my parents, Kitty and Dick, as well as the living presence of my patient, tolerant, and loving wife Evelyn, and our daughters, Kathy, Liz, and Noreen, I dedicate this effort. In years to come, I can only hope that my grandchildren and their children will enjoy this narrative. For their sake, I propose to inject humor and relevance and not take myself too seriously. The title *Decades* may seem somewhat pompous, but includes the 1930's through the present with appropriate timelines injected in the interest of historical perspective. The initial chapters will rely heavily, if not exclusively, on my father's earlier work and hopefully provide the continuity or stream of Irish Catholic identity and ancestry of which I am immensely proud. An acknowledgment of good health and the Lord's many gifts bring with it my prayers for an accurate memory and His inspiration as I compile and complete this labor of love.

CHAPTER ONE

THE THIRTIES

They met in the romantic setting of an Irish Boat Ride and Hudson River Day Line cruise on the SS Americana on June 9, 1932. Whether it was love at first sight or a relationship that grew gradually into the indissoluble bond of marriage until death did them part, we will never know. The six-foot, raw-boned immigrant from the strife-torn urban environment of Ulster was captivated by the warmth, the smile, and the figure and dark good looks of the farm girl from Mayo in the West of Ireland.

Richard (Dick) O'Prey had landed at Pier 60 in New York City aboard the S.S. Andamia on March 6, 1928. His father, Patrick met him at the pier, inquired whether he had funds sufficient to purchase a bottle of whiskey and told him that he had a job waiting for his son at the Atlantic and Pacific Grocery Store, starting on March 27, 1928. The O'Prey family was reunited when his mother Elizabeth O'Prey and seven-year-old sister Ellen arrived on January 30, 1929. Dick worked at various food stores and lived on the West Side of Manhattan, in effect supporting his family until his father died of silicosis, or miner's lung, on August 11, 1931. From that time on Dick was the major breadwinner and head of his family.

A twenty-year-old Kitty Duggan had left her farm home in Mayo in 1928 on somewhat of an adventurous lark. Returning from taking a nurses' examination in Dublin, she found that one of her neighbors or cousins in Ballygarry had developed last-minute fears of traveling to America. Offered his ticket, Kitty arrived in New York in July 1930 and initially took up residence with her cousin, Nora Munnely Hegarty, in nearby Greenwich, Connecticut. She found employment as a maid or domestic servant with a variety of families, including that of the World War One Ace, Eddie Rickenbacker.

From today's perspective, the Thirties were neither an auspicious time to marry nor to raise a family. The decade began with the Great Depression and culminated in the onset of World War II on September 3, 1939. On June 16, 1935, Kitty and Dick were married by Reverend Father Klug at St. Luke's Roman Catholic Church, 138th and Cypress Avenue, Bronx, New York. Joseph Taylor, a native of Bohola, County Mayo, served as best man while Peggy O'Malley was a bridesmaid. The honeymoon was a week in duration and spent in Syracuse, New York. Times were hard during the Depression, but Dick's employment record at the Park Crescent Hotel was continuous from September 11, 1931, until April 1, 1937; a conspicuous feat when jobs were scarce, layoffs frequent and dismissals arbitrary. On April 14, 1937, Dick was appointed Toll Collector on the Henry Hudson Bridge, working for the New York City Parkway Authority. His salary was $1800 per year. Tolls at that time amounted to five cents per vehicle and gave the driver a smooth connection from Manhattan to the Bronx over the Spuyten Duyvil on the scenic Henry Hudson Parkway. Whether there is any correlation between this pivotal job change and my conception, neither I nor posterity will ever know! The job did get Dick into the uniform of a police officer; a uniform he would wear proudly the remainder of his life.

Washington Heights is situated on a high, rocky and wooded promontory at the northern end of Manhattan. Drawings from the Revolutionary War depict two forts facing each other across a valley which is now Broadway and Inwood. Fort George faces the Harlem River to the east and overlooks Spuyten Duyvil (Dutch for Spitting Devil), a maelstrom of currents where the Harlem meets the majestic Hudson. To the west lies Fort Tryon, a fortification named for the last English governor of New York. Adjacent to Fort Tryon Park stood St Elizabeth's Hospital, a five-story structure with magnificent vistas of the Hudson and the recently (1935) constructed George Washington Bridge. Prior to the opening of the Golden Gate Bridge in San Francisco, the George Washington claimed the highest and longest suspension dimensions in the world. Beneath it, dwarfed by its soaring towers, stands the "Little Red Lighthouse," rendered obsolete, but famed as a child's story. In 1776, Washington led his defeated colonial army across the river to Fort Lee, New Jersey, surviving to fight another day. A towering, aesthetically delightful, symmetrical structure, the George Washington Bridge, in my memory, is more than a landmark; it serves as a symbol to me of all that is good about New York City and all that remains of a pleasant, warm, but necessarily fuzzy memory of early childhood.

According to my Aunt Helen, labor was prolonged and difficult for my mother prior to my arrival at 1:30 p.m. on December 2, 1937. I was a "breech birth;" feet first. My father was told that I would be lucky if I could ever walk normally. Whatever complications may have existed, I was baptized shortly after my arrival by Father Wall as there were apparent doubts about my survivability. In that day and age, the Roman Catholic Church taught that unbaptized infants could not enter heaven, but were placed in Limbo, a state of neither pain nor joy. Although I obviously had no choice in the matter, I do remain profoundly grateful for the gift of my Catholic faith and for my recovery as well.

Subsequently, I received full sacramental Baptism at St Elizabeth's Church, 187th and Wadsworth Avenue from Father Stewart on January 2, 1938. My Godparents or sponsors were my Aunt Helen and her first cousin, John McCahey. John is the son of my father's Aunt Minnie and her husband John, whom I remember as a lively and raucous World War One veteran. Mom came home from the hospital nine days after my birth, while I remained for sixteen days. On December 18, I arrived at 521 West 182nd Street and given my medical history, must have been some Christmas present! I had mastoids or ear problems and caught every childhood disease raging at the time. Otherwise, and providentially, I had no long-term physical disabilities. I reflect upon the blessings of being born into a loving expanded family. My grandmother, Lizzie (Nanny) and her daughter, Helen lived with my parents. Consequently, I never lacked for either affection or attention. Like most new babies, I must have been somewhat of a novelty and, until my brother Richie and Ray's arrival, enjoyed two years of non-competitive, monopolistic affection.

Actually, I have very little memory of these early years; Mom was always there for me as were Helen and Nanny. Helen attended George Washington High School; a year behind a somewhat guttural Jewish refugee kid named Henry Kissinger, who graduated in 1939. Nanny always had treats, toys, candy or ice cream. I have an extremely vague recollection of being pushed around the New York World's Fair in 1939. Several pictures exist from those days of being wheeled through the environs of Fort George, Fort Tryon and Riverside Drive as well as enjoying life in a laundry wicker basket on the roof of our apartment house with the family dog, Buddy.

The Thirties was truly a blissful time for me but a portentous one for the world. I have no personal memory of the events leading up to World War II; the rehearsal that the Civil War in Spain provided; the arguments pro and con for US isolation; the annexation of the Sudetenland etc. My entire family were strong, working-class Democrats, who would probably have followed Franklin Delano Roosevelt anywhere. As Irish immigrants, they bore a strong mistrust of England offset undoubtedly by a fierce pride in the status and welfare of their adopted country. The crucible of the on-coming world conflict would hasten and solidify the legacy of American patriotism passed on by my parents to me and my brothers.

CHAPTER TWO

THE FORTIES

By any conceivable measure, the Forties stand alone as the most significant, event-laden decade of the Twentieth Century. The fact that my entire generation and I could grow from toddler to teen secure from the far-removed violence, destruction, starvation and butchery of World War II is testimony itself to the validity of American exceptionalism. More to the point is the debt we owe to the unflinching sacrifice of our soldiers, sailors and marines. The totality of the war effort, the unanimity of the American people, and the patriotic efforts of Hollywood served to install military men as permanent childhood heroes.

Movies were unabashedly patriotic. I recall several assemblies at Incarnation School where "The Fighting 69th", "Sergeant York" or "The Fighting Sullivans" would be shown to the unanimous cheers and pleasure of the young audience. Our heroes were Patton, Bradley, McArthur, Nimitz and Halsey from the war fronts and actors like John Wayne, Gary Cooper and James Cagney who kept up morale on the Home Front. At the time, there was absolutely nothing good to be said about our treacherous, cruel and inhuman enemies, the Japanese and the Germans. While an Axis ally, Italy was widely regarded as a joke; not to be taken too seriously and was rarely the target of the vitriolic, stereotyped cartoon propaganda that depicted their partners.

This was a fight to the finish, the goal of which was the total, conclusive and unconditional defeat of our country's enemies. The totality of the conflict was apparent across American society. Commencing in 1940, my toys became model airplanes: Spitfires, Flying Tigers, B-17s and B-25s, as well as warships and tanks. Playing "War" with other kids was a popular pastime largely replacing Cowboys and Indians. In choosing sides, the loser of the coin toss was obliged to play the enemy. Collecting paper, old metal and toys was an enthusiastic civic duty in which kids could demonstrate their commitment to final victory. Reminders of the war effort were ubiquitous; coupon points or discs were required to purchase meat, eggs and dairy products that were being rationed for the war effort.

For the driving public, pleasure trips came to a virtual halt as gasoline was constantly rationed, in short supply or available only on the "Black Market." Complaints about inconvenience, scarcity or price brought the predictable retort, "Don't you know there's a war on!" The sinews of war; tanks, trucks, convoys etc. crossed the George Washington Bridge daily on their way to overseas battlefields. The most poignant of these early memories, however, is that of the Blue or Gold Star medallions which were hung in apartment windows. The number of stars indicated the number of family members in military service; Blue was for the living and Gold signified those who had made the supreme sacrifice and would not be coming home. It would hardly be an exaggeration for me to cite the formative background of World War II as the strongest exterior influence upon my subsequent value system, political outlook, and ultimate choice of a military profession.

The political and social background of the early Forties provides an appropriate time to briefly profile the most important and influential people of these young years, my family members. Their memories are vivid and uniformly positive. Their presence remains irreplaceable and their love ever abiding over the years. I feel as if I fully imbibe the spirit of each, but most particularly that of my father, whose accomplishments and defects I have replicated, consciously or otherwise. This being said, the very core or heart of our family with respect to love, selflessness and care, was my mother, Catherine Marie Duggan O'Prey. Let's begin with her.

CATHERINE MARIE DUGGAN O'PREY

There is not a person in my memory, consciousness or experience more loving, tender, caring or selfless than my mother, Kitty Duggan O'Prey. Her loving presence, cool touch wiping my feverish brow during the chronic illnesses of my childhood and her comfort during many sleepless episodes are now misty and vague memories. Mom's personal comfort or pleasure always took a distant back seat to the loving care and presence that she constantly bestowed on her children. If my praise is too lavish, it is small compensation for my failure to thank her frequently or to demonstrate my loving appreciation to her during her all too brief lifetime of 59 years.

Her photographs reflect an attractive dark-haired woman with a ready smile and a pleasant disposition. At a height of 5' 8", she was solidly built and tended to retain weight. Like her husband, a heavy Lucky Strike smoker, Kitty, like many of her contemporaries, believed smoking would keep her weight down and was a harmless, nerve-settling pastime or habit. She demonstrated little patience with anyone who ballooned or inflated their perceived accomplishments or as she put it "tooted their own horn." If there is one lesson I remember from her, it is to be humble. If you earned it let others sing your praises rather than be a blowhard. In today's milieu, I strongly suspect that she would be solidly on the side of accomplishment and actual deeds as opposed to the "touchy-feely" self-esteem practitioners.

Kitty had the instincts, skepticism and character of an Irish peasant, a reflection of her rural Mayo heritage. Her patience with phonies, buffoons or self-inflating egomaniacs was minimal. She could snort in indignant rejection of transparent liars or pompous fools. She dressed simply and spent her money resourcefully. Many hours were spent at her Singer sewing machine and her willingness to create shirts and trousers for us provided visible evidence of her industry and domestic thrift. We wanted for nothing but used what we had. Our table was always full and mom's cooking was wholesome and delicious. As a further household ethic, our rewards were earned rather than bestowed with profligacy.

Mom retained a memory and a fair singing voice for Irish songs and romantic verse as well as the popular music of the time. *"Believe Me If All Those Endearing Young Charms"* by Thomas Moore got equal billing with *"Maize Doats"* and *"South of the Border."* She would croon the Irish ballads while washing dishes. One could detect the sadness and nostalgia for her family in Ireland and for Ireland itself. The Emerald Isle from my early consciousness was always more than a spot on the map. It conjured the image of saints and scholars, heroic struggles of legendary heroes, and the mysticism of paganism converted to the enduring Holy Faith of Roman Catholicism. The Irish pride was welded firmly to a militant, defensive and non-compromising acceptance of Church doctrine and practice. The Jesuits, or was it their famed renegade Voltaire, who asserted that if they control a child's education for the first seven years of life, they will make him a Catholic forever. My mother did this job for them! Religious statues: the Sacred Heart, St. Patrick and Mother Cabrini, were prominently displayed on mom's dresser. A small holy water container hung at our apartment door, Roman missals, rosaries and holy pictures were always visible around our four-bedroom, two-bathroom apartment. The base of Mother Cabrini's statue served as an alternate spot for storing petty cash. "The money is under the statue" was a statement I overheard frequently. Mom taught me the Hail Mary and to revere the mother of God. Taken from a picture that hung over our kitchen table, I recall one of the first poems I learned:

> *Lovely Lady Dressed in Blue;*
> *teach me how to pray.*
> *God was once your little boy,*
> *and you know the way.*

The portrait of an angel escorting a young child across a narrow plank bridge dispelled any fear of the dark or reluctance to go to sleep.

Mom would frequently visit the park on Riverside Drive as well as Fort George. I suspect I took my first steps in the lush green grass of Fort Tryon or along Henry Hudson Drive. It was Mom's guiding hand, infinite patience and unconditional love that nurtured these steps physically, psychologically and spiritually. Again, no expression of thanks would be sufficient. I delight in the realization that her legacy lives in the character of my wife Evelyn and Kitty's grandchildren, Kathy, Liz and Noreen.

RICHARD BENEDICT O'PREY

The persona, character, sense of responsibility and fierce

patriotism of Richard Benedict O'Prey defy contemporary description. Raised, in effect by a single parent, my grandmother, in the hostile environment of Ulster, his unspoken love, generosity and wry sense of humor gave him the courage to be a pillar of strength during family emergencies and the uncertain anxieties created by our childhood illnesses. Having no role model in his own experience, he was instinctively a strong, appreciative, decisive and most influential presence in our young household. A "family man" par excellence, his police uniform, genial good humor and ability to separate the nasty realities of his police work from his home life were, in my belief, his strongest contribution to our early character formation. As a somewhat sickly toddler with mumps, chicken pox, scarlet fever, et al, I treasure the memory of him "looking in on me" as I fought the various fevers in my parents' bed. His calm reassurance as well as that quizzical look of helplessness that fathers experience when their children are ill and a mother's presence is the preferable and effective healing option in the eyes of the patient! Yet his care, concern and support were always there.

Dad had a very practical bent of mind and the instincts of a person who anticipates and plans in detail for the future. On the evening before my first day of school at Incarnation, he gave me my first lesson in classroom protocol, telling me to raise my hand if I had any questions for the teacher. This mental preparation may seem trite, but at the time it allayed a substantial part of my five-year-old's apprehension of entering a new and mysterious environment. In September 1943, nursery school was a threat my parents used to encourage obedience rather than a preparation for elementary education! In any event, his advice set me at ease and prefigured academic success in primary, high school and college.

Dick O'Prey would stand out in any crowd; 6'1", flaming red hair, genial, polite and humorous in disposition. He loved anecdotes and was confident enough to laugh at his own foibles. His job as a patrolman involved working three rotating shifts: 8 to 4, 4 to 12, and 12 to 8. He would, when the evening shift required, come to the dinner table in his boxer shorts, undershirt and gartered black socks. Richie, Ray and I bestowed the name "Big Garters" on him. Dad just smiled pleasantly and explained that his unconventional dress mode was a precaution to avoid spilling any liquid or food on his uniform. He would place a dish towel over his bare knees and simply enjoy his dinner. On one memorable evening, Mom spotted one of our apartment's ubiquitous cockroaches on the wall and swatted it to the floor. Totally nonplussed, Dad peered down as if to examine the insect and proclaimed, "My God, Kitty, it's a female!"

Riverside Drive from below Grant's Tomb up to the George Washington Bridge is both a scenic and a historic delight. I recall the hikes that Dad would take us on, entertaining us as we walked with historical anecdotes about New York City and the famous people who were celebrated, e.g., the Soldiers' and Sailors' Monument from the Spanish American War. When we tired, Dad would, in turn, provide a piggy-back ride to the weary. As the eldest, I weighed the most and recall envying Richie and Ray for getting longer rides on Dad's shoulders. I distinctly recall Ray's trusting gullibility as Dad related the tale of the talking fish from the Hudson River who would converse with him during the long midnight to 8 a.m. shift! I believe he imparted to each of us his deep love of history, specifically the lore and background of New York City, the Revolutionary War and the Civil War. That seed of interest has borne abundant fruit in each of his three sons. In later years, his memories turned more to Ireland; his tales more abbreviated and his narration more cryptic as alcohol became more of an accomplice to his natural storytelling talent. On my tenth birthday I received a call from Dad asking me to meet him and Mom on Riverside Drive. I still thrill to the memory of him peddling my very first two-wheel Schwinn bicycle and presenting it to me with the caution to be careful.

At times I suffer the conceit of believing Dick O'Prey is partially reincarnated in me. I am blessed to be articulate as he was, despite his life-long chronic stutter. Like him, I esteem honesty in myself and others and have replicated paths of career destruction by willful overindulgence. Yet, his premier qualities of honesty, familial affection, responsibility and good humor are just part of the priceless legacy he has given my family. His memory, familial devotion and presence during minor and major crises affected each of us positively. He was always there for us, and it is with humble gratitude and pride that I acknowledge his accomplishments and honor his memory.

ELIZABETH LENNON O'PREY (NANNY)

Stern of visage, short and definitely plump, Lizzie O'Prey's appearance belied an inward softness, love and fierce affection for her family. Widowed in 1931, she lived with my parents throughout their entire married life. While this served to divide the authority my mother would have otherwise enjoyed over the household and its members, she was nevertheless a loving, indulgent grandmother. She was our first and only babysitter; waiting patiently for our parents to leave for a movie or dance and then treating us to the "surprise" of both staying beyond our bedtime and having the additional treat of ice cream and cake. We responded to her affection, thoughtfulness and love with childish and sincere appreciation as well as obedient behavior. I believe I held the inside track of favorite grandson. To me this seemed to go with the turf of being the eldest.

During my frequent illnesses, Nanny would administer medicine; cod-liver oil, Argyrol, cough medicine and other vile concoctions, with her encouragement to "be a good soldier and kill all those rotten Germans and Japs down in your belly." The subsequent motivation to follow a military career may well have originated from this discipline!

I have never in my life been obliged to apologize for what I didn't say, the opposite, however, has never been the case! As a treat for my seventh birthday, Nanny was taking me downtown to see a movie at the Roxy or Paramount Theater. Boarding the familiar green and yellow Fifth Avenue bus at Fort Washington Avenue and 181st Street, the bus driver inquired whether I was younger than 7, the age under which a child could ride free. Just after Grandma asserted that I qualified, I innocently blurted out; "No, Grandma, today's my birthday!" I don't recall the sequel to this one, but Grandma and bus drivers, particularly Irish ones just didn't get along! On another occasion, she handed the driver a larger than the posted limit of a $5.00 or $10.00 bill. The driver pointed to the sign and with some testiness suggested that Grandma read it! Nanny's response was legendary, to the effect that the Irish bus driver might be capable of driving "Neddy's" donkey cart in the Auld Country but was way over his head in operating a bus in New York City!

Her tongue could be sharp and devastating. However, we were rarely the recipients of her wrath. I was slapped one time by a Jewish mother for punching her son. Nanny was immediately on the scene loudly declaiming "How dare you hit a white child!"

Born during the reign of Queen Victoria, in Gargary, County Down on November 2, 1886, Nanny exemplified the mores, ethics and sensitivities of that bygone age. Things were right or wrong, proper or improper, decent or indecent, moral or immoral, etc., with no middle ground for equivocation. Elizabeth Lennon O'Prey upheld consistent, unflinching, and courageous principles with respect to politics, sex and workers' rights to organize. While she became a naturalized U.S. citizen in 1936, I recall the surprise I felt when she confided to me that she never really wanted to leave Ireland and had a special spot in her heart for Scotland. She regarded the United States as the Wild West with too much drinking, gambling and loose women. How much of this perception was based upon her experience with her husband's prolonged absence from 1912 to 1922 is anyone's guess. I recall asking her somewhat naively whether she hated the English; her response, to my young inquisitive mind, was surprising. Employed at the Slieve Donnard Hotel in Newcastle, County Down during World War I, she recalled the British soldiers training there as "fine young men soon to be shipped off to die on the Western Front in France."

Like her husband Pat, Lizzy was a staunch union member and an early labor organizer in the New York hotels where she was employed as a housekeeper and chambermaid. To her way of thinking, there simply was no compromise with management or the upper classes. Their wealth was based on the sweat and labor of workers like herself. Politically, she found a copasetic home in the Democratic Party. In the election of 1944, she never referred to New York Governor Tom Dewey as anything other than "Dog Face" due to his prominent mustache. In a more humorous, but questionable vein, Nanny claimed to be the recipient of substantial guest gratuities as a hotel employee. In one instance she was offered $20 to ignore a suicide threat. I asked her whether the man jumped. Her response was that she did as he wanted to "earn" her tip!

Her courage and bedrock Catholicism was put to severe test frequently in Ulster, where religion made the difference between keeping a job or being terminated. Like the American Negro, "last to get hired; first to get fired" was the operative ethic practiced against Catholic laborers in the linen mills and workplaces of the time. Lizzy never compromised her religious faith, refusing to eat meat on Fridays despite the threat of job loss for not doing so. To this day, I revere her principled courage and uncompromising belief. She was and remains a role model for me in the formation of principled character and religious fidelity. In this age of doubt, skepticism and situation ethics, her unwavering loyalty to her Faith remains part of a priceless legacy.

ELLEN MARIE O'PREY CLANCY

A mere fifteen years separate me from my godmother and aunt, Helen O'Prey Clancy. Attractive, vivacious, intelligent, and caring, she was one of the loves of my early life. Younger than Grandma and my parents, Helen seemed to have a greater aura of freedom about her; was less of a disciplinarian and more like an older, wiser sister than an aunt. Helen was always generous and loving, presenting me with lead pencils and encouraging my early penmanship efforts. During World War II she wrote almost daily to her fiancée-to-be, Joseph Francis Clancy. I would watch and pepper her with a range of child-like questions, begging frequently for a piece of chocolate or other candy that was being sent overseas. I have vivid memories of Christmas 1943, romping around our living room far beyond my normal bedtime while Helen and Joe waited patiently for me to retire so that Santa might arrive. The poignancy of this episode came years later when I realized they were together for their final moments before Joe shipped out to England with the 82nd Airborne Division. Joe would subsequently jump over Normandy on D-Day and be missing in action for two to three weeks.

My habit of engaging my mouth before my brain, albeit innocently, recurred when I announced Helen and Joe's engagement to the neighbors stating that they had met in Macy's and "had" to get married! With a nephew as mouthy as I was, it is a testimony to the closeness of our family that we can joke and revel in these tales of family lore. Helen was a very key part of my early life as a confidante and teacher. The first U.S. high school graduate in our family, Helen modeled good study habits, a variety of interests and an endless willingness to answer my continual questions about this, that and the other. She was always patient, truthful, loving, understanding and informative.

RICHARD JOSEPH O'PREY

The monopoly I had enjoyed with respect to my family's

affection came to an unconscious end with the arrival of my younger brother, Richie at 6 a.m. on February 15, 1940, at St. Elizabeth's hospital. Mary Kiernan, the only daughter of Peter and Mary Kiernan, was designated godmother. The godfather was Joseph Taylor, a native of Bohola, County Mayo, a life-long bachelor and Best Man at my parents' wedding. Joe was "The Godfather" in the eponymous sense of the word insofar as he was truly a "member of our family.' His sincerity, sense of humor, and willingness to carouse with us kids made him a frequent and most welcome visitor to 869 West 180th Street. His tales of Indian guides and hunting in Maine were adventures well beyond the daily experience of each of us. Joe's ownership and generous sharing of rides in his leather-seated, 1941 Buick convertible are cherished childhood memories. I have a distinct memory of him stopping along the Sawmill or Taconic Parkway in response to my dad's request for a call of nature. The problem and laughs began when Dad would walk back to the car and Joe would accelerate just enough to keep him from reaching us. After a quarter mile or so of these shenanigans, Dad rejoined us with some vivid and unprintable commentary on his experience!

My earliest memory of Richie is watching him stand in his crib pointing proudly at the mattress upon which he had recently deposited his bowel movement or "numbers" as my parents would call them. I believe I can trace my later fear and aversion to mathematics to this terminology!

RAYMOND KEVIN O'PREY

Raymond Kevin O'Prey arrived at 6:15 a.m. on April 23, 1941, at St Elizabeth's Hospital. His Godparents were John and Marie Taylor. John was Joe's older brother and a former member of the Irish Republican Army. They too were frequent and welcome visitors at our home at 869 West 180th Street where we had moved on May 1, 1940. I have little or no memory of my brothers during their years of infancy. Mom took us daily to Riverside Drive where we played in a sand pile, frolicked in the grass, and enjoyed the background of the "Little Red Lighthouse" a structure that predated the construction of the George Washington Bridge and became the topic of a popular children's book.

With no malicious intent, I recall releasing the brake on my brother Ray's carriage and watching the vehicle roll downhill and across a highway exit to the bridge. Our Guardian Angel must have been watching as there was no traffic and Ray remained safe in his carriage.

Dad's records indicate that he registered for the Selective Service on October 16, 1940. The Mayor of New York, Fiorello LaGuardia, subsequently determined that his need for police officers was as urgent as the U.S. Navy's for Shore Patrol and Dad was consequently deferred from the Draft.

I have a vague recollection of a road trip my folks took me on from September 15 to 23, 1941. Together with Ben and Pat

Murray and their son, Jimmy we traveled to Buffalo, Cleveland, Detroit and Pittsburgh. I recall spending a night in a one-room motel in which the privacy of each family was provided by a curtain. The Murrays were close family friends and remained so throughout our parents' lifetime.

The Japanese attack on Pearl Harbor is but a memory of my family gathered in front of the radio, in a very serious, grim, and determined mood. I can recall the subsequent air raid drills. All our lights were out, and black shades pulled full down over each window. Headlights on automobiles were painted black over their top half. Rationing was imposed on gasoline, sugar and meat. At the tender age of four, I had no recollection of any radical change of lifestyle. Richie, Ray and I enjoyed a long hallway in our apartment down which we could bowl, play games, and chase each other. I have the memory of pushing Richie into a wall corner causing an open wound which required stitches and left a scar. This remains as vivid as the release of Ray's carriage brakes! The fact that I bear these memories, but no recollection of punishment or severe chastisement, is testimony to my mother's forgiving nature.

As children, we heard nothing of the German spies who landed near Jones' Beach in 1942. Nor were we aware of the sinking of cargo ships by Nazi submarines within view of Sandy Hook on the Jersey Shore. Quite oblivious to these perils, we enjoyed summer vacations at Keansburg, New Jersey. The beach was littered with horseshoe crabs but lacked the violent surf of the main Jersey Shore. This made for an ideal locale for swimming lessons. These were extremely simple as they consisted of following my mother out to deeper water and then floating or striking out as required. Under her gentle encouragement, I was a rapid learner.

One of the most vivid and in retrospect, scariest memories of these young years was the visit we made to my Grand-Aunt Catherine O'Prey Tierney's wake in Brooklyn on December 29, 1943. She was the first dead person I had ever seen and her pale compaction, blond hair, and stillness in the casket remain fixed in my memory.

Earlier, in September 1943, I entered the first grade at Incarnation School. My parents had prepared me well for this event, but it was Sister Elizabeth's warm and loving welcome that made my learning a positive and productive experience. Throughout the first six grades, the Sisters of Charity, Sister Elizabeth and Sister Jean as well as Mrs. Slattery and Mrs. Faulkner encouraged my academic endeavors to the point that my grades were consistently at the top of the class. I developed an insatiable desire to read with distinct preferences for historical tales and anecdotes. On a heavier note, I recall reading volumes of a home encyclopedia set. In contemporary parlance, I could properly be described as a nerd! A series of childhood illnesses-measles, mumps, chicken pox and scarlet fever, were significant deterrents to developing athletic talents. I distinctly and painfully recall the disappointment and embarrassment of normally being the last "pick" in a choose-up game of softball or touch football. In the field of sports, my brother Richie was most prominent and chosen consistently to team with other players. The significant age difference of three and a half years with my brother Ray caused him to be relegated to the "Schmohoppers," a term my friend Jim Torrens and I used to label the undesired presence of our respective younger siblings, John and Ray.

Walking by the "lots" or "monastery", a vintage mansion a block away on Haven Avenue, I formed an early and lasting friendship with Jack Whiteside. Jack was walking his pet cat. We went on to become classmates through primary, high school and college; enjoying a closeness which only the geography of distance has dampened. Jack, Jim Torrens and I would celebrate our First Communion together at Incarnation Church on May 12, 1945, five days after Victory in Europe (VE) Day on May 7.

Our social lives were significantly expanded by joining Cub Pack 716 at Incarnation. Our Cubmaster, Mr. Edmunds, his assistant, Mr. Silva, and our volunteer, Den mother parents created a world of arts and crafts, woodwork, plastic key chains and daytime hikes to New Jersey. From age nine through eleven we progressed through the Cub Scout ranks of Wolf, Bear and Lion, earning silver and gold arrows and finally attaining the rank of Webelo. Our Cub Pack Song to the tune of the Notre Dame Fight Song went:

We are the Cubs of 716
We'll do our best and then show we mean
To show good will so here our cry
We'll all be Boy Scouts by and by
Always remember when we were nine
First as a Wolf Cub, then Bear and Lion
Loyal sons of Incarnation
Marching to Victory

One way or another, our Cub Scout programs, and the unselfish donation of our leaders' and parents' time introduced us to many new experiences. A tour of the Pepsi Cola Plant in Long Island City and to be television studio guests at Buffalo Bob and the Howdy Doody Show were particular highlights.

I recall a family picnic with mom in Coytesville, New Jersey. The three of us had sweated and were suffering from chaffed legs and backsides. Mom had us strip and lie sunny side up in the sunshine. There were no witnesses, and this treatment did provide some relief.

In August 1944, I was privileged to join mom on a New York Central Railroad trip to Syracuse, New York. This provided an early introduction to my mother's side of the family, the Lynns. We would subsequently enjoy visits from "Red Willy's" family, Bill and Nancy Lynn and my Grand-Uncle Willy, the latter was a younger brother of my grandmother in Mayo, Mary Lynn who was married to John Duggan in Ballygarry, County Mayo.

While minds far more ponderous than ours brought the

Manhattan Project to its successful conclusion at Alamogordo, New Mexico, our family remained blissfully unaware of it and untouched by the violence raging overseas. A milestone of Catholic education was achieved on May 12, 1945, with our First Communion at Incarnation Church. It is not without strong nostalgia that I recall the innocence of youth, the demands of inclusive, total obedience, the pageantry, processions and awesome Latin liturgy of my early childhood. While some of the Church's moral teachings may be considered by contemporary critics as "fear based," they made an indelible impression on my mind and were later to be reinforced by a heavy dose of Thomistic Philosophy. I recall the patience and loving interest my mother bestowed on my preparation to become an altar boy in the sixth grade. The memorization of the Latin Liturgy was an absolute must. She would play the role of the priest celebrating mass and I would respond with the appropriate Latin responses or activities. "Situation Ethics" was far beyond the scope of the definitive morality of the Forties. Virtually every transgression of the Sixth or Ninth commandment was a mortal sin meriting eternal damnation. Harsh perhaps, but you always knew precisely where you stood! These remain as pillars of my personal belief. What the Sisters of Charity, particularly Sister Elizabeth and Sister Jean, provided as a bedrock foundation was further promulgated by the Christian Brothers, particularly Brother Corbinian Joseph in seventh and eighth grade, and the Faculties of Manhattan Prep and

Manhattan College. My moral and theological debt to both religious orders remain undiminished even through the cataclysmic changes of Vatican II. One of my personal legacies from the Forties is that piety and patriotism run hand in glove.

The wild, sheer, patriotic and religious exuberance with which VJ Day was greeted on September 2, 1945, is forever etched in my memory as the epitome of pride in my country and thanks for her decisive victory over her enemies. New York City was a center of celebration as the famous photo of the sailor kissing his girl in Times Square indicated. Impromptu parties blossomed up and down our block; Old Glory with its forty-eight states was displayed from every windowsill while a victory march was organized by Alex Petridi, a young man whose father had been beaten senseless by Hitler's Gestapo some years before in Greece. From my seven-year-old perspective, I saw only the glory of victory and not the totality of the human sacrifice which was necessary for its achievement.

For our immediate family, the first fruit of allied victory was the heroic return of Sergeant Joseph Francis Clancy. He and his 82nd Airborne buddy Al Coz were preparing to embark from Marseilles, France to continue the battle in the Pacific when the atomic bombs at Hiroshima and Nagasaki canceled the need for their presence. Joe and my Aunt Helen were married at Incarnation Church on September 23, 1945, after a three-year engagement. The subsequent reception was held at the Audubon Ballroom, 165th and

Broadway in Manhattan, where Malcom X would subsequently be assassinated in 1965. The celebration was the joyous family event of the decade, if not the century! After receiving a visit from the entire O'Prey family at their honeymoon lodge in the Pocono Mountains, the newlyweds moved in with us temporarily and then moved two floors above, Apartment 32 at 869 West 180th Street. During the postwar period both jobs and housing were scarce due to the return of a few million veterans. As a side benefit of this, however, Richie, Ray and I enjoyed many house-hunting trips with Helen and Joe as well as picnics to Jones Beach and Harriman Park. Their love and concern for our welfare was always there and the discipline we were subject to with mom seemed more relaxed with Aunt Helen as well as Grandma Lizzie.

The saddest day of my childhood's recollection was February 24, 1947, and the only day I ever witnessed my father in tears. He gathered us to announce that our newborn, day-and-a-half old baby brother John had died of a cerebral hemorrhage at Mother Cabrini Hospital. Baby John's subsequent burial at Calvary Cemetery was on a bitterly cold February 28; a memory of a never known, but nevertheless loved brother. I recall making a resolution with Richie and Ray to somehow be better kids and, in that way, help mom get over her grief. Later that year, the birth of Ellen Clancy to Helen and Joe Clancy brought incredible joy to both families and provided the novelty of a little girl to the company of her three rough neck, "Black

Hand" cousins as my Uncle Joe described us.

Commencing in 1946, our summer vacations were spent at The Police Recreation Center at Platte Clove, New York. In the middle of the Catskill Mountains, the relief from the city's heat, abundant recreation facilities, pool, and abundant sports and social opportunities brought the decade to a pleasant and memorable end. I continued to lead my class academically at Incarnation, skin my knees frequently playing roller hockey on 175th Street. The Brothers' Department which was male students only after Sixth Grade provided the needed discipline for rapidly growing youngsters like myself and consistently provided role models of both proper behavior, good sportsmanship and, when required sarcastic or physical reprimand. Our Principal, Brother Andrew would visit every other week to distribute report cards. Any deportment or conduct grade of c or less would provide the offender with a choice as to whether he wanted his knuckles rapped by pointer on the palm or the back of his hand. We survived and developed character as a result.

Primary among the pleasant memories of my childhood was the training and subsequent three years of service as an altar boy at Incarnation Church. Commencing in the Fifth Grade, we received instruction from Father Edwin Conlon, a young, articulate and popular parish priest. To supplement practicing the Latin responses, my mother would play the role of the priest at a practice mass at the kitchen table. I would respond to the different cues as altar boys were expected to do. During my Seventh and Eighth Grades a benefit of altar service was to be released from class to serve a Solemn High funeral Mass or "Missa Cantata". This compensated in some measure for being scheduled to serve the daily 6:30 AM Mass at the Sisters' convent, a good 15 block hike from our apartment. To serve at a wedding or Nuptial Mass on Saturday would normally bring a generous cash tip from the wedding party. In a more spiritual vein, I can recall no other time in my life when I felt more innocent, more spiritual or closer to God. Altar service reinforced the rigorous, positive and uncompromising teachings of the Sisters of Charity, the Christian Brothers and the example and practice of my parents. Given these circumstances, it was not uncommon to ponder a religious vocation to either the Priesthood or the Brotherhood. To the extent that I could, I gave the vocation serious thought but ultimately reasoned that I would be unwilling to give up girls and the alternative calling of marriage!

In March 1948, Tommy Brady, a 16-year-old, good-looking, wholesome lad from our neighborhood was murdered indiscriminately by a crazed, anti-Catholic fanatic. Tom was on his way home from band practice at Power Memorial High School. His funeral at Incarnation was the largest in memory and the Power High School Band played with muffled drums during the subsequent St Patrick's Day parade. During his time at Incarnation, Tom had been photographed in the habit of a Christian Brother as a young man pondering a vocation to that order. The value of life and its tragedies was further demonstrated when the youngest brother of my classmate, Martin O'Sullivan was hit and killed instantly by a bus on Fifth Avenue. The death of a classmate's mother and a young Cub Scout pack member brought with them an appreciation for the tragic side of life and the consolation of the Catholic Faith in coping with these losses.

CHAPTER THREE

THE FIFTIES

The unique power, prestige, leadership and influence the United States enjoyed as the leader of the Allied Victory in World War II was abruptly and seriously challenged by the Soviet Union's detonation of a nuclear bomb in 1949. The Cold War heated up substantially in June 1950 when the armies of North Korea moved south and came within a hair's breadth of moving the U.S. Army and the Republic of Korea (ROKS) forces off the entire peninsula. The trial of Julius and Ethyl Rosenberg, the Jewish couple who provided our top atomic secrets to the Soviet Union, resulted in their conviction and subsequent execution. There were no tears shed around the O'Prey household over this verdict or outcome. As my father would phrase it, "Every Jew is not a communist, but every communist is a Jew!" a cryptic and heavily biased comment, but nevertheless close to the temper of the times. There was no doubt then or now in my mind of the righteousness of our cause in defense of the West and its freedom. General Eisenhower's book *Crusade in Europe*, the television series "Victory at Sea" and the gentle but convincing homilies of Bishop Fulton Sheen fueled my patriotic convictions and later beliefs in American "exceptionalism." We were and are the "house on the hill" spared by God from Europe's constant bickering and strife. The glaring exception to this smug sense of national pride was the recollection of our own tragic Civil War. Yet, even in this situation, Lincoln had the moral right of Emancipation on the Union side.

Our Apartment at 869 West 180th Street was on the ground floor and only a building away from Mr. and Mrs. Neidishes' candy store. An elderly, pleasant, friendly and hardworking couple, two of their sons, Steve and Jack had served in the U.S. Army Air Corps in World War II. Two of their daughters, Ida and Ethyl, were contemporaries of my Aunt Helen and represented, as we did, the first American-born generation of foreign-born immigrants. The Neidishes gave me my first job around 1949 or 1950. My task was to meet the newspaper delivery truck at 181st Street and Fort Washington Avenue between 8:30 and 8:45 p.m. and to carry the pre-ordered newspapers to the Neidish's candy store, a distance of four city blocks. My pay for this service was a princely $1.50 per week, a great recompense for an eleven-year-old kid. I did take great pride in this responsibility and on evenings where I was otherwise involved, Richie or Ray could fill in for me. I subsequently added Solomon's Candy store on 181st Street as a client with the same rendezvous time with the newspaper truck, but two or three times the number of papers. The additional $3.50 that I received for this service brought my total income to a substantial $5.00 per week. As long as my grades were not affected, my parents had no objection to my part-time endeavors, and I was proud to practice thrift by opening an actual bank savings account.

Additionally, this employment provided an introduction to an older Negro veteran named Dwight, who had served with the Regiment from Harlem in World War I. Dwight could recite phrases he had learned in France, was a good conversationalist, and the first real acquaintance I enjoyed with a member of a minority race. Incarnation and Manhattan Prep had no minority students at this time. Black youths were feared rather than accepted or tolerated. My brother Richie had the unenviable experience of being confronted and robbed by a gang of Black youth in Riverside Park. My friend Dwight exhibited an intelligence and dignity that was a welcome eye-opener; other black people in our neighborhood were building superintendents, poorly dressed, private and somewhat slovenly. A muscular black named Lee looked as if he'd just left the cast of Showboat and was playing the role of William Warfield singing *"Old Man River"*. Another black super was Eddie, who was rarely seen without his wine bottle in hand. Race relationships would be on a learning curve for me; I would be 15 years old at YMCA Camp before I made friends with a black fellow counselor named Eddie Adams.

In the social circuit of paper delivery people, I cannot forget "Herman the German". Herman owned a candy store kitty-corner from the newspaper truck stop. In cold weather, he did not like leaving his store and would complain in heavily accented German English "Vi vait for der bastard mit der shit papers!" For me, this was an improbable but humorous introduction to foreign language study.

Recollections of seventh grade are dim but enduring. Jim Torrens (RIP), Jack Whiteside, (RIP) and Frank Walsh (RIP) did not take to the Boy Scouts as well as we had to the younger Cub Scout program. I recall the pride in making Webelo in the Cubs but never got beyond Second Class in the Boy Scouts. Overnight hikes to Alpine Boy Scout Camp across the Hudson River in New Jersey were popular with Torrens, Whiteside, and me. Jim Torrens was possessed of a droll, laconic wit; in a pup tent in the process of being washed away with rivers of water running through it, all he could comment was "I think it's raining!" Jack Whiteside tended to wax overly enthusiastic with respect to his woodsman's lore. In cooking around a campfire, he would state, "My eggs came out the best!" Cynical little devils that we were, he was taunted by this phrase for many years to come. Shortly thereafter, we rigged a dummy with Jack's name and that quotation on it and hung the dummy for all to see from the roof of his fifth story apartment.

We expanded our friendships to nearby Cabrini Boulevard

where the DeEsposito brothers, Hank and Pat, lived as well as "Big Moe" Friedman, Victor Alonso, Tom Tozer, Bill Fogarty and Eddie Ryder (RIP). Not unlike *West Side Story*, our "gang" was more social than malevolent or violent and included the young ladies of the neighborhood, Annabel DeWitt, Muriel Sheridan, Margie Toughey, Dianne Palmer and Joan Pasco. What did we do? We hung around on Cabrini Boulevard in the local candy stores or at the "Roach Hole," a fast-food diner on Fort Washington Avenue where a comely, blond waitress named Josie served us coffee, doughnuts and pie from behind an oval lunch counter. A group of girls, classmates from the Girls' Department at Incarnation, began the practice of calling me at home (Wadsworth 3-3972) and chatting, as pre-teens might do, about who likes who and who is going steady with whom. My first girlfriend as a result of this process was a contemporary classmate named Mary Geraghy. A movie date would be arranged at Loewy's Movie Theater at 175th and Broadway on the basis of "Dutch treat"; and "I'll meet you inside." Her friends, Peggy McPartland, Mary Kelly, Eleanor Mahoney and Connie Kornheisel, would visit us on occasion on Cabrini Boulevard. "Going Steady" became a custom; harmless, fickle and usually of short duration. The idea was buttressed at the time by the popularity of Nat King Cole's hit *"Too Young to Go Steady."* My second young love was a pretty, smiling and friendly lass named Irene O'Neil. Her advantage was that she lived on Fort Washington Avenue next to where I had my newspaper pick up. Convenience and distance were always substantial factors in these early relationships!

Just about this time of awkward and rapid growth in the seventh grade, our parents enrolled the three of us in music lessons with the New York Police Department's Honor Legion Band. Richie, Ray and I would travel weekly to the Ballroom of the Park Sheraton Hotel on 57th Street. Under the tutelage of Professor Robert Gary of Manhattan College, Richie and I worked on clarinet lessons while Ray found a niche in the brass section with his trumpet. As the instruments were loaned from the Honor Legion Band, our parents suffered no financial loss when none of us responded to this benefit.

With respect to the NYPD Honor Legion itself, my father had received membership and decoration for subduing an armed robber at night in Riverside Park in 1948. He was a hero to each of his sons and esteemed to this day by we who remember his integrity, love and good humor. I distinctly recall attending a Police Department Holy Name Communion Breakfast with him at that time and having the temerity to ask if he minded if I smoked. His response was favorable and deeply appreciated if a little too tolerant from my mom's point of view. "I don't mind if you smoke or take a drink as long as you don't get any girl pregnant before you are ready to marry her." Needless to say, my mother's reaction when I lit up in front of her was neither as liberal nor as tolerant! Smoking and drinking were both favorite adolescent pastimes, normally done out of sight of parents, teachers or authority figures.

A departure from this scheme occurred on Thanksgiving Eve 1950 when my parents were socializing with Charlie and Winnie Whiteside, my friend Jack's parents. While the adults were enjoying cocktails in the living room. I decided to experiment or sample some of the wine and whiskey in the kitchen. The effect was, in retrospect, predictable. Not only did I vomit all over Whiteside's bathroom floor, but I also gave a repeat performance in our own bathroom at home! I had the lying effrontery to blame the episode on eating my mother's Thanksgiving turkey several hours earlier! As my bed continued to swirl, my father visited me and let me know that he did not believe my alibi. Further, when I was older, he would teach me to drink socially. At the time, I was deeply grateful for not getting walloped, restricted, or otherwise punished for this shameful incident.

From a chronological and emotional point of view, this is probably the most appropriate place to acknowledge the inordinate effect that alcohol consumption and to a lesser extent cigarette smoking have had on each and every significant event in my life. To drink merrily and to sing loudly was to be Irish American to its fullest extent. Smoking was the cool and social entry to young adulthood. My personal conceit was such that I could witness my father's inane overindulgence and tell myself that, with my education and sophistication, it could never happen to me! Quite to the contrary, I would, in time, replicate his overindulgence, resulting in professional disappointments and, most importantly, the alienation of a beloved wife and family. Accordingly, from here on out, any narrative recollection of my life would be incomplete, dishonest and specious without the candid and frank acknowledgement of alcohol's powerful role for the subsequent thirty-three years. My early capacity to "hold my liquor" created an impermeable and ego-centric denial system. I did not trust people who did not drink and numbered among my closest friends those who drank as I did. I do not regret this past, nor do I wish to ignore it.

From home to school to teenage socialization, alcohol seemed to be the normal, convivial and proper activity to fit in. Dances at Incarnation and later, the rowdy Irish dances at Manhattan Center, Rockaway Beach and Yorkville Casino attracted the best looking and most wholesome Irish American girls in New York City. Alcohol brought me the courage to ask them for a dance and suppressed any feelings of inferiority. With respect to visiting bars in Washington Heights and Inwood, virtually every member of our group possessed a phony draft card. I owned one at the age of 14, indicating that I was 18 and of legal drinking age in New York State.

Academically, I was at the top of my seventh and eighth

grade classes at Incarnation. During the very last semester, I slipped to number two. My friendly rival, Dennis O'Shea moved into the top spot by a few tenths of a point, and we received General Excellence Medals One and Two respectively at our graduation in June 1951. He, Buzzy Ronan, Jack Whiteside, Al Diaz, Jim Gavigan, John Keegan and several others were accepted by Manhattan Prep. At the time, Manhattan Prep was regarded along with Fordham and Regis High Schools as first-rate, prestigious Catholic High Schools. From an Irish Catholic point of view, to even consider going to a public school was virtually tantamount to abandoning the Faith! I recall the pride with which I reassured my mother that I would be able to continue to work and to pay my $20.00 per month tuition at Manhattan Prep. Despite this independent stance on my part, she chose to seek employment as a Nurse's Aide at Columbia Presbyterian Hospital. My mother-in-law Ellen O'Dwyer went to work there about the same time but they really wouldn't meet until her daughter Evelyn and I got engaged in June 1961.

High School presented a relatively easy transition due to the fact that about twenty of us came from Incarnation School. The imprint and life -long penchant for savoring History was stimulated and reinforced by Mr. Charles Weans, who taught Ancient History and spoke elegantly with a cultivated Oxonian accent. He also introduced a "mite" box which fined students for real or attempted profane speech. Mr. Ed Doyle had been teaching Latin at the Prep for 25 years and was highly competent but easily distracted by students asking him about his experiences as a band leader during the Twenties and Thirties. He furthered his entertainment reputation by appearing on Ted Mack's Amateur Hour on early television. My three years of Latin, Caesar's Gallic Commentaries in sophomore year, and Cicero in junior year created an affinity for both language study and the historical backgrounds against which they were spoken. Buzzy Ronan quickly established himself as an orator, patriot and class officer. In debate, his spirited and unflinching defense of Senator Joe McCarthy won many adherents. To this day, we share a deep and abiding appreciation for the principles of conservatism. Lest either of us appear over angelic, I am obliged to recall the evening of imbibing liquor too freely and Buzzy's subsequent removal from Manhattan Center, not once, but five times!

In a similar vein, I learned a painful lesson at a high school dance at St Alphonsus in lower Manhattan. Two known "rumblers," or gang members, Skinny Ennis and John McElroy, for reasons unknown to me tried to trip me on the way to the dance floor. I responded with anger and a willingness to step into the men's room to "duke it out." These guys were by no means Marquess of Queensbury types as two of their associates pulled knives and held me hostage to the kicks and punches of Ennis and McElroy.

I have never forgotten that beating and over the next few weeks pondered revenge. Good sense prevailed and I never saw or heard from either of them again. I also learned the lesson that I am not by nature a brawler or pugilist! Other than a wrestling fight on the subway with an Inwood guy named Pete McNulty, from which we both emerged unscathed and shook hands afterward, my instinct has been to avoid violent confrontations. It is somewhat ironic and very likely possible that, in years to come, I would choose and revel in the macho and hawkish role of a military professional possibly to mask the less commendable feature of being a down-deep insecure coward! The difficulty of looking back now at my advanced age makes me realize that this is pure speculation as I entertained no such thoughts or reservations at the time!

Throughout freshman year, September 1951 to June 1952, I continued to find my academic strengths in History, Social Studies and English. To a lesser extent, Science was not difficult, but math remained a real problem and academic concern. Ronan, Whiteside, Diaz and I would gather at my house and drill each other over geometry theorems, quadratic formulas as well as the wonders of advanced algebra and trigonometry. It was rote memory and the solution of model or practice problems that got us through, not by any means an affinity for the subject.

Working as a delivery boy for Herbert Danzig, a German-Jewish refugee during the Thirties, provided about $20 per week in income and tips. Along with the income came an introduction to German/Yiddish and an outsider or goyim appreciation for shtick or Jewish humor. Harry Levy, nicknamed by me "Harry the Goniff," was a source of humor as well as a cultivated lover of classical music. Neither he nor Herb appreciated my changing the station to Martin Block's Make-Believe Ballroom Time when they weren't looking! I held on to this job, after school on Fridays and all-day Saturday for the entire four years of High School. My only regret is that the job precluded my involvement in High School extracurricular activities which would have been academically beneficial such as Speech or Student Government.

The strength and depth of our English teachers at Manhattan Prep matched the acumen of the Social Studies and Science instructors. Harry Dupuy, a Marine Officer in the Pacific during WWII and John Gaffney, another USMC veteran recently returned from Korea were particularly noteworthy for their patience and forbearance in dealing with us noisy, prank-playing and inattentive freshmen and sophomores.

Our religion class required standing vocal prayer at the beginning of each period. Brother Raphael, FSC, wore a hearing aid which occasionally went dead. One fine spring day, when the ample lawn of the Manhattan Quadrangle had been freshly manured, one of the class wits announced, during the Rosary, that Brother Raphael "smelled like a horse." The entire class cracked up at the comment and our hapless teacher didn't have a clue as to why!

Obvious casualties of Charlie Winan's ancient history course, John Keegan, John Kilroy (RIP), Danny White (RIP) and I formed a small clique which referred to itself as the "Tetrarchy." We enjoyed hanging around at lunch and sneaking cigarettes in the bathroom afterwards.

During the summer of 1953, Big Moe Friedman from our "Cabrini Gang" managed to get Jim Torrens (RIP) and me hired as Counselors at Camp Talcott, a YMCA Camp near Port Jervis, New York. It was a novel experience; living in a cabin with six ten-year-olds, working as Athletic Director, and visiting my summer romance girlfriend, Eileen, in Port Jervis on my one day a week off. It was a light-hearted relationship and that together with enjoying rum cokes with the guys made for a pleasant summer and alternative to the heat of New York City.

Junior year at Manhattan Prep (September 1953–June 1954) was a watershed with respect to entering young adulthood. A torrid, but deeply serious relationship developed rapidly in the fall with Sheila Waldron, a good-looking, well-built, contemporary in age but several years ahead of me in emotional development. Sheila was a great cook, gracious hostess and suitable company for my "hallway commando" penchant for lingering at her door never wanting to say goodnight! In my youthful enthusiasm, I was far more serious than she was. Ultimately, I suffered the embarrassment of a break-up and being obliged to have my helpful brother Ray retrieve my high school ring. "Live and Learn;" and "Once Burned, Twice Shy," the experience of teen-age love soured my outlook on women for years to come. The appeal of "High pockets" Sam Huxley, a major character in the novel *Battle Cry* by Leon Uris was irresistible; I vowed no more serious relationships with the ladies, no matter what!

American Literature taught by Mr. Bill Reidy nurtured my respect for great acting as well as classic literature. He literally ran breathless into the classroom one day and announced that Pope Pius XII had just landed in New York City and that he was organizing a group to travel downtown to see him. Asking for a show of hands, the majority of students volunteered to join him. After generating much excitement, Mr. Reidy then announced that he had perpetrated a hoax! He made his point when he subsequently asked how many of us had made a visit to Our Lord in the Blessed Sacrament which was being exhibited and venerated in the nearby College Chapel.

A major change in our family's structure and relationships occurred in the fall of 1954 when my younger brother, Richie, following his vocation and the encouragement of his role models within the Christian Brothers Community, departed for the Junior Novitiate at Barrytown, New York. While my parents accepted his decision spiritually, my father drank more heavily at the "loss" of his son. Personally, I regarded Richie's decision as a heroic one and felt immensely proud of him for it. On the day he left, Ray, Dad and I accompanied Richie to Grand Central Station to connect with his train up the Hudson. Well-oiled by Schenley or Seagram's whiskey, my father expressed his grief by threatening to throw himself on the tracks! Curiously enough, when sober, he was a generous supporter of the St. LaSalle Auxiliary, the primary support group for the Christian Brothers. In retrospect, rather than being a support to my mother during this period, his drinking generated additional concern and isolation from the rest of his family. Richie's accomplishments at Barrytown, Troy and Catholic University were a great source of pride to us while Dad's behavior brought ever-increasing embarrassment. Personally, I had neither the inclination to chastise my father nor to condone his problem. I retained a somewhat neutral position, which, over time, let me deny the exorbitant role alcohol was playing in my own life. Briefly stated, my attitude was "this will never happen to me," a recipe for both denial and ultimate career limitation in the U.S. Air Force.

Having acknowledged the early influence of alcohol on my teenage years and subsequent life, it would be appropriate to similarly recognize my early attitudes towards sex, the ethos of which I retain, for the most part, to this day. At the age of eleven I recall asking my mother what a wet dream was. She explained matter-of-factly that while this appeared like bed-wetting, it was actually the release of semen in young, adolescent males. Satisfied with her explanation, I did not pursue the issue, nor do I recall my parents hosting a "birds and bees" session. The Roman Catholic Church, however, was quite explicit in the "dos and don'ts" of sexuality. Any venereal or "below the belt" pleasure for boys was an occasion of mortal sin for which one would earn the pains of hell for all eternity. The solution to any sexual temptation was to keep a healthy distance from girls, "leave room for the Holy Ghost", take a cold shower, and divert all that energy into sports. These were holy and wholesome precepts reinforced by segregated mission sermons, separate school departments after fourth grade and the modesty of the holy clergy in thought, word and deed. I learned most of the mechanics of sex on the street and later, in High School, received explicit instruction in the classroom. Like most seventh or eighth graders, I gave a little thought to becoming a priest or a Christian Brother but felt that any vocational impulse would be negated by sexual temptation.

One benefit of the rigidity of the Catholic Church's' moral teachings of the Fifties and Sixties was that you always knew where you stood with respect to your own morality. You were either in the state of grace and therefore, eligible for heaven, or you were not. Weekly confession, in some cases, became the norm. Otherwise, receipt of the Holy Eucharist would be a sacrilege. "Situation Ethics", or the supremacy of one's own conscience, awaited the turmoil of Post Vatican II. Like many of my male contemporaries, my sexual morality depended to a large extent on the moral restraint of my date! The fact that these young ladies were overwhelmingly of Irish Catholic background served to keep many of my baser instincts in check. From the feminine point of view, the fear of an unwanted pregnancy or the social stigma of being a loose woman served to keep all of us in line along with the threat of eternal perdition for violations of the Sixth and Ninth Commandments. The subsequent discovery of the Pill and the recognition of the human conscience as the ultimate arbiter of morality have produced a confusion, amorality and profound change of perceived morality from this previous age. In most instances, my preferences remain with traditional morality. That being said, my waggish inclination is to assert that without the Sixth and Ninth commandments I would have hardly ever felt the need to enter a confessional!

It is with fading but nevertheless smirky delight that I recall the occasional Sunday afternoon pilgrimages of the Cabrini Gang to Union City, New Jersey. Our destination was the weekly Burlesque Matinee which introduced us to the normally hidden beauty of the opposite sex, baggy-pants comedians, low-brow humor, and absolutely gorgeous chorus girls. Big Moe Friedman would announce loudly on the bus "Opera House! Everyone off the Bus!" We would pay for our tickets, resist the blandishments of the candy and card salesmen, and look forward eagerly to two to three hours of live entertainment of the same genre which had been banned from New York City during the mayoralty of Fiorello La Guardia. A carefully kept secret from our parents, it did serve as excellent material for the following week's mandatory confession! Where was "Situation Ethics" when we could have used it back in the Fifties? The jokes have been, for the most part, retold or long forgotten. However, the memories of Blaze Starr, Evelyn West the "Treasure Chest", and Lily St. Cyr are vivid, if no longer inspirational.

Senior year at Manhattan Prep, September 1954 to June 1955, remains a pleasant, if somewhat relaxed memory. My major academic efforts were exerted in Math, Advanced Algebra and Introductory Calculus. More than a few evenings were spent cramming for midterms or finals in our kitchen with Buzzy Ronan, Jack Whiteside (RIP) and Al Diaz. One beneficial output was to convince me to avoid a college major in Engineering, despite my mother's encouragement to enter that field. As it turned out, Jack, Buzzy and I entered the Liberal Arts Program, while Al distinguished himself in the Business School.

Getting accepted into Manhattan College was a relief for each of us. I had entertained the hope of being accepted into the United States Air Force Academy's first class and pursued a battery of academic, aptitude and physical exams for that purpose. Ultimately, after pressing our congressman's office, I was informed that I had passed the tests but "not high enough." Since all my high school buddies were going to be Jaspers at Manhattan College, I shrugged off my first instance of military rejection and resolved to earn a commission through Air Force ROTC, a 700-member, all-male cadet corps at Manhattan.

On the social scene I enjoyed a senior prom date with a lovely young lady named Pat Bayard. Jack Whiteside and I were double-dating and I recall the misgivings and apprehension we felt when his father Charlie and my dad drove us to the prom site in mid-Manhattan. Another memory is the hours we spent reading and taping a brilliant satirical play written by a classmate Ron Young. He assigned roles for each of the faculty members at Manhattan Prep against the historical gospel accounts of the Lord's Passion and Crucifixion. While it may well have verged on the blasphemous, the character depictions and quotations were totally in character with the classroom mannerisms of each faculty member portrayed. Hopefully, the Ampex tape upon which this masterpiece reposes may surface some day in the future!

Shortly after graduation in June 1955, I checked into the Police Recreation Centre, a Catskill Mountain resort for New York Police Department members and their families. I worked as a waiter for the entire summer season, enjoyed the partnership of Hughie Gilmartin and saved about $500 for fall tuition. East Durham and Cairo were a drive down the mountain where Irish American music, beer, booze and good- looking, mostly Irish American girls were in residence. I recall working hard and playing hard that summer.

Socially, however, the wait staff, cooks and entertainment people were not without their cliques. My economic success in the dining room and propensity to quote freshly earned high school poems made me a suitable target and hapless defendant in a "Kangaroo Court," a pseudo mob scene which chastised my "excessive bullshitting" charge with a preordained guilty verdict and a volley of raw eggs. I was totally humiliated but took the experience in stride. To this day, I acknowledge my personal penchant for too much talk, comment or otherwise irrelevant, boring observations. Knowing the perpetrators of this incident, I am also convinced that a partial motive was the resentment of our aggressive and effective service in gaining tips in the dining room. I may never fully know the underlying reasons for being chastened, but my big mouth would continue to create similar resentment in others throughout my life's experiences. I would return to the Police Recreation Centre for the next four summers, enjoying a reprieve from New York City's heat, the opportunity to earn college tuition and the always alluring prospect of summer romances.

With respect to summer romance, the vision of Helen Walsh comes to mind. By any conceivable standard, Helen was a knockdown beauty with flowing natural blond hair, enticing short white shorts and a figure to compete with Marilyn Monroe, whom she strongly resembled! A fellow waiter and Fordham rival, Paul Phelan, asked her for a date. Her response was: "Fine; as long as Bernie can come with us!" Helen and I went swimming at Hogan's Hole, a secluded, rustic and beautifully landscaped flowing stream. The memory endures as does that of Gail Fortrell, Diane Abramowitz and several other summer guests. None of these dalliances endured through the fall but did make for a varied and romantic summer.

The Fall of 1955 brought the realization that we were in college now even if it was on the same campus as Manhattan Prep! Ronan, Whiteside and I entered the Liberal Arts Program, and I soon realized the time demands that reading placed upon my seventeen-year-old life. To keep an unrequested promise to my hard-working mother as well as to assert late teen economic independence, I obtained a part-time job at the A&P market store on Sherman Avenue in Inwood. The job consisted mainly of cutting and cleaning crate upon crate of chickens, breasts, legs, thighs, giblets, etc. The boss and fellow workers were pleasant people, and I took perhaps inordinate pride in using my earnings to pay my college tuition which was partially defrayed by receipt of a New York State Regent Scholarship of $1200. Manhattan College tuition at the time was about $20 per credit. At any rate, the downside of the job was the distaste I developed for my mother's fried chicken when she served it for dinner.

The Liberal Arts Program at that time was innovative, challenging and addictive. It was the basis for a commitment to life-long learning and a love of knowledge for its own sake. Our theme or core-curricular courses were History, Philosophy, Theology, Language, World Literature and Fine Arts with electives in Math, Psychology, and the Sciences. The biggest threat to my academic longevity (college survival) was the required Math course in Introductory Calculus and Statistics. At my father's suggestion, I sought the advice of a treasured family friend, John Trainor, who with patience and academic brilliance demonstrated the relationships between conic sections, hyperbolas, parabolas, etc., and the equations from which they were derived. It was truly an aesthetic experience, a teachable moment where something within my mind clicked and enabled me to appreciate the phenomena. Practically speaking, it enabled me to raise my grade from a D on the mid-term to a B-plus on the final. As John Keats more succinctly expressed it: "Beauty is truth; truth, beauty."

The theme courses themselves were unified by history; Freshman Year covered Greece and Rome; Sophomore Year, the Medieval Period; Junior Year; Renaissance and Reformation; and Senior Year, the Modern Period. The framework was similar, if not a direct offshoot of Mortimer Adler's Great Books program, The Syntopicon, a most respected reading of the classics, popular in academic circles at the time. To my abiding dismay, the Manhattan

Liberal Arts Innovation would ultimately be axed by the inroads of political correctness and an expansion of the program to African, Asian and minority themes during the Seventies and Eighties. The life-long learning impulse remains with me to this day whether the genre be history, military history, historical fiction or the luxury of watching the "Great Courses" on a DVD.

One of the attractions of Manhattan College's ROTC Program was the opportunity to earn a commission in the U.S. Air Force upon graduation. As a high school senior, I had applied for admission to the Air Force Academy and passed the physical and entrance exams only to be told by the Congressman's Office: "You passed, but you didn't pass high enough!" No grades were published but my instinct told me that the Academy was looking for football players, not part-time A&P employees! At Manhattan, I was proud to wear the uniform as AFROTC was mandatory for the first two years and afterwards on a contractual basis for Juniors and Seniors. Call it "Gung Ho" or whatever you wish, I spent six weeks pledging for a military fraternity or club, the Pershing Rifles. This group took pride in military bearing, drill, and precision marching. After vigorous marching and drill instruction, I and three others failed to be selected for membership. No reason was given; I chalked it up to not being able to reach their marching standards. Years later a good friend let me know that it was a personal dislike on the part of the cadet commander that kept me out. "Win a few;

lose a few!" However, this was a disappointment at the time and remains a painful memory. Perhaps it was something I said? Meanwhile, the standard AFROTC curriculum was exciting with great audio-visual presentations, Air Force history and customs of the service. Compared to the more rigorous academic requirements of the theme courses and other electives, AFROTC was a pleasant, delicious and alternative "piece-of-cake." One of the most memorable moments was a faculty piloted flight in a C-45, taking off from Mitchell AFB in Hempstead, Long Island and cruising the length of Manhattan Island under starry skies.

One of the concomitant learning lessons of the Liberal Arts Program was receiving an "A to Jaeger, F to you!" as a grade on a philosophy paper. The professor, Al Dilashia, explained that he knew what Werner Jaeger had to say in his *"Paideia"* opus; he wanted to know what I thought of it rather than a regurgitation of the author's thought.

Required reading in World Literature included *The Iliad*, *The Odyssey*, and *The Aeneid*, as well as Greek and Roman poetry. Brother Anthony's vivacious reading of selected passages in their original language displayed both his erudition as well as his love of his subject. The same could be said of Mr. Swift, a stuttering but insightful World History professor, taking us through the major events of the classical world that served as background for the Literature and Philosophy courses. The "icing on the cake" was provided by Professor Dan Woods in his Fine Arts course which depicted the ancient age in sculpture, painting and architecture. In a true and humble manner, I owe an unpayable debt to these men and to the subsequent faculty at Manhattan for the legacy of respect and desire for life-long learning and their acknowledgement of the human dictum: "As a man, nothing is foreign to me!"

If I were obliged to single out the professor who had the most effect upon my future intellectual development and career interests, it would have to be Dr. Edmund Tolk. Selecting the German language as my required course, the subsequent three years were marked by his unique pedagogic methods, erudite lectures and fascination with his progressive, inclusive and stimulating subject matter. His materials include mainly "run-off" papers on a wide variety of subjects. Beginning with the story of Snow White, we launched into sight translations and cognate activities, learning word origins in English and German as well as the vicissitudes of German grammar. Danish by birth, Dr. Tolk taught German to American GIs during World War II. He himself was a "drei-sprach-mancher," a scholar familiar with Greek, Latin and Hebrew. When Freshman year came to a close in June 1956, I recall him finishing his last class, wishing us a pleasant summer, and taking off for Saudi Arabia to study Arabic! As a faculty representative at a school dance, he amazed us and the young ladies present by his ability to dance the Tarantella. An "Old School" world gentleman, Dr. Tolk was a model of sophistication, sincerity and intellectual diversity. I recall his contributions to my diplomatic interests fondly and frequently.

My enthusiasm for German carried over into the social dating scene with excursions to Deutsche Halle, a genuine German bar and restaurant in Yorkville on Manhattan's upper east side. With the motive of impressing Evelyn, I ordered drinks and dinner in what I believed to be impeccable German. At the conclusion of the evening, I requested the check by stating "zahle bitte" or "check please." The waiter smiled, thanked me for the tip and stated that he was a Scotsman and didn't understand a word I was saying! "Win a few, lose a few!'

With respect to Philosophy and Theology, both these disciplines were heavily loaded in favor of traditional (pre-Vatican II) doctrine and scholastic philosophy. Thomism, the teachings of St. Thomas Aquinas, was the philosophy of the Roman Catholic Church and, to reinforce this emphasis, six credits were required during Junior year. Dr James Mullaney was particularly intense in his lectures on Scholastic Philosophers, imparting a life-long bias towards Realism and Faith. Brother Luke Salm, FSC, shocked our sophomoric sensitivities by proclaiming that he personally was indifferent as to whether we carried our rosary beads, made pious novenas, etc. Our grade in his Theology courses would depend upon our abilities to "regurgitate" the academic content and interpretation of his lectures. Somewhat heavy set, blessed with a lively and occasionally irreverent wit and an abiding sense of humor, he reminded me of a well-fed and benign medieval monk. He was one of the few, if not the only, Christian Brother to earn a Doctorate in Sacred Theology, a most formidable and highly respected accomplishment.

The legacy of these gifted educators is my appreciation for Catholic doctrine and tradition, Aristotle, Aquinas, *et alia*, as well as the historical foibles of the Church through its checkered and present existence. Thankfully and humbly, I retain a belief in the "Real Presence" as well as a respect for the teachings on morals and doctrine. Whether this is due to Latin piety, gravitas, fear of the hereafter or Celtic obstinacy is open to question!

Socially, the Tea Dances held on Sunday afternoons at the Cardinal Hayes Library provided the venue to meet, dance and date college girls from nearby Mount St Vincent's, Marymount Tarrytown, Marymount Manhattan and Manhattanville. These were all college girls of similar backgrounds, mostly BIC's, or "Bronx-Irish Catholics." This was a whole new world of manners, restraint, and best-foot forward behavior. I don't recall any serious dating relationship from this time but did enjoy comparing notes with Buzzy, Jack or Al Diaz.

June 1956 brought another round of pleasant summer employment at the Police Recreation Center in the Catskill Mountains as a recently legalized, 18-year-old drinker. A return to

Manhattan College in September brought with it the pseudo sophistication of a "seasoned" sophomore or freely translated from its Greek origin, a "wise fool." This was a year of immersion into all things medieval, along the now familiar framework of our theme courses: Philosophy, History, Fine Arts and World Literature. After exploring the depths of St. Augustine's *City of God, Confessions*, et alia, and Occam's Razor, I was more than ready to explore the lighter side of medieval society in the company of the Goliards, the minor clerics of the day, who lived by their wits, both holy and profane, earning their meals by song, poetry, and merriment. The popularity of the movie, *The Student Prince* with Stewart Granger singing in Mario Lanza's voice "Eins, Zwei, Drei Vier lift your stein and drink your beer" coincided with the cultural contributions of the Green Leaf, an Irish Bar proximate to the campus, frequented after class and sometimes in between classes by a good number of fellow Jaspers. I found Goliard verse, penned in the Middle Ages, much to my 20th century lifestyle, taste, and sentiment. A fading memory of mine can still recall a sample of their light-hearted, faintly whimsical, faintly theological fragment:

> *My intention is to die*
> *In the tavern drinking;*
> *Angels when they come shall cry,*
> *At this sot still blinking;*
> *Spare this drunkard, God he's high.*
> *Absolutely Stinking!*

The ribald and semi-blasphemous verse of the Goliards would find a modern counterpart in fraternity songs, chants, scurrilous limericks, and sacrilegious jokes. In my belief, these could only flourish in a Catholic or believing environment. This was truly the "Age of Faith," but as *The Canterbury Tales* also indicated, not all of its inhabitants were, by no means, saints, as my younger, unsophisticated imagination had conceived them to be. The full reading and theological allusions of Dante's *Divine Comedy* brought this point home even more emphatically. This was a year of intellectual, emotional, and social growth, a debt I owe to the structure and faculty of the Liberal Arts Program.

Given my negative experience freshman year with the Pershing Rifles, I was skeptical and somewhat reluctant to pledge for a "real" fraternity, Alpha Sigma Beta, Manhattan's oldest and finest, whose motto was "Semper Primus." John Annicelli, a year ahead of me at Manhattan Prep, was a persuasive recruiter and a conscientious sponsor. The pledge period consisted of six weeks of pure harassment, occasional instances of sadism, meetings at noon each day, shining the shoes of fraternity brothers, accomplishing seemingly impossible pledge assignments, a hell weekend, and many social activities. Buzzy Ronan and I supported each other and, with fifteen other pledges, were inducted as ASB Brothers. These became the closest and most exclusive group of men with whom I associated then and with whom I maintain contact to this day. My pride in being selected wiped the board clean of resentment, self-doubt or failure due to the Pershing Rifle episode.

The social benefits of ASB membership were overwhelming; to wear a blue blazer with the fraternity crest and to participate in the ASB sponsored Fall Barn Dance and Spring Boat Ride to Bear Mountain were but a few of these warm and cherished memories. In the Spring Semester of 1957, Buzzy and I were delighted to welcome Jack Whiteside, Jim Gavigan, Mike Bette, and Bob Semple into our select group of ASB Brothers.

Given the fraternity activities, a part-time job at the A&P and normally a weekend involving two or three dates, I began to appreciate the proximity and convenience of Inwood as a dating base for young ladies. Joan Mahan and Patricia Cunningham from Arden Street come to mind as other attendees at Manhattan Tea Dances. Amid this diversity of interests, I was able to maintain a 3.0 GPA and stay on the Dean's List for Second Honors. I attribute this, not to academic brilliance, but rather to the discipline of hitting the books and keeping up with the voluminous reading assignments from Monday through Thursdays. Dad had purchased a 1955 Ford and, when I could negotiate its loan, a visit to the Whitestone Drive-In Theater or to the New Rochelle Barge were popular dating destinations.

I realize today that the academic dice were heavily loaded in favor of Aristotle and Thomas Aquinas and, despite the ranting of existentialists, nihilists, socialists and Marxists, have left me with my Roman Catholic Faith and personal belief in philosophical realism. From the matured and seasoned perspective of old age, I am privileged to look back on 1957 as the pivotal and most significant year of a long and mufti-blessed life. The fall term at Manhattan focused on the Renaissance and Reformation, a period which still commands my attention in history books, magazine articles and television presentations. Each of our theme courses provided insight into the thoughts of Erasmus, Descartes, Bacon, Hobbes, etc., and the tragic history of the internecine religious conflicts of that age. Anticipating an Air Force Commission at graduation, I "signed on the dotted line," which provided me entrance to the Advanced Corps of the AFROTC, a stipend of $27 a month from the government payroll and an obligation to serve three years of active duty after graduation.

Don Theobald, a neighborhood educator, U.S. Marine Corps Pacific combat veteran and business partner of my uncle Joe Clancy in selling Catholic family bibles, obtained part-time jobs for Jack Whiteside and me as "Health Education" teachers in the Hunt's Point section of the Bronx. The job itself was to supervise teenagers as they played basketball, volleyball or harmonized in singing groups on the most popular rock and roll songs of the era. In general, the students, mostly Black and Hispanic, were well behaved and enjoyed the independence of minimal direction from me in choosing sides and playing their games. I was obliged to eject troublemakers and to head off any potential fights. The Director of the Recreation Center at Public School 75 was a Black gentleman, highly professional and possessed of great acumen in judging teen behavior. Winston Robins had the charisma and ability to persuade one young man to surrender his "piece," an illegal pistol. I learned a lot working for and with Winston and gained insight into the ethics and values of the minority community.

One rarely anticipates when a most significant and consequential event is about to take place. Mary Teresa Ryan, Joe Hilly and I stopped by 137 Nagle Avenue to pick up Joe's date, a very winsome if not gorgeous, Kathleen O'Dwyer, Mary's student-nurse classmate from St Vincent's Hospital. While being introduced to the O'Dwyer family, I was privileged and delighted to meet her attractive and enticing younger sister, Evelyn. She was dressed in a housecoat and, like Cinderella, busy sweeping and cleaning the kitchen floor. Her shapely figure and eyeglasses subsequently became items of life-long interest, while, for the moment, I was successful in obtaining her telephone number. It was hardly love at first sight but rather the beginning of a life-long courtship and competitive campaign which endures to this day!

Shortly thereafter, I called and asked for a New Year's Eve date. Evelyn already had a date for the evening but was willing to get together during the day on December 31. Hoping to inject an aura of mystery while simultaneously completing a term paper assignment, I briefed Mrs. O'Dwyer on my plan to visit the New York Public Library on Fifth Avenue for that purpose. Evelyn was to bring along two sandwiches and an apple for lunch. While riding the bus downtown, she compelled me to reveal my plans. Evelyn had previously indicated that she understood some French. I had intended to exploit that talent by citing some French titles on my term paper bibliography on Marie Antoinette. Evelyn suggested that we alter that plan and visit the Central Park Zoo where we could see the animals and enjoy our sandwiches in the sunshine. We subsequently visited the Metropolitan Museum of Art as well as a brief trip to the New York Public Library. I managed to temporarily impress Evelyn with my dilettante knowledge of "Frontality" in Egyptian statuary and other intellectual nuggets from my liberal arts background. It was a pleasant date for both of us and the beginning of a merger of two widely diverse temperaments.

By December of 1957, I was no longer a teenager and the most influential person I would ever know and love had just entered my life. By the Spring of 1958, Evelyn had accepted and wore my fraternity pin as visible evidence of our committed, loving and occasionally stormy relationship. The pin would be returned to me on several occasions, but my persistence and Evelyn's patience brought us back together and ultimately into the state and commitment of marriage.

At the conclusion of Spring Semester in June 1958, Mike McDonald, Jake Honan and I were enroute to AFROTC Summer Camp, a month-long training session at Plattsburgh AFB, New York. A driver had stalled his car under a shaded bridge on the New York Thruway near Newburgh. We plowed right into him at about 40 MPH. Mike sustained a fractured knee; Jake was unharmed; and I had a broken left ankle after bracing for impact. We subsequently took a Greyhound bus to Plattsburgh where Mike and I received casts at the base hospital. After the cast had hardened, the young Air Force medical technician continued to apply ice bag treatments on top of the cast. When I questioned him about it, he responded to the effect that no one had given him orders to stop! Since there was no way that we could complete the training program, we were released, and my parents drove me back to New York City with a knee length plaster cast over my left ankle.

The good news was that I could travel down to the Jersey Shore and date Evelyn on and off while she was waitressing at the Monmouth Hotel in Spring Lake. It turned out to be a relaxing summer of reading books, trips to the Shore, and sharing good times with Evelyn's classmates and co-workers, Jeanne Hickey, Sally Campbell, and Ann Daley. The top hits of the day remain a romantic memory: *"One Summer's Night," "Under the Boardwalk," "Volare," "Come Go With Me,"* etc. My cast became a badge of honor as I claimed to gullible female admirers that I was a Marine Corps veteran of the incursion into Lebanon!

As the lazy days of summer 1958 came to their inevitable close, Senior year commenced at Manhattan College. The challenges of Twentieth Century Literature, Art and Philosophy made for another heavy-duty reading year. The exposure to Nietzsche, Dumas, Existentialism, Dada, William James, Soren Kierkegaard, *et alia*, was fleeting but adequate for us as undergraduates. The compliment I shall always cherish was that of Brother Abdon Lewis, FSC, to the effect that he was surprised I was going on active duty with the Air Force rather than pursuing graduate work in Literature. Knowing that active duty awaited, I sat in for only one job interview with Proctor and Gamble. Military service was inevitable for most males of my generation and a commission in the U.S. Air Force was vastly preferable to being conscripted or drafted.

In the Fall of 1958, my family was obliged to move from our apartment at 869 West 180th Street to 358 Wadsworth Avenue, about a mile north and four flights up at 190th Street. The move was generated by the construction of the Cross Bronx Expressway and the addition of a lower level to the George Washington Bridge. Until his last day, my father would condemn Robert E. Moses for this radical demolition clear across northern Manhattan and the Bronx. The site of our former apartment in which we lived for 18 years, is today transited by a circular approach ramp to the George

Washington Bridge.

In January 1959, as an AFROTC Cadet Major and Wing Information Officer, I entered the Flight Instruction Program (FIP) at Westchester Airport. After several hours of instruction, I accomplished a solo flight and felt on top of the world. I had the misfortune of ground-looping my Aeronca Champ aircraft. This resulted in my elimination from the program, a failure I took in stride as another opportunity to be a pilot might present itself in the future. My status with AFROTC was reclassified from Pilot to non-rated Officer Candidate.

Senior year rushed by in a flash, the most memorable part of it being the disagreement and break up between Evelyn and myself over her unilateral decision to travel with her classmates to Fort Lauderdale, Florida for Spring Break. In retrospect, I believe I was overly possessive and could have handled the situation differently. As it turned out, I joined Bob Martin, Buzzy Ronan, Jim Gavigan and Joe Williams, all ASB Brothers, in Florida. We drove down there for one memorable beer drinking and boozing party of a week's duration. Buzzy and I hitch-hiked back to New York with three attractive young ladies who were students at Manhattanville College.

Graduation Day at Manhattan College occurred on June 9, 1959, a few days after the AFROTC Cadet Review where my name was announced as one of the future-to-be-commissioned Second

Lieutenants at the completion of Summer Training. To this day, I cherish the photographs of my parents, grandmother, and me on that occasion. Evelyn thoughtfully presented me with an engraved set of rosary beads which I also treasure but use rarely. I had, once again, received my fraternity pin back as she planned to waitress at Bear Mountain and the Jersey Shore. Neither of us was enthusiastic over long-distance romance. I would be spending a month at Lockbourne AFB, Columbus, Ohio for military training, marching, academics, physical training, reveille daily at 0600 hours, survival school and rotating leadership roles.

Lockbourne AFB was a SAC Installation, home to an RB-47 Bomb Wing and KC-97 Tankers. We enjoyed a refueling mission as well as an orientation flight in the T-33 Thunderbird. My Cadet role was that of Color Bearer as the more challenging positions went to the college Juniors who constituted the vast majority of the cadet corps. Never an outstanding athlete and limited to some extent by my still swollen ankle, I went along with the training, kept my big mouth shut for a change and received the gold bars of a Second Lieutenant on July 10, 1959.

At Lockbourne I had developed a new friendship with a fellow senior cadet, Timothy J. McGrath, a likable but somewhat obsessed military martinet. He had been Cadet Wing Commander at NYU and was given to finding picayune faults with the Staff and Cadet Leadership cadre. He paid the price of walking demerit tours while I enjoyed being swept off base our first free weekend by a platinum blond Sherry in her convertible. Win a few, lose a few, but the benefits of keeping a low profile were obvious but not always practiced personally. Tim and I were both in the aerie atmosphere of a newly-found freedom which only twenty-two-year-olds can experience. As yet, we had no job responsibilities and accordingly spent a few more weeks in Columbus, partying and pursuing the fleeting romances of summer. Our Cadet Mess Hall had been serviced by attractive, college-aged girls employed for the summer as waitresses. Predictably, dating opportunities emerged after the first two weeks of training. Tim dated a young lady named Sabre and I pursued a winsome blond named Sally. A romance would develop between Tim and Sally which resulted in their marriage in January 1961. I had met and enjoyed the company of a contemporary, young, head-turning platinum blond named Sherry. One of her major advantages was ownership of a convertible which provided transportation for two. As she had been married and divorced, nothing serious was contemplated on my part.

Orders for active duty in September arrived in due course. I very much appreciated the car-buying advice of my uncle, Joe Clancy. I ended up purchasing a powder blue Buick Century convertible for the princely sum of $770. The funds came from a timely payment of damages previously incurred in the auto accident in the summer of 1958. The most memorable moment of the transaction was when Manny, the used car salesman, stated that such a low price given to me was agitating his ulcer, but that I could have the deal, nevertheless.

The four-day drive to San Antonio, alone and in beautiful Fall weather, was an adventure in itself, driving through Washington D.C., Virginia, Skyline Drive, Northern Georgia, etc. Stopping overnight in a hamlet named Rising Dawn, Georgia, I was appropriately proud of the "Blue Bitch," my Buick with New York plates and the attraction she was to the rustics who came to gawk at her! We arrived in San Antonio, signing in at Lackland AFB early in the afternoon of September 23, 1959, a significant date insofar as all service commitments as pay and dates of rank were calculated from that time. My first culture-shock occurred shortly thereafter. After checking into an off-base motel, I felt that a liquid refreshment reward was in order. Stopping in at a nearby bar, I ordered a Seagram's 7 & 7. The bartender informed me that he could pour me a drink, but Texas law required that I provide my own bottle! No bar back East had any such requirement. It was easily resolved as I purchased a Fifth at a nearby liquor store and returned to the bar to have it poured and consumed. No, this was not the beginning of a notorious, destructive drinking career; that had begun in High School, been fostered in college, and would continue unimpeded for another 21 years. It was, however, my first exposure to Texas ways and local idiosyncrasies.

Reporting into Lackland, I was interviewed by a senior master sergeant with respect to possible job or career field preferences. I responded to the effect that my History/Political Science college background should qualify me for Intelligence duty. "We don't have any Intelligence outfits down here, Lieutenant; Have you ever fired a rifle?" I replied that I had, and his response was that I could choose between the Security Police or the USAF Marksmanship School. I elected the latter and was subsequently assigned duties as Assistant Range Safety Officer at Lackland or nearby Camp Bullis, a U.S. Army range north of San Antonio. One of the primary missions of the Marksmanship School was to train and hone the skills of competitive USAF shooters in pistol and rifle competitions in order to defeat their Soviet competitors in the upcoming 1960 Olympics. It seemed to me that the NCOs who ran the ranges were both far more experienced and competent than I as an inexperienced "butter bar" was or was ever likely to be. Unlike the Army, which used NCOs, the USAF required a commissioned or Warrant Officer to be physically present when firing was taking place. Most of the NCOs respected this reality and were patient and understanding with the "new" Second Lieutenant. A glaring exception occurred when an Army Master Sergeant, putting me to a test, fired at a light bulb over my head, extinguishing the bulb and giving me a menacing smirk. My response was to comment sarcastically to the effect that I thought this was the Range Safety

Office and to leave it at that. To this day I speculate whether this response was preferable to attempt "chewing out" or preferring court martial charges against a Korean War Combat veteran, a senior NCO with a loaded rifle.

My reporting officer at Lackland was a First Lieutenant, Donald E. Grigsby, an Alabama-born former SA-16 Albatross pilot. Don counseled me frequently on customs of the Air Force, non-fraternization with enlisted personnel, etc. While I respected his experience and sought his friendship, he managed to record my early learning deficiencies, use of beatnik slang and defensive attitude when counseled into my first Officer Effectiveness Report, concluding: "He might, in time, develop into a typical effective and competent officer." I had no idea whether effectiveness reports were honest, objective evaluations, but rather inflated documents and testimonies to the writer's command of the English language. I was somewhat assured that lower or "average" ratings were normally bestowed on Second Lieutenants as they were new and inexperienced officers. I didn't become aware of these comments until several years later and simmered and bristled over this less than promising forecast of my future value to the Air Force. In retrospect, today, I may consider his comments somewhat deserved. My judgment was certainly deficient when I suggested to Don that he could do himself a great benefit by pursuing a college degree! While well-intended on my part, I believe it was received as malicious. At any rate, Don was willing to endorse a fresh application for Pilot Training, which I was delighted to see was approved with a class date at Moore Air Base, Mission, Texas on 3 March 1961. Don was right on two counts: the Air Force and AFROTC did not communicate with each other and, secondly, I would ultimately "wash out" because I didn't think rapidly enough to react and control a landing aircraft!

A bachelor oriented social life revolved around our rented residence at 119 Lansing Lane near South Zarzamora Street in San Antonio. Second Lieutenant Steve Lauer, an Assistant Boy Scout Master, Second Lieutenant Marty McLoughlin, Holy Cross '58, and Second Lieutenant George Kawas, Fordham '58, occupied this modest residence with me and partied heartily virtually every weekend. With a counterpart group of young ladies, we referred to our abode as the "Zoo" and theirs as the "Sow House." Steve didn't drink or smoke and was more involved with his Boy Scout activities over a given weekend. Marty, George, and I more than compensated for Steve being the resident "Straight Arrow." Marty had an explosive temper with or without booze. George was nicknamed the "Beast" after a contemporary comic strip character featured in Prince Valiant in the Days of King Arthur. Dark bearded and dark complexioned, with penetrating blue eyes, George was of Syrian parentage and resembled the camel dealer from the Hollywood epic Ben Hur. During our residence at Lansing Lane,

Pat McDonald, a classmate from Manhattan College, and Tim McGrath, my old sidekick from summer camp, would occasionally enjoy our hospitality. Persnickety as Tim tended to be, he was critical of our hospitality, and asserted that if we didn't take better care of him, he just might leave. To this incredible "threat" as he wasn't sharing our rent payments, Marty quickly responded: "Should I slash my wrists now or wait until you're gone?" Overall, we got along well, had similar New York backgrounds and similar tastes for drinking and female companionship. Tim would go straight to Navigator Training at James Connelly AFB in Waco, Texas, while Pat and I would go to Primary Flight Training at Moore AFB in Mission, Texas.

During late 1959, I met and frequently dated a pleasant, attractive, and intelligent redhead, Mary Jane O'Hara, and enjoyed a home-prepared meal with her and her single mother. Nothing too serious as we both were aware of my imminent move to South Texas, but good company, nevertheless. Taking a holiday leave for Christmas and New Year's Eve, Evelyn and I parted decisively and amicably. I entertained the pleasant memory of Evelyn's mother reassuring me that I would always be welcome in her home.

In retrospect, the Fifties constituted the apogee of American military power, sage diplomacy, and economic stability. I think of it as the "Age of John Wayne," a larger-than-life American Hero, a morally upright fearless exemplar of battlefield courage

(Sands of Iwo Jima), and unabashed patriot (The Alamo). His co-star was the beautiful, intelligent, and wholesome Maureen O'Hara (Fort Apache). Together they exemplified the unquestioned ideals of the American West and the heroism of the U.S. Cavalry. Our country was at the top of the world due to hard work, sacrifice and the inspired vision of its Founding Fathers.

I was privileged to begin my military service in the United States Air Force and specifically in Strategic Air Command (SAC), the organization whose unprecedented military power ensured that hegemony. The irony of the SAC motto "Peace is Our Profession" emblazoned upon the fuselage of a B-47 or B-52 bomber was not lost on me. The U.S. military preserved our national ideals and offered its protection to less fortunate allies gathered under our nuclear umbrella. I took immense pride in our country and found its critics rare and mostly inarticulate. Aided by these convictions, I grew more confident in my choice of an Air Force career as the opportunity to serve in the protection of this unique American "House on the Hill" heritage.

Bernard as a baby in 1937.

Dick, Kitty, Helen
and Bernard at their
apartment on West
180th Street, 1938.

Bernard, age one,
1938.

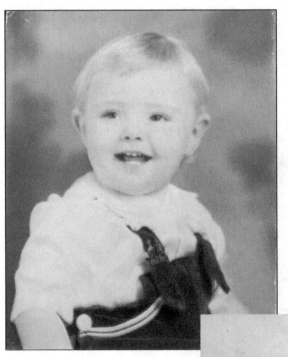

Bernard and his father Dick,
1939.

Ray, Richie, and
Bernard, circa 1942.

Ray, Richie, and
Bernard, circa 1945.

Bernard's First Communion with his mother Kitty and friends Jack Whiteside and Jimmy Torrance.

Bernard, Ray, and Richie, circa 1950 taking the Circle Line around Manhattan.

Bernard at his 8th grade graduation with his grandmother, Lizzie O'Prey.

8th grade graduation from Incarnation.

Camping with
the family.

Bernard as a camp counselor, 1953.

Benard's graduation
photo from Manhattan
Prep, 1955.

Benard's
graduation photo
from Manhattan
College, 1959.

Junior Prom, Manhattan College, 1958.

Marymount Snow Ball, 1960

CHAPTER FOUR

THE SIXTIES

Few suspected that the new decade of the Sixties would present the cusp of a cultural revolution: Flower Children, Hippies, and obscenities elevated in the writings of the Beat poets, Jack Kerouac, Allen Ginsburg, *et alia*. The Roman Catholic Church would initiate reform under the auspices of Vatican II and my hard-learned altar boy Latin would become useless. The near catastrophe of nuclear war was narrowly averted with the positive resolution of the Cuban Missile Crisis. The prolonged conflict in Vietnam would challenge our nation's patience and ultimately its will to win. Fortunately, the future is hidden from us, and one is reduced to writing what my memory tells me rather than the fantasies of what could have been! I entered the decade of the Sixties as a somewhat carefree bachelor and exited as the husband of a loving wife and soon to be father of three healthy and beautiful daughters.

We were labeled the "Silent Generation" in the Fifties as we tended to conform and accept reality as we saw it and refrained from the liberal constant penchant for change. Early on, Mario

Savio and his ilk founded the so-called "Free Speech Movement" at Berkeley, encouraging riots, profanity, sit-ins and violent student demonstrations. His opponents were my heroes: S.I. Hayakawa and Governor Ronald Reagan. The demonstrators, in my opinion, were spoiled brats, convinced that the world owed them a living and that traditional beliefs in God and Country were outdated. Most of my contemporaries worked their way through college and took pride in that fact. The Flower Children of San Francisco rejected traditional sexual morality as well as anti-drug laws and thereby formed the cutting edge of social, cultural, moral and political rebellion in the early Sixties. Ultimately, the Civil Rights Movement, while morally justified and overdue, would be seriously conflated with the anti-war movement and the violent actions of H. Rap Brown, the Black Panthers, the Students for a Democratic Society, and the burning of our cities. At the time and to the present day, I retain a pride in the fact that I was entering a profession diametrically opposed to the rhetoric of revolution, constant change, and the violent upheaval of America's traditional values. I would be strongly influenced by Edmund Burke's opus, *Reflections on the Revolution in France*, as well as the candidacy of Barry Goldwater in 1964. I had taken a solemn oath to preserve and protect the Constitution of the United States as an officer in my chosen Air Force profession and would continue to serve with pride, if not always with distinction, toward that worthy goal.

The inebriating whiff of fresh orange blossoms and their surrounding groves greeted the Blue Bitch and I as we arrived with her top down at Moore Air Base, Mission, Texas in early March 1960. Warm and verdant by comparison with chilly and wet San Antonio, Moore AFB was run by civilian contractors with traditional support activities. These included a base theater, gymnasium, athletic fields, and a dining facility that would be the envy of South Texas, also known as "The Magic Valley." I was delighted to find Pat McDonald and Mike DeAngelo as classmates, both Class of '59 at Manhattan. Pat and I did a lot of flight training studying as well as other extracurricular activities together during our brief interlude at Moore. We were introduced to the T-34, a tandem-seated, single engine trainer. My initial flight instructor was a gentle-spoken and encouraging B-24 veteran of WW II named Elmer Sellars. He was the kind of instructor who generated the desire to excel and determination to not disappoint or let him down in the flying phase: takeoffs, landings, spins, unusual attitudes, etc. Under his tutelage, I managed to solo after about twelve hours of instruction. Unfortunately for both of us, Elmer was grounded due to permanent ear damage from the T-37 (Tweety Bird), the new, two-engine primary jet engine trainer. By luck of the draw, I was assigned to a heavyset gent named Ed Walker, a former Navy Pilot and Crop Duster. Ed was more accustomed to chewing out fledgling aviators like me rather than encouraging them. For one reason or another, my in-flight performance deteriorated, and I entered the infamous "washing machine," a series of check rides which ultimately resulted in my elimination from pilot training. The coup de gras to my aviator aspirations came with a final check ride with Tex Melugin, the popular and well-respected chief pilot at Mission Aviation. My takeoff and spin procedures went reasonably well. When requested to shoot landings at the Auxiliary Field, I was quite chagrined at being unable to find it! "Division of Attention" was one of my major problem areas; I could do one activity or another but not at the same time. Spins were one thing but keeping track of the aircraft's position was another. The icing on the failure cake occurred when returning to home base, I entered the traffic pattern in the opposite direction from aircraft that were taking off! That flight convinced me and the Air Force that I could fly but not safely enough to meet USAF standards. The prevalent claim was that the Air Force could teach a monkey to fly but it was a matter of how much time they were willing to invest in the process. Although bitterly disappointed by my failure, I was obliged to accept the verdict. It was a "pilot's Air Force" and, at best, I would be playing second fiddle as a navigator. If I chose, I could have fulfilled my service commitment in three years by entering law school and a different career. I muse to myself today that had I made it through successfully, I would have chosen the F-105 Thunderchief and would likely be reposing on "Thud Ridge", a graveyard for many U.S. pilots near Hanoi.

Brief as it was, the social scene at Moore was characterized by many bachelor gatherings featuring rum and cokes and Oscar Brand's LP's *The Wild Blue Yonder, Volumes 1 and 2.* Nearby Mexico was a popular destination for wild times and cheap booze. The base theater would issue warnings when rattlesnakes were spotted near its entrance at night. One had to be careful and not wander around without a flashlight. The Main Gate to the base would display a dozen or so recently killed six-to-eight-foot reptiles. Our morale was substantially enhanced by a visit from Evelyn's sister, Kathy, and three of her recently graduated classmates from St Vincent's Hospital in New York City. Their welcome presence provided for a weekend of partying as well as the company of "Anglo" females. Many of the Hispanic young ladies at the base would date us young lieutenants only on condition that their fathers not see them because he "didn't like Anglos." With Doyle Ruff, a future Thunderbird, we took the girls on a side trip to Mexico.

By the time I was eliminated, my class had been reduced by 31 percent with Pat McDonald among the "wash-outs". We were able to console each other. A combination of enjoying Air Force social life and the lure of flight pay as Navigators enticed us to opt for Undergraduate Navigator Training at Harlingen AFB, about sixty miles east down the Rio Grande. We were assigned to Class 61-04 K, scheduled for nine months of training with graduation and the awarding of Navigator wings in March 1961. In addition to the constant menace of Physical Training (PT), Navigator Training emphasized academic learning, Dead Reckoning, Polar Navigation (Grid), Weather, Radio, Loran, Celestial, and Radar. The gradual application of these areas and techniques were incorporated into 300 hours of flying time in our flying classroom, the two-engine prop, T-29 Aircraft. Unlike pilot training, the skills required were thought and practice as opposed to the manual dexterity required in pilot training. While social life was most convivial, it lacked the aggressive elan and fiery spirit of pilot training. About halfway through the program I gave some serious thought to dropping out and shared this inclination with our Tactical Training Officer, Captain (Major Selectee) Bobby Albeck. His advice was to go party in Mexico over the weekend and if I felt the same way on Monday, to come back and see him. I took his advice and the thoughts of quitting vanished! In addition to Pat McDonald, I added new friends to my party and drinking circle, Scott Ryder, and Chuck Caldwell. We drove to Monterrey, Mexico, a virtual metropolis when compared to nearby Matamoros and Padre Island.

As the Navigator Course progressed, I found I could handle the various problems and electronic systems with pacing and practice. It was just a matter of keeping up and ahead of what the aircraft was doing. Speed and pacing did remain drawbacks throughout my flying career which encompassed 6500 hours. I could do it; it just took me a little longer in a T-29, KC-97 or C-141!

Christmas of 1960 brought a visit back to New York and another parting from Evelyn. Returning to Harlingen in January, the final phase of Navigator training whizzed by, and we graduated with our long-sought wings on March 3, 1961. By pure luck of the draw, I was able to select the very last "operational" assignment available; KC-97 tankers at McGuire AFB, New Jersey in the 305th Air Refueling Squadron (SAC). After two years in the training command (ATC), I was now a member of the Air Forces' "First Team" in SAC. I was pleased to be assigned close to home and to be in occasional touch with Evelyn. However, prior to arrival at McGuire, I faced a month-long combat crew training course in the KC-97 school at Randolph AFB, San Antonio, Texas. Together with two other Harlingen classmates, we rewarded ourselves with the purchasing of a TR 3 Triumph sports car. Mine was jet black, shiny, two-seated, and flashy. The academic and flying training program was challenging. I learned how to conduct a mid-air refueling rendezvous with the B-47 bomber and how important crew coordination was in this process. However, my most distinct and cherished memory from the Spring of 1961 was receiving a long-distance call from Evelyn at the Randolph AFB Officers' Club during which she told me she loved me. What could I respond to top that other than "I love you too!"

Driving back north in my new TR-3 was a great adventure.

After settling into the BOQ at McGuire AFB, I made the first of many visits to Evelyn's and my parents' homes. Summoning up my courage after four years of active pursuit, I have the cherished memory of asking Jack O'Dwyer for Evelyn's hand in marriage. His terse but most welcome response was: "Ahh, go ahead, I'm going to bed!" With her sister Kathleen's crucial assistance, an engagement ring was purchased by her friend Jerry Peppercorn and our engagement was publicly announced at Evelyn's Graduation Party in June 1961. This was truly an unforgettable event and the first social opportunity my parents, Kitty and Dick, had to meet Ellen and Jack O'Dwyer in addition to the key members of their large family. Evelyn's paternal Aunt Nora was in tears describing to my father just how much she missed her deceased husband. Dick politely inquired: "How long has he been gone?" Nora's tearful response was: "30 years". The O'Dwyer family lore attributes this to the rumor that Nora and her brother, Jack, were both baptized in whiskey. This disposition was by no means confined to the O'Dwyer family as the O'Preys had a traditional love for "the creature" on the paternal side. In my father's pithy, but realistic estimation, it was "a good man's failing."

I felt very much at home in the O'Dwyer household. Ellen O'Dwyer could not have been more loving and solicitous for my comforts or taste palette. On one occasion, she asked what my favorite meal was, and I truthfully responded to the effect that it was lobster. Passing around the table on a Friday night (lobster qualified during days of abstinence from meat) Jack O'Dwyer rejected the offering claiming that it was "unnatural"! I felt close to Jack insofar as he would escape from time to time and invite me to join him for a drink at McGoldrick's, one of the ubiquitous Irish bars in Inwood. Evelyn's Uncle Jim and Aunt Julia Browne were equally warm and welcoming, and I felt privileged to be joining such a large, loving and deeply Irish American family. Let me not forget Evelyn's maternal Uncle Bart Hayes and his Mayo born spouse, Nance.

Impeccably dressed and meticulously on time, Jack served as an Usher weekly at Sunday Mass at Our Lady Queen of Martyrs Church, two mere blocks from their apartment house. I distinctly recall the glare he gave Evelyn and I on the occasional late arrivals for Mass. This was the Pre-Vatican II Church, replete with "thou shalt nots" fasting and abstinence, separate religious retreats for men and women and a high esteem for the veneration of Mary, which placed her on a pedestal hardly lower than that which held her Son, Jesus. I retained my Faith as the legacy of my Irish Ancestors but did not always comply with its moral imperatives and teachings.

In April or May,1961, SAC required additional crew training at Randolph AFB. I was obliged to entrust my shining TRW to the mercy of my brother, Ray, who was delighted to accept the task.

Returning to New Jersey for the summer, Pat Mc Donald and I shared a cabin in Browns Mills from which I subsequently upgraded to more modern housing at Country Lakes, about five or six miles south of Fort Dix/ McGuire AFB. At the time, I was qualifying to "combat ready" status in the 305th and full-time crew duty mostly involving home alert. During one weekend dinner visit to the O'Dwyer household, the phone rang, and I was obliged to return 80 miles back to McGuire due to a no-notice SAC alert. I had been reveling in the dispensation active-duty military had from not eating meat on Fridays. The alert convinced my in-laws that SAC was serious business. Our social introduction to the 305th was impressive. Captain George Dersheimer and his wife Marge hosted us as guests in their home in Cherry Hills and the Squadron Party provided plenty to eat and drink. Our commander's nickname was "Whiskey" Willy Wilson and he and his wife demonstrated how they earned it. The 305th claimed few career success stories, a combination of WWII veterans, mid-career captains and young Lieutenants like me. Following my college and Training Command preferences, I choose to associate with the rowdy, fun-seeking and drinking party people. To myself I conceded that I drank too heavily but had the situation "under control."

Evelyn had secured employment as a 22-year-old Math teacher at George Washington High School in my parents' neighborhood. She was an immediate success and would continue to be so until family responsibilities arrived in 1966. Meanwhile, nuptial planning was new to both of us and the help we received from her sister Kathleen and her bridesmaids Jeanne Hickey and Pat Reynolds was deeply appreciated.

A life and the decades which constitute its span, contains ups and downs, triumph and tragedy, victory and defeat for each of us. On the positive side, I recall with pride the trip to McGuire AFB arranged by my brother, Richie, for approximately 20 minority students from St Augustine's School in the Bronx, where he served as a Christian Brother. The kids really enjoyed the tour of my KC-97 Squadron and the modest picnic that was provided. The darker side of life's reality occurred on February 9, 1961. My father, whom I loved deeply and whose memory I revere almost 50 years after his passing, had lapsed into the realm of alcoholism. This was a gradual process for him; mom refused to attend the County Down Ball and other social events as his blathering and staggering would be an embarrassment to her and all concerned. The most hurtful comment she made is engraved on my memory. It was to the effect that she should have entered the convent rather than marrying a drunk. The widening of this parental gap was painful to observe, and I chose to "remain above the battle" as I no longer lived at home. The climax to Dick O'Prey's drinking came on April 9, 1961. As a uniformed NYPD Sergeant, he got involved violently in an altercation with a "Peace" demonstrator outside of the United

Nations building. Dad was drunk, definitely in the wrong and subsequently suspended with forfeiture of three months' pay. Providentially, he managed to keep his job and through the intervention of the Police Chaplain, Monsignor Dunne and Alcoholics Anonymous, achieved seven years of total sobriety. Driven by grief over my mother's death on March 4, 1968, he tragically reopened the bottle and subsequently died on February 6, 1969. I reflect today, with supreme irony, how I entertained the resolution to never repeat this failure in my own Air Force career, only to ultimately discover on June 12, 1983, that my denial mechanism had led me into the same trap. Retrospect always trumps foresight! My ego told me that I was too intelligent to repeat my father's mistake and had to learn the hard way, that alcoholism is cunning, baffling, powerful and patient!

Saturday morning, June 30, 1962, dawned brilliant, cloudless, and warm. I had spent my "last night of freedom" at my parents' home, 358 Wadsworth Avenue, and enjoyed jostling and joking with my brother, Ray, the Best Man in the Wedding Party. Jack Whiteside and Buzzy Ronan served as Ushers or Groomsmen. Other members of the Bridal Party, Maid of Honor, Kathleen McAdam, and bridesmaids Pat Reynolds and Jean Hickey arrived on time at 10:00 a.m. My cousin, Joseph Clancy, and Evelyn's younger brother Edward served the Nuptial Mass celebrated by Father John McEnroe at Our Lady Queen of Martyrs Church. After the obligatory photos were taken, Evelyn and I were driven to the RSHM Convent on Isham Street where we visited Evelyn's sister, Mary Joan. As a professed religious person in 1962, her convent rules prohibited attendance at weddings. Our wedding reception was a joyous and memorable event hosted by the O'Dwyer family at the Birchbrook Inn in Westchester County. We hosted about 125 guests at a dinner and provided setups, rye, scotch, soda, and ginger ale, at each of the ten tables. People were generally well behaved and Jackie Roache's Irish Orchestra, a five-piece band provided a lively and pleasant selection of American and Irish music. Audience participation was enhanced by Lil Damann's rendition of *On Top of Old Smokey*; John O'Dwyer's singing of *Sean South of Garryowen* as well as Uncle Jim Browne's soulful and moving *Boulavogue* or the *Boys of Wexford*.

The only regrettable part of the great day was missing the party after the reception at O'Dwyer's. Calling from our hotel room at Idlewild Airport, we both listened to the merriment. As it was, I got involved depositing wedding checks and our honeymoon commenced. We boarded an Eastern Airlines flight to Nassau the next morning and enjoyed a week at the Montagu Beach Hotel, a luxury site with 30 or 40 fellow honeymooners with whom to share the social events. e.g., a Limbo Contest. Upon our return to NYC, we enjoyed the hospitality of the O'Dwyers and packed up our few possessions for the trip to our new home in Mount Holly, New

Jersey. Although only 80 miles away, the impact of Evelyn's leaving hit her mother emotionally as she began to weep as we said goodbye.

Our newlywed rental residence was 210 Robin Lane, Mt. Holly, New Jersey. I had repainted the bedroom and cleaned up a bit, but Evelyn made the place truly presentable. Our newly purchased bedroom furniture set with its "wormy chestnut" from the blight of 1919 and other furniture didn't amount to a lot. Yet, when it came to socializing with the movers when on-base housing became available in November, Evelyn was appalled at the lack of packing progress achieved while she was off teaching at Northern Burlington High School. As my father would have felt, the movers would enjoy a drink or two; they did but Evelyn definitely did not!

By the Spring of 1962, I had upgraded to combat-ready status and was thereby eligible to pull alert duty, initially at McGuire AFB and later "reflex" status at E. H. Harmon Air Base in Newfoundland. Our crew consisted of Captain Bob Andrews, Aircraft Commander, Lieutenant Paul J. Reinman, Copilot, Tech Sergeant Willy Williamson, Flight Engineer, and Tech Sergeant Mike Skierkowitz, Boom Operator. As a crew we were required to take leave at the same time and the absence of more than one primary crew member would invalidate our combat-ready status. Bob Andrews was a clean-living teetotaler whose idea of a crew party was to gather at his home, drink iced tea and make ice cream by churning a machine! Paul was moderate in all his habits and together we enrolled in many correspondence courses the Air Force offered at the time, e.g., German I and II as well as background courses in the Intelligence career field and Squadron Officers' School. Willy and Larry Hurley, Mike's replacement as boom operator, enjoyed a stiff drink or two and I was pleased to provide them at our home after the ice cream party. We more than made up for the libations we had missed at the ice cream soiree. The Summer of 1962 brought beach trips to Manasquan and Spring Lake and closer friendships with Bob and Nancy Matus, Paul and Nancy Reinman, and Al and Pola Romig.

These carefree days soon passed into the "Missiles of October" where SAC went to a wartime alert posture, and we were prepared to blow Cuba off the face of the earth. With 26 aircraft and 36 aircrews, we crowded head to toe in the alert facility (Mole Hole) when one astute crew member observed that 10 crews were superfluous, and the alert schedule could be adjusted. Accordingly with some scheduled time off, Ev and I exploited this opportunity by hosting a Halloween Party where five of eight couples came dressed as Fidel Castro! In my 28-year Air Force Career, this was the closest our country came to nuclear war, and I can now express my gratitude that it never came to pass.

In January 1963, the 305th was scheduled for a three-month rotational tour at Lajes Field in the Azores. The entire squadron of

500 deployed and the trip across the Atlantic was a fascinating and valuable learning experience for me; Loran, Celestial, Pressure Pattern and Radar were essential over water aids and totally unlike our training missions across New York State or down the Allegheny Mountains. Captain Carmine Parella was a patient, experienced Instructor Navigator and subsequently a good friend and tour guide in Madrid. Deploying 500 crew members and 26 airplanes to a mid-Atlantic Island was just phase one of a three-month adventure. Our mission was to rendezvous and refuel B-47 bombers redeploying to the U.S. from Europe. The KC-97 could not safely land given a cross wind component of 25 knots or greater. Lajes Field was notorious for winds increasingly out-of-bounds and our alternate airfields were Santa Maria in the Azores or 600 miles away at Torrejon Air Base north of Madrid, Spain. Our Squadron operated a weekly incentive flight to Brize-Norton RAF Station in the U.K. and enjoyed long weekends in London. It was most ironic to visit Speakers' Corner in Hyde Park to listen to the "Ban the Bomb" speeches of Bertrand Russell and observe B-47 Crew members in civilian attire wearing peace emblems on their jackets during their weekend off alert from our SAC bases in the U.K. In addition to England, we had alert commitments at Moron, Zaragoza, and Torrejon in Spain as well as Ben Guirre, Nouasseur, and Sidi Slimane in Morocco. I managed a week at Sidi Slimane, Torrejon, and an R&R on St. Patrick's Day at Palma Majorca.

Social life in the Azores consisted mainly of flying missions and partying at the Officers' Club Stag Bar. At 25 cents each, drinks were cheap and, in time, some of our older squadron members introduced me to the trick of blowing flame. This was accomplished by squirting lighter fluid into one's lower lip and blowing it out over an open cigarette lighter flame. On my very first attempt, Major General Eugene LeBailey, Commander, U.S. Forces, Azores, walked into the bar, caught my act, and proclaimed that I was the culprit who had been terrorizing his club over the past few weeks! After a non-stop chewing out, we made it back to the BOQ where the word of the incident spread like wildfire. The next morning, we found ourselves standing in braces before our Squadron Commander, Colonel Roy Broyles, and being warned in unmistakable terms that any repetition of this conduct would bring far more serious consequences. Back at McGuire, Evelyn heard about the incident within a few hours of its occurrence. The next day, a redeploying B-47 crew stated they would take their briefed offload of fuel but wanted to make the last three thousand pounds lighter fluid! In my saner moments, aided by a bottle of Rose Mateus, I kept up an almost daily correspondence with Evelyn, was delighted at her reciprocation, and returned home to her when the deployment ended in March.

The 305th began a new alert commitment, this time to Goose Bay, Labrador, a colder version of Harmon AFB in

Newfoundland. November 1963 brought with it the tragedy of John F. Kennedy's assassination. Evelyn was teaching at Northern Burlington High School, and I was scheduled for a refueling mission the evening of November 22. On our flight to the refueling area over the Alleghenies, we monitored the radio calls of Air Force One in the traffic pattern at Andrews AFB with the bereaved Jackie, LBJ, and the remains of JFK. Evelyn and I spent the weekend in New York as Jeanne Hickey married Jim Shevlin on Saturday and we witnessed Jack Ruby shoot Lee Harvey Oswald on TV on Sunday. My brother-in-law, John O'Dwyer, felt obliged to travel to Washington, D.C. for the funeral which we watched along with millions of other bereaved Americans.

1964 brought the rumor followed by the news that the 305th would be disbanded later that year. Other than the personal friendships acquired, no copious tears were shed as few of the field and company-grade officers were experiencing rapid career progression. The outlook for most was to continue the tanker mission in the more modern and more rapid jet tanker, the KC 135. Evelyn and I flew to San Juan, Puerto Rico in April for a week's vacation. In the fullness of our youth and exuberance we toured the Bacardi Distillery and sipped more than our share of frozen daiquiris at their spacious hospitality center. We rented a car, toured the El Yunque Rain Forest and sampled more Mai Tais at the Ramey AFB Officers' Club eighty miles to the west. We managed to drive back to San Juan, somewhat inebriated, through torrents of tropical rain. Thank you, Lord, for your Protective Hand during those carefree and careless days of yesteryear! An additional highlight of my week was being hosted for lunch by a U.S. Coast Guard skipper aboard his cutter in San Juan.

In June 1966, I was privileged to serve as best man at Buzzy Ronan's wedding to Roberta Sabatini (RIP). Fortified by a cocktail hour of martinis at the New York Athletic Club, my ASB cronies and I "wiped out" Frank Goodman, got thrown out of the planned rehearsal dinner restaurant in Yorkville, and substituted a traditional, heavy drinking stag party. I assured Mrs. Ronan the next morning that her son was safe at the home of his prospective in-laws. She responded to the effect that she was "mortified" that Buzzy would do this. Over time, she recovered as did Jack Whiteside from being "rolled" on the subway home by an opportunistic Black thief. The wedding went off, however, without a hitch. It was perhaps providential that SAC alert duties prevented me from performing similar rites at the weddings of Jack Whiteside (RIP), Al Diaz and Mike McAdam (RIP)!

One of the recurring missions flown in 1964 was the delivery of our KC-97s to the "Boneyard" at Davis-Monthan AFB in Tucson, Arizona. With thousands of other obsolete aircraft, fighters, bombers, transports, tankers, etc., from all the armed services, these planes were placed into long-term storage aided by the constant dryness of the desert climate. During one of these missions, our crew was introduced to Mr. Dean Burch, at the time the Chairman of the Republican National Committee. The locale for this privileged meeting was Pinnacle Pete's Restaurant, an establishment where wearing a tie would normally result in having it cut in two by one of the attending pretty waitresses. At any rate, following my own instincts and acknowledged conservative bias, I had voted for Richard Nixon in 1960 and would bestow my ballot on Barry Goldwater in 1964.

Social life went on merrily at McGuire AFB with young officers and their pretty spouses. Hardly a week went by without a party at one place or another. Dick and Jackie Kato celebrated the arrival of the Beatles with a memorable party at their home. The Officers' Club, the Cherry Hill Mall or Country Lakes, Brown's Mills were often party destinations. In this post Cuban Missile Crisis time, it amounted to a sigh of relief and legitimate pride in the role we had played as SAC combat crew members; SAC's motto, "Peace is our Profession," somewhat ironically decaled on a B-52, Minuteman Missile or B-47, nevertheless signified that our strength had truly prevented WW III. During our frequent visits to NYC, Evelyn and I enjoyed Broadway plays, courtesy of the USO, dining at Mama Leones' in the Theatre District, riding a stagecoach down Broadway with Bob and Nancy Matus, and enjoying Camelot with Ev's sister, Kathleen. One might call these the halcyon days of yesteryear, no tragedies, and all pleasant, enduring memories. Our biggest problem then was how to share the holidays equitably with our two families. This always worked out for the best. The love and understanding lavished upon us by both our families were exemplary. While I preferred my mother-in-law's cooking, my mom saw to it that I was supplied with boxty, or potato pancakes delivered personally by Jack Whiteside to us at McGuire AFB. The only discordant note was sounded by my grandmother, Liz, who asserted loudly that the only reason that Evelyn and Pat Kennedy, my brother Ray's wife, were going to Marymount was to "catch a husband." As I continued to be grandma's favored grandson, this statement was almost as predictable as the praise she gave me for my get-well card while my brother Ray's portage of her heavy oxygen bottles up four flights of stairs was hardly recognized! At the time, grandma was prone to fomenting arguments with my parents, threatening, and fulfilling a promise to pack up and live with the Clancys in Long Beach. In time, she would recover from her "huff" and return to our home at 358 Wadsworth Avenue. My father could read her like a book having lived with her his entire life. My mother attributed her own hypertension or high blood pressure to grandma's antics. Nevertheless, I believe a strong bond of love and affection existed between the three of them, difficult to accept one another at times but always amenable to reconciliation.

In early 1965, the 305th Air Refueling Squadron was

officially disbanded, and I received orders assigning me to the 384th
ARS at Westover AFB in Chicopee Falls, Massachusetts. I was able
to obtain a thirty-day leave or delay enroute. Ev and I flew space-
available (free) from McGuire to Frankfurt, Germany where we
rented a car with a young Marine couple and drove down to Munich
for Fasching, the German pre-Lenten celebration. Driving through
the Alps foothills, each town and village presented children dressed
in cowboy and Indian costumes as if it were Halloween. We
witnessed bakers and tradesmen marching in a big, colorful parade
with numerous brass bands and the populace enjoying their steins
of beer. We were told that during Fasching, German judges refused
to hear any court cases involving adultery, basically, a Teutonic
version of the Latin Mardi Gras. Retiring to the fabled Hofbrau
Haus, we joined in the singing and arms-linking celebrations. I
engaged in a conversation with an older gentleman and his frau. He
asked Evelyn what she would like; Evelyn responded, "Ein Bier
Stein." He was back within minutes with a souvenir Bier Stein Pin!
I was able to get along reasonably well with my college German,
and we found the Germans we met to be most friendly and
welcoming with an uncanny fluency in English.

After touring the impressive Technical Museum in Munich,
we succeeded in catching a space-available hop to Evreux Airfield
in France, a short train ride from Paris. We toured Paris on foot for
the next few days taking many 35mm slides with my Argus C-3 and

savoring the many sights of that beautiful, historic, and romantic city. We stayed at the Hotel DeLittre, a military contract hotel in central Paris, a block from the Champs d'Elysee. Our old picture albums provide ample evidence of our visit, the locales, and our mutual enjoyment of just being fascinated tourists.

The "Boat Train" brought us from Paris to Dover and on to London. In addition to sightseeing, London brought a reunion with my cousin, Jack Duggan, my Uncle Bernie's son who was four years old when we visited Mayo in 1948, seventeen years previously. Jack and his German girlfriend, Ursula, were good company for dinner at the Columbia Club on Baychester Road.

On what is probably our most unforgettable water journey, the overnight ferry from Fishguard, Wales to Cobh, County Cork, Ireland remains primary. Having experienced seasickness as a lad of ten sailing on the Mauritania from NYC in May 1948, I had no inclination to repeat the experience. I went to the bar on deck and found that drinking Guinness and swapping stories with the "boyos" forestalled any illness or nausea. Evelyn was not so fortunate. She remained in our cabin all evening, chronically seasick. We were later informed that the Irish Sea in that area is one of the roughest bodies of water in the world. She still blanches at the thought of that particular voyage.

We arrived in Cobh on March 10, 1965, in bright, comfortable sunshine, rented our Morris Minor automobile and proceeded north to Limerick to visit Evelyn's relatives. What a delightful coincidence it was to spot Evelyn's Uncle Jack Hayes riding his bicycle and ask directions to his home. Evelyn recognized him immediately and we subsequently enjoyed his and his wife's, Aunt Moll, warm hospitality. As a remarkable incidence of Irish hospitality, we were given their main bedroom and showed us where the restroom facility was located in the backyard. We naively inquired why they wouldn't have a toilet in the house. We were told: "We wouldn't have the dirty thing in the house, and it was used mainly by visiting Yanks in the summertime!" The warmth of their hospitality was reflected in other members of the Hayes family, Aunt Molly, Ned Callahan in Ardpatrick, and in Jack O'Dwyer's fewer relations in Kilfinane.

On March 12, it was time to head north to Mayo and enjoy the privilege of a reunion with my grandfather, John Duggan, his brother, Bernie Mor, and my Uncles Anthony, Bernie, and Jack and Aunt Madeline Boyd, her young family and husband, Alec. To make our reception even more cordial, I provided two bottles of Jim Beam Bourbon which were greatly appreciated and quickly consumed. In response, I was trusted sufficiently to partake of a drop of poteen, the illegal hooch distilled from potatoes and heather.

Witnessing Evelyn's discomfort, Aunt Baby (Maude) Duggan offered to show her the "facilities." Leading her out to the barn, she slapped a cow on the rump and indicated a corner of the cattle stall! We occupied the same bedroom that my brothers and I used in 1948. Things hadn't changed much; water was still drawn from the well, and the hob and turf fire still warmed "delicate" chickens. The only real change was the addition of a singular light bulb, installed a week before our arrival. Once again, the warmth, genuine sincerity and closeness of family ties superseded any discomfort at the disparity between Irish and American living conditions. Mayo and Limerick remained "must stop" locations for subsequent visits in years to come, with the addition in future trips to my father's family in County Down. Evelyn and I felt privileged to enjoy the love and closeness of our Irish relatives and family.

We drove back to Dublin and flew to London to celebrate St Patrick's Day since in Ireland it was primarily a parade and a religious holiday. We located my Uncle Seamus' modest apartment where he and his wife Mary kept a bathtub still for the distillation of poteen! The youngest of the Duggan brothers, Seumas evaded British taxes by claiming Irish citizenship, was a scab (non-union) plasterer by trade, who owed no taxes to Ireland either as his income and residence was in England! An intriguing study in either event, when he passed on years afterward, his mass card bore his photo with a cigarette dangling from his lips.

In London, the theater was a "must" and with the recommendation of Jackie and Dick Kato, good friends from

McGuire AFB, we went to see "Our Man Creighton." We enjoyed a double treat in going backstage to meet David Kernan, one of the actors who was also a cast member in the contemporary hit movie "Zulu."

The flexibility of youth was truly amazing when, at Evelyn's Uncle Davy's invitation, we left London for Merthyr-Tydfil, Wales on March 19. We had met Evelyn's cousin John Hayes in New York City. John, a retired Royal Navy person, possessed a booming singing voice, a ready wit, and a contagious sense of humor. Requested by his father to wallpaper the guest room for Evelyn's sister Michaeline's visit, John made a modest attempt. However, after a few swigs of whiskey, he proclaimed that "he now knew how Hitler went mad!"

The entire Hayes family, Sheila, John Vincent, Danny, Paddy Goggin, Philip, Eileen and others, treated us like visiting royalty. The highlight occurred when we visited the Merthyr-Tydfil Labor Club for an evening of vaudeville talent imported from London which included a menacing, vociferous "bouncer." With the best of intentions at the bar, I proposed a toast to the late Winston Churchill. This was greeted by a profound but deafening silence. John let me know that the Welsh had yet to forgive Churchill for turning the troops out on the coal mining strikers. Well-oiled by whiskey and ale, John and I were negotiating the steep stairway on the way out. We tripped, tumbled down together, and discovered the next morning that John had fractured a rib. The Welsh hospitality of the Hayes family was every bit as close, memorable, and sincere as that experienced in Ireland.

Driving back to London on March 22, we went sightseeing and touring for our remaining four days. London is a fascinating city which we resolved to visit in the future. Evelyn's records show that we spent a total of approximately $1000.00 touring from February 23 to March 26, 1965, a bargain definitely, but the memories are priceless. A Charter airfare of $200 brought us back to New York City without incident on Friday, March 26, 1965.

Entering a new phase of my Air Force career at Westover AFB, Massachusetts in April 1965, it is helpful and perhaps illuminating from the perspective of full background disclosure, to introduce some of the characteristics of the Air Force's career progression program. Hand in glove with these, however, is acknowledgement of my incredible failure to deal with what others might well regard as a "drinking problem." Alcohol was part and parcel of the Irish American social and cultural scene in New York City. This was strongly reinforced by the collegiate atmosphere at Manhattan College and, for the most part, endorsed by the active social encouragement of all the military services. While my father had been obliged to get sober by the NYPD in 1962, my "intelligence" would spare me from falling into any similar fate. For years, however, I entertained the fear that someday, somehow, I too would share a similar humiliation. For the time being, having a few drinks was an affirmation of a proud Irish American culture, a God-given right widely celebrated by The Clancy Brothers and Wolfe Tone ballads popular at the time. It is my intent to include future incidents where my naivete and denial mechanisms eroded my finest professional accomplishments and career plans, bringing humiliation to myself and deep disappointment, if not heartbreak, to my beloved spouse, Evelyn. It is with a profound sense of gratitude to her and to sobriety that I can look back on these incidents in calm, positive reflection rather than the resentment with which I regarded them at the time.

Career management or the promotion system for officers in the Air Force was based upon an "up or out" policy. As a regular Air Force Officer, I had a 70% promotion opportunity over a four-year time span to be promoted to Major or Lt. Colonel. The system, however, was not without its anomalies; my good friend, Dick Kato from McGuire AFB, received his Silver Star for heroism at relieving Khe Sanh and his second pass over to Major within the same week! The effectiveness reports themselves appeared very logical on the surface with numbers 1 through 9 across the top with 9 being highest and 1 through 4 on the bottom indicating the timing of the promotion. The problem came when it was realized that in a hierarchical, competitive system, there had to be failures. Ultimately, inflation ran the numbers and if everyone was outstanding, who among them were the true leaders? Sponsorship, a general officer's endorsement, and level of assignment, Squadron/Wing/Numbered Air Force/Headquarters, became critical factors. It was said and widely believed that promotion Boards were looking for reasons to pass people over as this made their work far easier than distinguishing top performers. There were additional factors, including the rater's command of the English language, and the tendency of the "Ring Knockers" or service academy graduates to support their fellow alumni, etc.

I was entering the mid-phase of my career and was doing all in my power to be "competitive" in this process. As a Combat Crew Navigator, I had accumulated 2000 hours of flying time and the equivalent of 20 college hours from correspondence courses, Intelligence Career Courses, German, Squadron Officers' School, and Command and Staff were a few of these subjects. Yet, the numbers from performance reports received while at McGuire AFB were mediocre by comparison with those at a similar squadron at Westover, the 384th ARS. After moving into on-base quarters at Westover, I was privileged and delighted to meet my new aircraft commander, Captain Ned Duffield, an up-front practitioner of "lead by example" and a man of flawless integrity. I did think it a bit odd that he required all five of us to wear ironed flight suits, but, then again, each of us has his own quirks! We did achieve recognition as crew of the month for July 1965 and shortly thereafter were informed that the 384th would be deactivated with the phase out of the B-47 weapons system and all crew members would be reassigned. Since I had less than a year on station, I was ineligible for reassignment and would remain at Westover assigned to Base Flight. A non-entity job, I sought an assignment to Squadron Officer's School, but this was disapproved by the Personnel Gurus, who controlled such matters. As an alternative, I worked my way into the 99th Bomb Wing, Targets Division, acquiring increased Top Secret Code Word clearances and entry into a secondary career field in Intelligence. Duties involved maintaining SIOP mission materials, given an Emergency War Order from SAC. On the less serious side, the entire unit would adjourn each Friday afternoon for fried clams in Chicopee Falls, the unofficial Polish capital of the United States. I enjoyed a positive and productive relationship with my supervisor, Major Don Fagerstrom, a B-52 Electronic Warfare Officer, and Lt. Colonel Bob Ahlborn, who would introduce me to the Battle Staff duties in PAACS.

In May 1966, I was assigned to the Eighth Air Force Command Crew as Navigator on a VC-97, a luxury Aircraft built especially for Governor Tom Dewey, who ran for president in 1944. Our mission was to fly the Eighth Air Force IG Team as well as distinguished civilian VIPs to various U.S. Air Force installations on orientation/goodwill visits. These trips included Peterson Field,

Colorado, Homestead, Florida and Ramey AFB, Puerto Rico. This "plum" assignment terminated in May 1967 when I was assigned as a Target Planner on the Eighth Air Force Post Attack Command and Control System (PAACS). Our aircraft, an air-refueling capable EC-135 was the eastern link of Looking Glass, SAC's constantly airborne flying command post. Our duties involved hard alert and prolonged 18-hour training missions, generally across New York State. The communications capability was such that we could establish an airborne telephone link with our wives at home while cruising or orbiting at 35,000 feet.

As a master's degree was a definite career enhancement, if not a tacit requirement, I enrolled in the new on-base Master of Business Administration Program, sponsored by Western New England College in September 1967. One could attend classes while on alert and, among other subjects, the program was my introduction to computers, behavioral science, and statistics. The course required 36 Masters Level Courses but no thesis. Accounting, Advanced Math, Personnel and Financial Management and Linear Programming were new, fascinating, and useful disciplines to acquire. Most providentially, I was able to complete the course requirements and obtain my MBA just prior to my departure for Saigon in June 1969.

At the risk of jumping too far ahead, this is probably as good a time as any to introduce the "darker" and less commendable developments of the late sixties. In both the Command Crew Assignment and PACCs assignments, my drinking earned me less competitive ratings than what I had hoped for on performance reports. Lt. Colonel John Harris just "could not bring himself" to give me the very top rating due to my drinking off-duty. Lt. Colonel John Cowart, my supervisor on PACCS, gave me a blunt, honest, and direct answer when I queried him on my rating: "Because I had to replace you on alert when you got drunk, fell and broke your ankle." The ultimate effect of both ratings was a first time Passover to Major while enroute to Vietnam in June 1969. While I resented and was stung by both ratings, neither caused me to reflect seriously on the root cause of the problem, my own drinking and refusal to moderate or abandon the habit.

We did form new and enduring friendships at Westover. The New England restaurants, the Yankee Pedlar, etc., were new dining experiences and the fall foliage was magnificent. Ned and Ruth Duffield went on to a C-130 assignment in Tennessee; Lt. Neal Monette, our co-pilot, was killed in action flying his FAC mission in Vietnam. Joe and Inez McElroy share a California friendship with us and the Duffields, which is sustained by an annual lunch in nearby Riverside, CA.

I believe it was early December 1965 when Evelyn announced she was "expecting" the coming August. My ego-driven, unwarranted, and inconsiderate message throughout her pregnancy was: "You had better have a boy; otherwise float the infant down the Connecticut River!" Having the privilege and good fortune to administer gas and to witness the delivery at the Westover Base Hospital, I cringe at the memory of every blaming pair of eyes looking at me while Evelyn, the brand-new mother, cried out: "But he wanted a boy!" Bringing our beautiful and healthy baby girl, Kathleen Maura, home a few days later, we discovered her welcomed by a big pink bunting on our house proclaiming: "Welcome Home Moses O'Prey!" Kathleen's Christening in mid-August was a major social event for both family and friends. It took place at both a buffet at the Officers' Club and a backyard lawn party. These were memorable days indeed; Evelyn did most of the work with our new daughter, ably assisted by both grandmas and her sister, Kathleen. I continued to do most of the celebrating with the dawning realization of how inappropriate my expectations for a male heir had been. Having taken some baby care classes with Evelyn, I found myself several months later giving Kathy a bath in ice water to keep her fever down. Thank God she survived my short-term care! Having a baby around the house was a new experience for both of us, but our neighbors, Tom and Pat Mooney, Don and Eileen Murphy, Stu and Bobbi Coleton, Jack and Judy Sutcliffe, and Dave and Bernice Cohen, were all new parents too.

Christmas 1966 was a joyous occasion in Cranford, New Jersey, where we joined Mike and Kathleen McAdam and their new daughter, Mary Jo, to celebrate their first holiday together. 35 mm slides of both young ladies on a rug in the living room remain vivid in my fondest memories as do both healthy infants fitted together into the seat of a commissary shopping cart at McGuire AFB. Later, Evelyn and I were in Holyoke, Massachusetts for a St Patrick's Day Parade and I retain a photo taken with my Argus C-3 Camera of Ted and Joan Kennedy, a glamorous young couple there for the occasion.

Memories of the summer of 1967 remain strong, mainly of the vacation trip we took through New England with Jack and Ellen O'Dwyer, Ev's kid sister, Joan, and our soon-to-be one-year-old, Kathleen. Jack's lungs were failing as we climbed up the Flume at Franconia Notch in New Hampshire. Lake Winnipesaukee was easier on all of us as we had a lakeside cabin. We visited the playground and beach at Bar Harbor Maine and Cape Cod, Massachusetts. Baby Kathy's lobster dinner debut was a classic with parts, claws, sauces, and bibs tossed indiscriminately in all directions.

In the Fall of 1967, I joined the Knights of Columbus in Fairview, Massachusetts and was proud to have my father in attendance at the Third-Degree Rites. We began to realize that my mother's blood pressure, hypertension and uremia problems were increasing. Under constant medication for one problem or the other, she tired easily and became lethargic in movement. She and

Dad continued to take short automobile trips and his sobriety was an asset to both of them. When we visited both families of grandparents in December 1967, Jack O'Dwyer and Kitty O'Prey's failing health was obvious and of concern to all.

The cycle of birth, death, hope, and despair spun around both of our families for the next two years. Jack O'Dwyer's exploratory lung surgery at Jewish Memorial Hospital confirmed a case of inoperable lung cancer. Bedridden towards the end, even his tracheotomy forestalled his passing away at home on October 18, 1968. Jack was waked at Finan's Funeral Home on Sherman Avenue and buried at Gate of Heaven Cemetery in Westchester County, New York. As his son-in-law, Jack treated me fairly and, in retrospect, was most tolerant of my penchant for Irish Rebel Songs. As a young man, Jack had served as Sergeant Major in the Irish Free State Army during the Irish civil war in the Twenties.

My mother was in and out of Columbia Presbyterian Hospital several times in the Fall of 1967 for her hypertension and uremia conditions. Believing that dad could not emotionally confront her medical situation, I took it upon myself to let her know her illness was fatal. This was the closest and most loving conversation that I had with her in my life. Her initial reaction was not of anguish, but a deep concern for the effect on my poor father and whether he could handle the situation of being a widower. She expressed her thankfulness that God had allowed her to witness the growth of her three sons into healthy adulthood. The very next day, mom described me as the "amadan" who told her she would die; a statement of hers, not in rancor, but in cheerful denial of her medical prognosis.

Christmas 1967 was spent visiting both families and enjoying the rural perspective of my parents' recently purchased home in Piermont, New York. My dad had a sign made stating in Gaelic "Rath na Rogue" (Home of Kings). The three-hour drive back to Westover in our 1965 Pontiac LeMans convertible was uneventful. Shortly thereafter, the New Year of 1968 brought the blessed and safe arrival of our second daughter, Elizabeth Ellen, in the early hours of February 13, 1968. My sister-in-law, Kathleen McAdam, did a fantastic job, taking the call from the hospital and letting us know that mother and daughter were well and would see us during regular visiting hours in the morning. With extreme pride, we brought Baby Liz home a few days later and let her sister, Kathy, cradle her in her arms. I was silently grateful for her safe delivery and for the fact that this time out, I kept my big mouth shut regarding boy or girl preferences.

New England is notorious for cold winters. Accordingly, I was delighted to be at McCoy AFB in Orlando, Florida on March 4, 1968. Evelyn contacted me at the BOQ with the sad, but not unexpected, news of my mother's death that evening. I called my father and found that his grief was overwhelming, and he had already taken solace in a whiskey bottle unopened for the past seven years. After flying home commercially, Evelyn had the bags packed and we were consoled greatly by Grandma O'Dwyer as we stayed with her, and she cheerfully babysat Kathy and Liz. I managed to be the first family member to arrive at Connor's Funeral Home for my mother's wake. The mortician politely asked how my mom looked. My terse response was to the effect that I had not seen her dead before. Shortly thereafter, the arrival of my father, grandmother and brothers etched an indelible memory of the grief on their faces. Three days later, mom was laid to eternal rest at Calvary Cemetery in Queens, New York, atop her infant son, my brother John, and her long-buried father-in-law, Patrick O'Prey, who died in August 1931.

All guests were invited back to dad's home where the liberal dispensation of alcohol toasted mom's memory and where I and my brother Ray imbibed too freely. With pangs of weltschmerz, I insisted on playing "A Mother's Love Is a Blessing," an appropriate, but perhaps too maudlin, selection. Ray objected to the selection; I took the opportunity to express my disapproval of his furnishing liquor to Dad on their way to the cemetery. Today, I am apologetic and grateful to my brother, Richie, for stepping in between us and preventing a potential drunken brawl between Ray and myself. I vaguely remember hugging each other in tears of previously unexpressed sorrow for the loss of our mother. Dad complained all night of his inability to pee. Richie took him to the hospital early the next morning where he was catheterized and underwent prostate removal. Once again, being three hours away by automobile, Richie and Ray were of unique benefit to the family than I could be throughout this entire period.

Our infant daughter, Elizabeth Ellen, named for her great grandmother, Elizabeth Lennon O'Prey, was quietly baptized at Our Lady Queen of Martyrs Church on Arden Street. Returning to Westover AFB and a new job in PAACS at Eighth Air Force, we settled down with Kathleen and Liz as I resumed alert duties and my MBA studies. Evelyn continued to perform a magnificent role as a new mother. In the Summer of 1968, we vacationed with Evelyn's sister Joan at Cape Cod and enjoyed the drama of the Democratic Nominating Convention, held in Mayor Bill Daley's Chicago. Evelyn's brother-in-law, Mike McAdam, who had a medical history of heart trouble, experienced a heart attack in September and another fatal heart attack on November 29, 1968. This was a tragedy which affected Mike's widow, Kathleen McAdam, their numerous friends, neighbors and the close O'Dwyer family. It is most poignant to note that her young children, Mary Jo and Michael, were roughly of the same age as our Kathy and Liz. Evelyn provided comfort and assistance to her bereaved sister. However, the pain and anguish of losing a young father at 35 years of age was pervasive and remains to this day. Our family connection became even closer as we celebrated a subdued Thanksgiving and Christmas holiday in each other's company.

My father meanwhile found himself quite incapable of caring for my grandmother. She had remarked to me at my mother's wake that it was she who belonged in the casket, not my 59-year-old mother! Always in all matters highly opinionated, Grandma Lizzy was never reluctant to express her views. Her modus operandi was to get in an argument with her son, Dick O'Prey, and depart in a huff to her daughter Ellen Clancy's home in Long Beach, Long Island. On one, in retrospect, humorous occasion, believing she was on her death bed at Clancy's, she called Evelyn into her room and apologized for all the nasty things she had ever said about her! Ultimately, my father faced the reality that, in the absence of my mother, he was incapable of providing proper care for his mother. Most reluctantly, he had her placed in a full-care facility in Pomona, New York. A week or so after this event, we stopped by to see her and I, for one, was shocked at her appearance. Physically restrained, pale and teeth chattering, she had nothing but criticism for the facility, the staff and my father for making the terrible decision to have her institutionalized. They had been together all his life; how could he ever do this! On the positive side, I took great pride in presenting her great granddaughter, Liz, her namesake. Making polite inquiries with the staff, I was informed that Grandma was in the habit of roaming around the facility at all hours, ate little, and was a very uncooperative patient. I inquired whether there was a Catholic Chaplain on the premises and a priest appeared to hear her last confession. Moments later we left promising to return on Monday. My father was informed the next morning that Grandma had died peacefully in her sleep. If ever a person had earned "the grace of a happy death," eternal salvation, it was Elizabeth Lennon O'Prey. Her hardships and unshakeable Roman Catholic Faith have been a source of inspiration and emulation to me. She was waked, as my mother was, at Connor's Funeral Home, 207th Street and Broadway. Her remains rest above my mother's at Calvary Cemetery, Long Island.

A subdued and saddened Christmas in December 1968 was spent in Cranford, New Jersey with Kathleen, Mary Jo and Michael and the company of Sister Michaeline O'Dwyer. Returning to Westover with her, Evelyn recalls a "random act of kindness" whereby a motorist in the car ahead of us paid our toll on the Merritt Parkway in Connecticut. I got a good laugh at Michaeline's response when I offered to have her sample a martini at the Officers' Club. She responded to the effect of "thanks but make it weak."

My personal strong weakness for the drink took an adverse turn. When leaving a well-stocked bridal celebration, I slipped on the ice and sustained a broken right ankle. Assisted by Captain Pete McCullough, I made it home and checked in to the base hospital the next morning. True, the accident or injury could have happened sober or drunk, but the second condition prevailed when the slip occurred. Fortunately, the Doctor ruled it a "line of duty" injury. A thigh cast had me grounded from flying duties and alert for about six weeks; a reality which would impact substantially my forthcoming efficiency report.

Each of the family bereavements, while deeply sad, could not be described as a surprise since serious health issues were diagnosed and played out in each instance. This was not the case with the sudden passing of my father, Richard O'Prey, in the early afternoon of February 6, 1969. A delivery boy from the local liquor store was making his second stop of the day at my father's residence in Piermont and found Dad dead in his own living room. I remain indebted to my brother Richie in particular for being on the scene in a few hours and describing it as "not a pretty sight." It would take me another fourteen years and a timely intervention to realize just how deadly the disease of alcoholism is, particularly to people like me, who deny it most vehemently.

With my left ankle casted and Evelyn driving, we made it to O'Dwyer's' on Arden Street and, once again, to Connor's Funeral Home at 207th and Broadway. Dad was laid out in his New York Police Department Sergeant's uniform without a single strand of gray in his red hair. His numerous County Down friends and police co-workers spoke most highly of him and managed to travel through a blinding snowstorm to pay their respects. I made it a point to place an Irish Tricolor flag in his casket before it was officially closed, and dad made his final journey to Tir An Nog. He was given an "Inspector's Funeral" at Incarnation Church. Adverse weather and freezing ground delayed his internment at Calvary Cemetery for about ten days. Once more, Grandma O'Dwyer's hospitality and TLC got us through this sad situation.

One of the prime motivators for me to pursue a full military career was the excellent and free medical care available to members and their dependents. Our daughter Liz had been born with a minor defect, a hemangioma, growth or disfigurement of her right hand. The attending physician at Westover got her a consultation at Wilford Hall, the Air Force's top hospital facility in the country. Evelyn was designated Medical Attendant and I non-medical attendant, which enabled both of us to accompany Liz on her round-trip medivac flight to Texas in February 1969. One year old at the time, she was an excellent patient. Evelyn and I enjoyed an excellent reunion with Bob and Nancy Matus, our closest Air Force friends from McGuire AFB and the 305th. The physician's recommendation for Liz was to defer surgery for another ten years and operate at that time. This was accomplished successfully in good time, but the reassurance that my family would be fully cared for while I was in Vietnam was probably the primary morale factor I brought with me.

Returning to Westover, a not unexpected assignment to Vietnam awaited me. The assignment was to the 1131st Special Activities Squadron, in Saigon, RVN for the standard one-year, unaccompanied tour. At the ten-year point in my Air Force career, the focus of SAC had turned from the hard alert and readiness mission to prevail in a nuclear conflict, to the employment of the B-52 weapons system, reconfigured with "iron bombs" as airborne artillery. The bomber portion of this program received the name "Arc Light," while its necessary tanker component was known as the "Young Tiger" program. A single B-52 would be loaded with 100,000 pounds of ordinance from bases in Guam, Okinawa, and Thailand. Combat sorties were launched in formations of three to six bombers against targets mainly in South Vietnam. To my surprise, my assignment carried "duty and travel restrictions" which precluded flying for the entire one-year period of duty. Most of my contemporaries from SAC received flying assignments to KC-135 Tankers, C-130 transports or gunships, the AC-130 or AC-47 (Puff the Magic Dragon). Due to the Top-Secret clearances, I held at Westover, I could get killed but not captured!

This appeared to be a similar situation with my co-workers in PAACS; Captain Calvin Smith was going to Saigon; Captain Jack Wrabel to U-Tapao Royal Thai Air Base and Major Jerry Alley to Nakhon Phanom Air Base, Thailand, each of us to an intelligence billet. Knowing that a Southeast Asia assignment was inevitable, my reaction was to feel grateful that its timing had enabled me to be home for the previous year and a half to attend family funerals. In addition, I chose not to seek the delay of a medical profile due to my still healing but cast-free right ankle. For the same reason, I was privately relieved not to have a flying assignment as I hardly felt sufficiently fit to endure the rigors of attending Survival School at Stead AFB, Nevada or Jungle Survival at Clark AFB, Philippines. Win a few, lose a few; it all comes out in the wash!

March, April, and May of 1969 flew by rapidly. Evelyn had decided to spend the year I'd be gone near her sister Kathleen in Cranford, New Jersey. Our young children would be near each other, and Evelyn could help Kathleen through the loneliness and heartbreak of early widowhood. I managed to complete my MBA requirements by late May 1969 and helped my young family move into 19 Parkway Village, Cranford, New Jersey soon afterwards. I was delighted to see the facility was well-populated with new friends for Kathy and Liz as well as for Evelyn and myself. Captain John Post, USMC, and his wife Mary were particularly helpful as he was a recently returned JAG Officer from a one-year tour in Danang, RVN.

We were together with Kathy, Michael, and Mary Jo at the Jersey Shore when I called the Personnel Office at McGuire AFB and confirmed the fact that I had been passed over for Major. While not an absolute surprise, the hurt was deep, enduring, and painful.

However, having accepted a Regular Officer commission back in 1962, I would be entitled to five more promotion opportunities in the years to come. Somewhat consoling, but I had little or no control of the future but resolved to let the chips fall where they may. Vietnam presented a new opportunity to heal the "injustices" of the past. My views regarding the war itself were of unstinting support for our political and military objectives. I entertained an absolute contempt for those who chose to protest while their countrymen were being killed in combat. These views have been consistently right-wing but have not changed over the many years. The irony of my departure was that during the same week, President Nixon was announcing his program of "Vietnamization"!

The saddest day of my young life was June 24, 1969, when I held Kathy and Liz in my arms and kissed them and Evelyn a tearful good-bye at Newark Airport and boarded a flight to San Francisco and Travis AFB, California enroute to Saigon. Captain Kay Yingling and his wife hosted a mini 305th reunion at their on-base quarters with Don Vollette, Skip Fawcett, Jim Toland, and I enjoying the hospitality and swapping stories. Saigon was predictably hot, humid, and rainy upon our arrival. Catching up from jet lag, I enjoyed a full night's sleep at the in-processing facility at Ton Son Nhut Airbase. As a matter of fact, I managed to sleep entirely through a Viet Cong 122 mm rocket attack that very evening!

In-processing was routine; I was given an M-16, poncho, bedding, a supply of malaria pills and a BOQ assignment at the PAX BOQ as I reported to CICV, the Combined Intelligence Center, Viet-Nam. This was a low-level, hands-on cooperative venture with our ARVN allies which involved posting combat incidents, e.g., mortar attacks, terrorist activities and hostile engagements, on a map for subsequent analysis and targeting purposes. The Center itself, like MACV Headquarters, was located adjacent to Ton Son Nhut Air Base as was the Joint General Staff Headquarters of the ARVN. My quarters were about a mile from the base and my first roommate was a USMC combat veteran, John Clancy, pleasant company but reluctant to discuss his previous experience in I Corps along the DMZ. June was the wet monsoon season with daily drenching, the heaviest showers at 6:00 a.m. and 6:00 p.m., coinciding with the beginning and end of the duty day at either CICV or MACV!

Captain (Major Selectee) Calvin Smith, a good friend from PAACS at Westover, had preceded me by a few months and was assigned to J-2 Targets Division at MACV Headquarters. Cal was of key assistance in getting me assigned to that organization, a significantly higher-level assignment, with U.S. Army, Navy, and Air Force personnel only. Under the supervision of Lt. Colonel Charles (no middle initial) Hope, USAF, and the coaching of Captain David Jan Allen, U.S. Army, I soon qualified as an Arc

Light (B-52) Target briefer. Lt. Colonel Hope had given me a well-deserved, competitive rating on my effectiveness report at the end of September 1969. He was succeeded by Lt. Colonel Clay Blanton, U.S. Army, a seasoned and well-respected combat veteran, who, in turn, rated me high and competitive. He completed his tour in late February 1970. I made my chronic mistake of celebrating too freely at his accustomed farewell party. Equipped with a classic hangover, my speech sputtered and coughed and was an embarrassment to all present. My unconvincing apology was to the effect that I had a cold! My supervisor, Lt. Colonel Hal Bamford, USAF, another PAACS Officer from Westover, chose to have this regrettable, one-of-a-kind incident reflected in my June 1970 effectiveness report. Based upon his judgment and our personal friendship, our higher-level Director, Colonel James Provan, USAF, upgraded the offensive rating and in all probability rescued my Air Force career. Again, however, I take myself to task for wittingly or unwittingly letting alcohol exercise its proven devastating effects. I began privately to suspect fear might be a more appropriate verb, that I, in turn, like my father before me, would pay a heavy price for my failure to moderate my drinking habits.

As in so many other matters in life, hindsight is always perfect. During the one-year tour in Saigon, I did earn a Bronze Star and a Joint Service Commendation Medal as well as an Air Force Commendation Medal from Westover. Overall, I performed a credible job at MACV, holding down a two briefing, 24-hour shift every third day and evaluating target nominations on off days. In this process, we were most ably assisted by our NCOs, Master Sergeant Ed Schaeffer, Tech Sergeant Jim Nettles, and Tech Sergeant Lee Young. It's amazing, but indicative of our mutual respect and shared experience that Lee Young and I remain in touch via social media.

While I resided on the sixth floor of the Newport BOQ, most of my off-duty evenings were spent at BOQ 2, an air-conditioned Field Grade hotel where Major Cal Smith and Major Bob Rafferty, two colleagues from Targets Division resided. Drinks were a quarter each; floor shows with disco dancers were a weekly event. A poker game or crap game was available to those who chose to pass their time gambling, which was not my particular cup of tea. Captain David Jan Allen and his Vietnamese War Bride, "Maggie," introduced me to Vietnamese restaurants. My culinary tastes were fully satisfied by the Officers' Mess at BOQ 2 with full western entrees served by cute waitresses. Thanksgiving and Christmas meals were particularly nourishing since these were served along with card greetings from COMUS/MACV, General Creighton Abrams, himself. Even more appreciated was the full salami and cheese package which Joe and Helen Clancy had so thoughtfully sent me. On the home front, their gracious hospitality and TLC was deeply appreciated by Evelyn and our daughters during my long absence. She definitely bore the heavier responsibility in being the fantastic mother and caregiver to Kathy and Liz. Her letters and tapes were a tremendous morale booster to me throughout the entire year. Just to hear one of the girls I forget which one, say "Stupid Daddy!" was a prize and humorous event. One of the available benefits in the war zone was free mail and I remain most thankful to Evelyn for her liberal use of the privilege!

The decade of the Sixties came to its end with our country, despite the sacrifice of its soldiers, airmen and sailors stuck in the quagmire of Vietnam. The future would reveal that Ho Chi Minh's analysis was correct; the United States would ultimately lose patience and withdraw, leaving South Vietnam to its own fate. In my opinion, he was ably assisted in this purpose by the American Anti-War demonstrators at home.

One of the sadder recollections of this period was the death of Captain Carmine (Pappy) Parella, USAF. He was enroute to Taiwan when the C-130 he was on as a passenger crashed into a mountain in Taiwan. His widow, Jo, contacted Evelyn as she was the last mutual friend he had talked to at Travis AFB.

The Seventies would bring its own triumphs and tragedies. As 1969 receded into history, I looked forward to an R and R with Evelyn in Hawaii and a gratitude for her indispensable role as a mother on the home front. With six months to go, my "short time" calendar was filling in slowly but relentlessly. In 1973, the Arc Light

Program would ultimately bring Hanoi back to the peace talks in Paris. The 1969 holiday season in Saigon was characterized by GIs randomly firing their M-16s into the air to welcome the New Year of 1970 and the new decade it brought. The friendships made at MACV Headquarters, J-2 Arc light Division, would sustain us through the holiday in the absence of loved ones and family.

Those of us who served our one year in Vietnam kept the faith in our ultimate victory. However, ultimately the tragic waste of time, lives and technology was enormous. Politically it raised doubts among our friends as to whether they could remain close or trust our foreign policy. I do not, for an instant, regret my service there, either in the staff position at MACV Headquarters or on the subsequent 78 combat-support missions flown in the C-141 Starlifter transport. At the same time, I retain nothing but contempt for the American Left, the demonstrators, draft dodgers, spoiled college students and outright cowards who refused to serve or took refuge in Canada. Conversely, I retain a grudging, but reflective respect for our determined enemy, VC or NVA, whose determination never wavered and who kept their courage and faith in their nationalistic, if flawed cause.

Compared to an Army or Marines year in the bush, Saigon was a plush assignment with maids (mama sans) laundry service, free postage, first run movies and cheap drinks. The duty day ran from 7 a.m. to 7 p.m. but did provide an occasional day or afternoon of free time. One could visit food markets and street vendors who carried a range of U.S. goods from military shovels to Zippo lighters. One could also visit the Catholic Cathedral or any one of the more numerous and exotic Buddhist temples. Saigon was a city at war and, as such, was choked with the exhaust from Army trucks and the motorized bikes the Vietnamese rode called cyclos. Like all courses of its kind, I found the Circle Sportif Golf Course most challenging as far as it had mine-warning signs throughout. My round was witnessed by a pretty, black pajamaed female Vietnamese caddy!

What I found most ironic were the occasional U.S. Army visitors who felt extremely uncomfortable in the terrorist urban environment of Saigon and could not wait to get back to their APCs (Armored Personnel Carriers) where they felt more secure with their superior weaponry and ability to spot the enemy from a distance!

June 1969 to June 1970 was a relatively quiet year in Saigon. The Tet Offensive of 1968 had been effectively blunted at great cost to the enemy. The VC/NVA remained furtive and resourceful. One stellar example occurs to me - Nui Ba Din, the "Black Virgin Mountain", near Tay Ninh City. The bottom of the mountain was owned by the U.S. Army's 2nd "Tropic Lightning Division, the middle by the NVA, and the top by the 509th Radio Research Group, a U.S. Army unit. In the area below were the celebrated

Tunnels of Cu Chi, an underground network which contained a VC hospital. The B52 Arc Light program during my tour prevented the enemy from massing in numbers sufficient to mount a successful attack on U.S. or ARVN Forces. However, despite our best efforts and targeting, the enemy continued to infiltrate South Vietnam via the Ho Chi Minh Trail. I looked forward to Richard Nixon's decisiveness to bring the war to a successful conclusion as the Decade of the Sixties closed out.

CHAPTER FIVE

THE SEVENTIES

As 1970 arrived predictably and on time, the realization began to dawn on me that my tour was nearly half over, and that February would bring our long- anticipated reunion with an R & R in Hawaii. After deplaning at Hickam AFB in Honolulu and enjoying a prolonged hug and a kiss, Evelyn commented to the effect that I was the only guy getting off who had not lost weight. We spent our first three days at the Outrigger Hotel in Honolulu then three days at the Surf Rider Hotel on the Island of Kauai. As thirty plus honeymooners we enjoyed the Hawaiian Cultural Center in Oahu and the wild Pacific waves crashing on the mountainous, pristine beaches of Kauai.

Returning from my one-year tour in Saigon in June was a joyous event for a reunion with Evelyn and my two young daughters, Kathleen, and Elizabeth. For many of my countrymen however, the occasion was not so joyous as they were jeered and spit upon by the "oxygen thieves" and political cretins who constituted the anti-war faction. In effect, the Vietnam involvement ultimately tore us apart as a country and perhaps President Gerald Ford had the proper foresight to declare a general amnesty for those who had fled or deserted their country during this prolonged conflict.

Returning to 19 Parkway Village in Cranford, Kathleen was initially a bit shy in recognizing the dad who moved back in with her mother; Liz was more accepting with genuine hugs and exclamations of "Daddy, Daddy, that's my Daddy!" My sister-in-law, Kathleen McAdam hosted a welcome home party for 30 plus people at her home in Cranford. She had been widowed in November 1968 and Evelyn's company complemented her two children, Mary Jo, and Michael with those of our daughters who were of similar age. During this same summer, we enjoyed a visit with Joe and Helen Clancy at their home in Long Beach, Long Island and experienced the terror of losing Liz for an hour or more at the beach. One of my cousin Jim's friends, hearing Liz mention the name Clancy, returned her to us at the Clancy home. To this very day, my relief is palpable! By mid-July, we were ready for our first cross-country trip; planned across the central part of the U.S. Saying good-bye to Aunt Kathy, Mary Jo, and Michael generated tears but we were reassured that once we got settled in California, they would be our first visitors.

Our first overnight after leaving New Jersey was at a motel along the Pennsylvania Turnpike. Liz expressed her exuberance over motel living by bouncing off the bed and incurring a few stitches on her forehead due to impact with a chair or couch. Moving across

Ohio, we visited Paul and Nancy Reinman in Dayton, Pat McDonald in East St Louis. We then headed west to Denver where we met Evelyn's sister, Joan (15) at the airport and adopted her for the remainder of the summer. Heading southwest through New Mexico and Arizona through Raton Pass we stopped at Hoover Dam, Las Vegas and moved on in the summer heat to Disneyland in Los Angeles. Driving up Highway 101, we enjoyed a hearty breakfast in Morro Bay. Resuming our journey north, Evelyn expressed her delight in a still-life, fruit painting that caught her eye in the restaurant. Totally out of character, but delighted to be back with my young family, I swung the Ford Station Wagon around, drove back to the restaurant and presented Evelyn with the painting she admired. We proceeded up the beautiful, scenic Coast Road, past Big Sur and San Francisco and arrived at our destination, Travis AFB in early August.

Our reception at Travis was substantially enhanced by the invitation of Captain Kay and Lois Yingling to stay with them for about a week while waiting for modern, on-base quarters. Additionally, their hospitality provided a gracious introduction to California Wine Tasting as well as trailer camping. We moved into 121 Lamb Street and were very pleased with the modernity of the Quarters (Capeheart) compared to the older (Wherry) housing we lived in at Westover. My assignment was to the 86th Military Airlift Squadron (MAC), 60th Military Airlift Wing. Commanded by Lt.

Colonel Thomas C. Long, the Squadron and Wing itself were committed mainly to airlift operations in support of Southeast Asia; a down-range mission to Woomera, Australia, and a Fall commitment to Reforger, an annual deployment to Europe in support of NATO. Compared to the static responsibilities of SAC alert in the old KC-97, the on-going vitality and flexibility of MAC Operations was awesome to behold as well as be an active and involved participant.

Ground School for Navigators in the C-141 was held at base level with approximately one month of training and ground missions. I began flying actual flying missions in September/October 1970. Compared to the slower KC-97, it felt like going from the Stone Age to the Jet Age in the C-141 Starlifter. It took me a good while to adjust to the faster pacing requirements of the aircraft itself as well as the newer MAC procedures as a combat crew member. Once my waiver of Duty and Travel Restrictions came through, I was subsequently able to accumulate 78 Combat Support Missions and qualify for two Air Medals at 35 missions each.

The MAC System comprised a constant flow of transport aircraft through the Pacific area. Our missions to SEA (Southeast Asia) would originate at Travis AFB. The Aircraft Commander and Navigator would meet at Base Operations three hours before takeoff; flight plan and attend a weather briefing prior to meeting the rest of the crew for a "bag drag" at the aircraft itself. Together with the Copilot, Flight Engineer, and Loadmaster an individual pre-flight would take place. My navigator duties involved checking the sextant, the radar, loran system and loading the coordinates of our route into the ASN -24 airborne computer. This routine would recur at the beginning of each mission throughout a normal two-week deployment. Our crew duty day would normally maximize at 16 hours when a 15-hour period of crew rest would commence. The aircraft and its cargo never rested while the mission and flight schedule were picked up by a freshly rested crew.

Normally, a flight originating at Travis would arrive 5 or 6 hours later at Hickam AFB, Hawaii, and crew rest on-base or, depending upon non-availability, downtown at Waikiki. The next leg would transit Guam and crew rest at Clark Air Base in the Philippines. From Clark, the crew would normally fly shuttle missions into Vietnam, usually Tan Son Nhut (Saigon, or Danang in the north of the Republic of Vietnam (RVN). Many support missions were to bases in Thailand in support of fighter (F 4, F105), tanker (KC-135) or bomber (B-52) operations. At the conclusion of our shuttle schedule, we would redeploy through Kadena, Okinawa to Yokota Air Base, just north of Tokyo, Japan. In nearby Fussa City, one could find a wide selection of hi-fi equipment, tuners, amplifiers, tape decks etc. as well as pachinko machines and Japanese souvenirs.

The most challenging flight for Navigators was the North

Pacific Flight redeployment (Northpac 1) redeployment from Yokota to Travis, depending upon the time of year and the prevailing winds, the flight was of 11 to 14 hours duration. For the lone navigator, this involved combined and selective use of celestial, radar, loran and dead reckoning techniques. The objective was to split the ADIZ or entry point for aircraft entering U.S. airspace 200 nautical miles off the Pacific Coast. Failure to hit within 20 miles of this point could result in the scramble of a fighter interceptor and a substantial fine for the Aircraft Commander! It was always refreshing at this phase of a long overwater mission to hear the reassuring voice of the ground radar controller confirming our aircraft position exactly where I had us on my chart.

While the missions in support of Southeast Asia constituted the majority of our efforts, the desired break from this routine came with missions to Australia, Pago Pago and Kwajalein Atoll. The annual Reforger Exercise provided our West Coast crews the opportunity to familiarize ourselves with North Atlantic Operations and to visit bases in Germany, United Kingdom, Norway, Denmark and Iceland. I was totally fascinated by the variety of missions themselves and the flexibility of the aircrews flying them.

The Credo of flying the "MAC Line " was to work hard and to play hard. After a full 16-hour crew day we would enter a 16-hour crew rest period observing the maxim "12 hours between bottle and throttle." After a few weeks of flying and partying, it was always a pleasure to return home with souvenirs for Kathy and Liz as well as a gift for Evelyn. The most well received of these, in my belief, was the Thai Four Seasons Bracelet, virtually solid gold carvings which Air America pilots used to buy their way out of captivity in Laos. During our two-week break at home base, we were kept occupied flying airdrop training missions over Central California. It is relevant to note that the C-141 Airdrop mission itself was never executed in Vietnam; that perilous and often deadly mission fell to the C-130 Hercules, our smaller, propeller driven "trash hauler."

Operational flight schedules did not always flow as timely or accurately as planned. Weather, maintenance and unforeseen problems at the destination could and would alter our flight planning. Of all the varied missions, none was more critical or rewarding than the Air Evacuation Flights carrying severely wounded combat casualties back to the U.S. for treatment. On one Air Evac mission with Captain Chuck Niemeyer, a close friend from Travis as Aircraft Commander, we took off from Clark AB, Philippines enroute to Hickam AFB, Hawaii. About two hours from Andersen AFB, Guam, our number three engine was shut down at 39,000 feet due to a fire warning indication. We were obliged to descend through a typhoon to maintain flight. Chuck did a cool and highly commendable job with the assistance of Joe Watson, our Copilot. I took over radio communications with Guam and navigated our way through thunderstorms to a safe landing at

Anderson AFB. Once we reached the Billeting Office, the entire crew had an appropriate and well-deserved celebration even though it was 4 AM local time. There were many such memorable missions; a crosswind landing by Lt. Colonel Harry Bush in Christchurch New Zealand was commended by the local newspapers for its audacity and success. Flying a U.S. Navy resupply mission from Clark AB to Diego Garcia, British Indian Ocean Territory and navigating south of the Equator was always an adventure in lonely aviation as there would never be other aircraft or traffic on the route. One of the key memories of Diego Garcia was the warning to avoid swimming barefooted and risk stepping upon the highly poisonous sea urchins. For such an injury, there was no known cure, and the nearest hospital was in Mauritius, a 7-hour flight distant.

As a MAC Line Navigator, I accumulated over 2000 hours of flying time in a time period of little over two years. By comparison, it had taken 9 years in SAC (KC-97), given alert duty, to log an equivalent number of flying hours. In retrospect, flying the MAC Line was an exciting and adventure filled experience, not unlike an international fraternity party! On the downside, being away from home and hearth on birthdays, holidays and family celebrations was a fact of life. Evelyn's flexibility, understanding and loving care of the girls was exemplary and more deserving of the Air Medals awarded than I was. There were many young wives and children at Travis AFB and both Evelyn and the girls made good friends easily.

One of the most sought-after missions in the Wing was the so-called "Embassy Run." Originating at Travis with an augmented crew, this comprised a six-day trip completely around the world. Hickam AFB, Guam, Philippines, Vietnam, Thailand, Karachi, Pakistan, New Delhi, India, Dharan, Saudi Arabia, Torrejon, Spain, Charleston, South Carolina and Travis AFB. Having our own aircraft and available pallet positions, I brought back hand-carved wooden screens from India as well as paintings and furniture from Madrid which decorate and are used in our home to this very day.

The holiday season of 1970-1971 witnessed the planting of a two-foot Colorado Spruce on our front lawn and also brought a major event into our lives when Evelyn announced that she was expecting a child that coming August. On August 9, 1971, Noreen Patricia O'Prey arrived at The Travis Base Hospital, not only on schedule, but during my lunch hour! She and Evelyn were a beautiful and healthy sight and the presence of her Aunt Kathleen McAdam with Mary Jo and Michael as visitors was very much appreciated. Later that month, she and my brother, Richie became Godparents for Noreen when she was baptized by Father Ricardo Hernandez at the Base Chapel. Over the many years, the closeness and love of the McAdam family has been the spiritual glue of our relationship with each. It was a busy summer for visitors. In addition to Richie and his band of traveling Christian Brothers, Ed O'Dwyer, Joe and Helen, Ellen, Jim, Michelle and Dan Clancy arrived at varying time periods.

Grandma Ellen O'Dwyer arrived to welcome our new addition. Aunt Kathleen proposed the name Noreen which fit perfectly as did the reception she received from her sisters who held her and hugged her ever so gently. It was only months later when Noreen was being potty trained that they would refer to her as "the Stink."

I continued to fly missions with Major Joe Benedetto and Lt. Colonel Jim Richael being my supervisors in the Navigator Section. The key to success was to refrain from developing colds and illness and going DNIF (Duty Not Including Flying) shortly before a mission and thereby generating, on short notice, a need for a replacement. We got along very well, and I continued to receive competitive evaluation reports. It was April or May of 1971 when my name appeared on the Majors' promotion list and the "sins of the past" were apparently forgiven and forgotten. I proudly exchanged my Captain's bars for a Major's gold leaves. I had always regarded rank more important than wings or accumulated flying hours. Pilots and Navigators were a dime a dozen. If one sought long range to a promotion and career progression, it would be necessary to develop skills or expertise in career fields other than Operations and also to avail oneself of the residence or correspondence courses pertinent to their particular rank or grade. I had selected Intelligence and, in SAC, completed every correspondence course available as well as College German. As a Major, it would be important, if not crucial, to complete Command

and Staff and Industrial College of the Armed Forces (ICAF) by correspondence as the Air Force did not appear to be inviting or soliciting me to attend in residence. These courses themselves demanded many hours of reading and test completion activities. I was pleased to take the material with me for consumption during the many available crew rest hours in the MAC System.

This decision and determination would ultimately pay off but in a manner modified by my propensity to enjoy drinking at the wrong time or at the wrong place. The Air Force promotion system was "Up-or-Out." I witnessed many of the most capable and competent aviators, both pilots and Navigators fail to make Major or Lt. Colonel due to their refusal to take these courses and rely exclusively upon their flying skills.

As a career Air Force Officer, I began to view the correlation of my activities with what was occurring in the larger world of international politics. The war in Vietnam went on through 1972 when, finally in December, President Richard Nixon ordered the bombing of Hanoi. I had flown several missions transferring a U.S. Marine Corps Wing from Iwakuni, Japan to Nam Phong, Thailand and other destinations in the Inter-theater Stage of Southeast Asia. Transiting Guam on 17 December, I enjoyed a reunion with Major Gerry Alley, a former Target Planner at Westover and now a B-52 Radar Bombardier. He declined my invitation to party stating that he was going to Mass in the morning prior to early takeoff on a bombing mission. He asked that I give his family a phone call after I had arrived back at Travis. Arriving home on December26 and calling his home at March AFB, Riverside, his young son informed me that his mom, Rosemary and other four children were at a memorial service for his dad. Gerry was classified MIA for several years, posthumously promoted to Lt. Colonel and confirmed KIA on his mission over Hanoi on December 18, 1972. He was the closest of the relatively few friends that I had lost during the Vietnam War. His widow, Rosemary, was not interested in keeping in touch; regrettable, but nevertheless her personal and unwavering decision. May Gerry rest in Peace! Richard Nixon brought Us combat involvement to an end shortly thereafter with Henry Kissinger's epic "Peace is at hand" statement; a positive effect of the ultimate sacrifice made by Gerry and his contemporaries in Linebacker II.

In late 1972, Lt. Colonel Floyd Dick Steiner, Chief of Plans at the 60ᵗʰ MAW offered me a position as a planner working for him on the Wing Staff. This job would be the busiest, most productive and most potentially rewarding of my Air Force career. At the same time, he recruited Captain Chuck Niggemayer and Lt. Colonel (selectee) Vince Hurtado for the same office. Each of us was assigned two or three war or contingency plans; the responsibility to keep them up to date and to prepare Wing Level briefings for each. My primary responsibility was for the 9439 Operational Readiness Plan which tested the Wing's ability to meet its wartime commitments when exercised by MAC Headquarters. I thoroughly enjoyed the prestige and visibility of briefing each of the three flying squadrons as well as the Wing Staff. This was a definite upward progression from the squadron level, and I thoroughly enjoyed the challenge. I owed a lot to the experienced advice of Roy Quint, a retired U.S. Army Lt. Colonel, whose expertise was in logistics. In a new career-broadening assignment, his guidance and support were invaluable. President Nixon's decisiveness to implement Linebacker II, the Christmas bombing of Hanoi ultimately ended the war in Vietnam. In the Spring of 1973, the return of our POWs from imprisonment in Hanoi was brought about. Vince Hurtado, Chuck Niggemeyer and I coordinated a reception center at Travis AFB where the returning POWs would meet with their service-assigned escorts, naming it the JSEC (Joint Service Control Center). This activity was staffed by our U.S. Navy, Army and Marine Corps counterparts. When the C-141 Flights arrived, there wasn't a dry eye on the ramp as one plane loaded at a time, bringing these heroes home to their families and loved ones. Evelyn and I had the privilege of hosting Captain James Lowe, USAF, whose name Evelyn had on her POW bracelet. Operation "Egress Recap" suddenly renamed "Operation Homecoming" was a joyous occasion and success for all parties involved. The Base Commander, Colonel McKee subsequently approved Joint Service Commendation Medals for Vince Hurtado and me. Chuck Niggemeyer deserved one too, but higher authorities decided to limit the submission to two.

By Easter of 1973, the NVA had mounted a full- scale ground invasion of South Vietnam. U.S. ground forces had been pulled out in accord with the Paris Peace agreement. I found myself at Clark Air Base in the Philippines as we were alerted to move an ARVN Division north to Quang Tri where the combat was taking place. As things turned out, the ARVN vs NVA, facing two more years of combat, ultimately prevailed as the U.S. withdrew all its support from the Thieu Government (RVN) in April 1975 and faced the most humiliating withdrawal in its history. I do not for an instant, regret my whole-hearted support for our effort in Vietnam. At the same time, I lament the lack of purpose and polarization of the conflict on the American home front. In the aftermath of Kent State, it was announced that we would go no more than 25 miles into Cambodia to come to grips with the NVA! Ho Chi Minh had it right when he asserted that America did not have the patience to fight a prolonged struggle and that victory would ultimately go to the Communist fighters. Our policy makers viewed Vietnam through a Cold War prism, ignoring the reality that a large part of the enemy's morale was a belief in Vietnamese nationalism.

The summer of 1973 brought more race demonstrations and riots to our country as well as a limited outbreak to Travis AFB. We were at a movie in the Base Theater at Travis when it was announced to return home, lock your windows and doors and remain inside.

The small group of Black demonstrators were rounded up and flown off base to other military installations. No violence occurred as it had on some U.S. Navy warships, but the incident was reflective of the racial divisions of the time.

Professionally, I had long entertained the prospect of being an Air Attaché or an equivalent position as a military-politico-affairs Staff Officer. This ambition caused me to generate a volunteer application for attaché' duty, also known as a dream sheet! A response from Air Force Headquarters at Fort Belvoir, Virginia indicated that I would be required to take and achieve a certain grade on the Armed Forces Language Aptitude Test (AFLAT). I completed the requirement but scored one point lower than the accepted grade. Citing 12-hour Workdays in the Plans Office I submitted a letter to the Chief of Personnel at USAF Headquarters requesting permission for a retake. This was granted and I was successful in achieving the desired grade. This generated a response from Air Force Headquarters that I would be considered for a post in Burma or Morocco.

Shortly thereafter, the posting was changed to Copenhagen, Denmark, generating an invitation to bring Evelyn with me for an interview at Fort Belvoir. My persistence had paid off! Evelyn and I were prepared to launch on the adventure of our Air Force career in a highly desired, cultural, and romantic overseas location. This was one of the very few Air Force assignments in which a formal interview was required. My recent completion of ICAF, the Industrial College of the Armed Forces and Evelyn's poise and positive image made the interview a success. Colonel George Gering, Air Force Chief at Fort Belvoir, commented after the interview that a "nice pair of legs never hurt" and he wasn't talking about mine!

On our return to Travis, I received an assignment as Plans Officer to the 435ᵗʰ Military Airlift Wing at Rhein Main, Germany which I felt prudent to decline as I would presumably never learn the outcome of the interview for Copenhagen. When confirmation came through in short order, our happiness and delight knew no limits and I even more deeply appreciated Evelyn's role as an Air Force wife. In the Attaché business, wives were gratefully referred to as unsalaried employees of the U.S. Government.

As the Fall of 1973 approached, so did the onset of the Yom Kippur War and our resupply of Israel. Our Plans Office was a hotbed of activity; briefings, updates and heavy airlift involvement in what came to be known as Operation Nickel Grass. C-141 and C-5 missions were routed through Sigonella, Sicily enroute to Israel with war supplies. Vince Hurtado was deployed there on temporary duty with the MAC ALCE (Airlift Control Element). Our boss in the Plans Office, Lt. Colonel Floyd Dick Steiner retired and Lt. Colonel Lyle Smith, a fellow Navigator from the 86ᵗʰ MAS became our new supervisor. A demanding but fair, participating and perceptive leader, his personal example and commitment to long hours and short-fuse suspense taskings from our DO, Colonel Tom Julian, left no room for complaint or argument from anyone. As Nickel Grass wore down, the Oil Crisis of 1973-74 arose when the oil supply to the West was cut off by the Arab nations in retaliation for the U.S. support of Israel. Our new task in the Plans Office was to devise and implement conservation measures for our vastly limited oil imports.

Having the Attaché assignment in hand and having successfully completed the extensive, rewarding but time-consuming course, Industrial College of the Armed Forces, I was taken aback in the Spring of 1974 by a request from Vince Hurtado. Stating that he had "filled most of his other squares," he asked me to give him my ICAF correspondence course questions and answers. I initially responded to the effect that I would "think about it." Sharing this request with Evelyn, she strongly responded to the effect that I did the work and should give him nothing! My response to Vince was negative. He then attempted extortion; threatening to reveal how often he had seen me drink too much and argue with Evelyn at the Travis Officers' Club. His conversation with OSI or any subsequent investigating authority was privileged information. He could tell them whatever he wished, but under no circumstances would I comply with his request. A year or so later, at the Bolling AFB Officers' Club in D.C., an OSI agent revealed to me that reports of my drinking had been received from my old base, Travis. He, the OSI had concluded that I was just a raucous Irishman and did not have a problem with alcohol. My conclusion was that Vince Hurtado had vindictively followed through on his threat. Threat or no threat, I would have been better advised, then and there, to modify my drinking habits. I chose the path of denial, reinforced by the conviction of Hurtado's contemptible extortion attempt. The reality was that my drinking habit could and would compromise a fairly promising Air Force career. I should be more judicious of the time and place for partying as well as my choice of drinking companionship.

The population of California has more than its fair share of unique, if not outwardly ridiculous characters; Hollywood types et alia, but no place in the world can rival it for its variety of breathtaking scenery. We deeply appreciated the wealth and grandeur of Hearst Castle, followed by the unique experience of driving U.S. 1 through Big Sur and Monterey on our way north to Travis in 1970. In the summer of 1971, we drove south down the newly opened Interstate 5 to Disneyland with the McAdam family. Evelyn was quite pregnant at the time, and I recall the funny look the desk clerk at Zaby's Motel in Anaheim gave me as we checked in with two families. My guess is that he took me for a Mormon Bishop! We went on to be tourists in Tijuana, Mexico and viewed the scenic ocean and environs of La Hoya, north of San Diego at the home of Jack Donovan, a neighbor of Kathleen's from Cranford.

After settling into our new home, 121 Lamb Street, Travis AFB, the benign climate and spectacular scenery provided irresistible motivation to visit and camp in any of California's state or national parks. At Kay Yingling's suggestion, we purchased a Coleman Folding tent trailer and learned the rudiments of towing it behind my LTDD Ford station wagon. Of all possible destinations, Yosemite National Park was primary. Shortly after the tent was set up, it began to snow. Evelyn insisted rightly that this was not the proper weather for infants! Accordingly, we spent the night warm and cozy at the Yosemite Lodge.

In the summer of 1972, I enjoyed a reunion with Dave Kuebler, my former roommate from Saigon and his vivacious, red-headed wife. Lynda. Dave was very helpful in introducing me to contacts in the Intelligence community who assisted in my application for Attaché duty. He also introduced me to a travel trailer which he proposed to sell to finance a new van. The price was right, and the camper trailer was a definite upgrade from the Coleman tent. Other travel destinations were Crater Lake, Lake Shasta and Lake Shastina, the latter with our Travis neighbors, Phyliss and Dave Hoffman, my personal dentist from the Travis AFB Clinic. In the early summer of 1973, we embarked up the California Coast to Oregon and Washington, visiting the giant Redwoods of Northern California as well as the Oregon Sand Dunes, Mount Lassen and the

Olympic Peninsula. Evelyn was highly pleased when we ferried across the Strait of Juan de Fuca to visit the beautiful Butchart Gardens in Victoria, British Columbia. One notable winter outing during this time frame occurred with Steve and Terry Kudriavetz when we rented a condominium at Lake Tahoe and got in some novel practice skiing. In addition, we visited Hoss and the crew of the Bonanza Ranch, a popular Western TV serial at the time.

Camping was, for all of us, part of the California experience, a most memorable, carefree and relaxing period of our diminishing youth. Closer to home at Travis, we explored Fort Ord, the Monterey area and Monterey Bay Area. With an eye on investment as well as a suitable retirement locale, we purchased a condominium in the town of Aptos, halfway between Carmel and Monterey. A year later in 1974, when the assignment to Denmark came through, rather than risk being absentee landlords, we sold and broke even. How were we to know that during our three years overseas, our investment would quadruple!

To transit the breadth of this great country in an RV is a pleasure and a privilege which few of my civilian contemporaries have ever partaken. It develops not only a deep appreciation for its natural beauty, geography and varied dramatic landscape, but also an abiding respect for our history and multicultural heritage. In early April 1974 we bid a fond farewell to our friends and neighbors at Travis AFB and headed south via a now familiar Interstate 5 to visit

Joe and Inez McElroy and their sons in Fountain Valley, a community about 20 miles south of Los Angeles. Their three sons were growing like weeds, and it was a pleasure to renew memories of being neighbors at Westover AFB, 1965-66. Their Basset hound growled and struck fear into our three-year-old, Noreen and was severely admonished by Inez for his inhospitable behavior. Our next stop in Southern California was at the Redlands home of Carl and Jan Swenlin, Air Force friends we knew and partied with often at Travis. On a previous visit, Jan had redone Evelyn's make up to the point that I initially failed to recognize her and asked who the gorgeous dish was in the living room!

With our travel trailer intact and a comfort to camp in, we headed east to the Colorado River, visiting KOAs in Arizona and New Mexico. We arrived at our intermediate destination, Carlsbad Caverns after two more days on the road. The stalagmites, stalactites and well-lit subterranean caves were awesome sights. The winds which assailed us at our campsite were strong, uncomfortable and unforgettable aspects of raw nature. On the road to El Paso, the headwinds reduced our mileage to about six miles per gallon as compared to the usual 10 to 12 MPG. It was a relief and a pleasure to enjoy the hospitality of Jan Allen and his bride, Maggie. Jan and I had spent the better part of a year together in Saigon, 1969-70.

When people tell you Texas is big, they hardly exaggerate. Heading slightly northeast over excellent and sparsely trafficked highways, we transited Odessa, Midland, Sweetwater, Abilene, Dallas and finally, Shreveport, Louisiana. Our three-day odyssey across Texas included a tourist stop in Sweetwater to visit the Rattlesnake Capital of the World. Souvenir wallets, belts and boots were easy to resist but the size and number of reptiles was truly remarkable. Louisiana from Shreveport to Vicksburg, Mississippi was predictably humid, rainy and moist but nevertheless, a better time to visit than the heat of mid-summer. It was a relief and a pleasure to camp and take a leisurely tour of the battlefield and scene of U.S. Grant's key victory in July 1863. As it was Easter Sunday, Evelyn stored Easter eggs for the girls to find. Noreen expressed her concern that the Easter Bunny might not be able to find us the next year since we were moving so often! Proceeding on to Jackson and Montgomery, Alabama, we viewed the carving of the Confederate leaders on Stone Mountain, Georgia, a vivid and highly visible monument to our nation's tragic Civil War. A similar comment would be appropriate for our subsequent tour of Petersburg, Virginia with its still visible trench lines. Andrews AFB, Maryland was a relatively short distance away with a trailer parking facility and a Visiting Guest House, a welcome relief to each of us who had spent approximately two weeks on the road.

It was now decision time for Evelyn and me. For our 15-month tour in the Capitol Area, should we locate in Maryland or Virginia? Our schedule called for 6 months of Danish Language instruction at the Foreign Service Institute in Arlington. Virginia and an additional five months at Defense Intelligence School in Anacostia, D.C. We opted for a Georgian style, two story rental in Oxon Hill, Maryland which featured an uphill parking space for our RV. Our landlords were a pleasant young couple, Mr. & Mrs. Bill Helmrich. In short order, we met our neighbors, Dick and Carolyn Slye on one side: Jim and Barbara Zampogna on the other. A family of Donaghues lived across the street and provided early friendships for our three daughters. Jim and Arlette Aanested lived around the corner and G. Gordon Liddy of Watergate fame resided a few blocks away. A standing neighborhood joke was that he had plenty of time on his hands in prison and accordingly could serve as PTA Secretary. When all was considered, 9103 Ivanhoe Road, Oxon Hill, Md was a pleasant, welcoming and warm neighborhood and made for a comfortable living style. Located about 10 miles south of the Capitol, it did require a daily commuter bout with the Beltway, something on-base living up until that point, had never required! This was resolved shortly thereafter by car-pooling with Lt. Ken de Graffenreid, U.S. Navy and Major Mike Fleming, USAF, who, like me, was a Jasper, an alumnus of Manhattan College. In the autumn of 1974, we were introduced to Fred and Susanna Ross, Air Attaché couple with whom we would serve two years of our three-year tour. We hit it off well; Fred had flown the F-106 Interceptor and Susanna had some experience as a schoolteacher. They were parents to two active sons just a little older than Kathy and Liz.

The three of us hit it off immediately. Ken was a Naval Aviator, a C-130 pilot, whose expertise with DIA was Spain and Portugal. Mike, like me, enjoyed a good party and Irish songs. He donated his reserved parking spot at Pomponio Plaza to our carpooling cause. Father of three sons, he also owned a sailboat which hosted my family and sister-in-law, Mary on one or two occasions. A few years younger than me, Mike was my ideal of a free-spirited Irish Romantic with a love for Irish music as well as "the creature" or Irish Whiskey. He had flown AC-47 gunships in Vietnam and possessed an enviable combat record.

In late April 1974, I reported into DIA Headquarters for Attaché Affairs in Pomponius in Arlington, Virginia and was informed that the originally scheduled, 6-month Language Program had been cut back by a month. Facing a 3-month gap in my training period, I exploited the opportunity to work as a Desk Officer and acquire an additional effectiveness report for the upcoming Fall, 1974 promotion board. The introduction and experience of working within DIA was invaluable, although, in some respects, ludicrous. I received good advice and assistance from Major Howard Hicks, U.S. Army, and Captain Frank Babbit, U.S. Navy. On the other hand, fruitlessly traveling the hallowed halls of the Pentagon, seeking a definitive statement on DOD's official position on canine medical experimentation in Germany was an education in itself! However, to see how a "purple Suit" or inter-service organization worked from an insider's perspective became an asset to be used in Copenhagen. In retrospect, the strategy of an extra report turned out to be futile when the first of many non-selections to Lt. Colonel occurred in November/December of 1975. In my opinion, this was largely attributable to the Air Force's implementation of the 1-2-3 system of enforced distribution by reviewing Officers. In effect, 50 percent of a field of eligible officers would receive average or "3" ratings; 30 percent above average or "2" ratings and the rare 20 percent "1", top bloc, fast burner or below the zone rating ensuring promotion. Fairly or not, it would take me 10 years in grade as a Major to gain promotion to Lt. Colonel. With the deck so stacked, my drinking habit generated a formidable additional obstacle to overcoming this system while I stubbornly refused to modify my habit or enjoyment of alcoholic beverages.

Throughout 1974-75, Lt. Colonel Phil Vollman, USAF and his wife, Jean could not have been more helpful in preparing us for the job itself in Copenhagen. Their practical tips on entertaining, modes of dress and solid advice on schools for the girls were warmly appreciated as they were completing the last of their three-year tour in Copenhagen. Their sponsorship was unique, frequent, detailed and always practical, particularly their recommendation that we succeed them as tenants at Trongardsparken 50, their California style rental in Lyngby, a suburb of Copenhagen. Phil was a West Point graduate and had served a tour at the MAC Command Post at U Tapao, Thailand. We commenced an enduring personal, professional, and beneficial friendship and remain to this day, Christmas card exchangers with his former wife, Jean.

In the early summer of 1975, I had the pleasure of meeting Major Stanley Pratt, U.S. Marine Corps who was designated incoming Assistant Naval Attaché in Copenhagen. Stan had the same schedule as Evelyn and me; Language School at Foreign Service Institute followed by Defense Intelligence School at Anacostia, Md. Stan and his red-headed wife, Donna had three daughters, approximately the same age as ours and we enjoyed a camping trip together with them in Northern Virginia. We attended the weekly USMC Retreat Ceremony with them at Marine Corps Headquarters, 12th and I Street in downtown Washington. Stanley had a most impressive combat record; Bronze Stars with V as well as two purple hearts for wounds in I Corps, Vietnam. I had every reason to anticipate three years of both friendship and cooperation during our mutual three-year tour in Denmark. This highly positive expectation came to a crashing halt when the language grades were announced at FSI. Evelyn and I had achieved the Commandant's List; the equivalent of 90 pluses or A's in the course while Stanley received a B. Visibly and emotionally shaken, he was obliged to excuse himself from the classroom. The people at Marine Corps Headquarters had constantly pressured him to be "Number One" and he had fallen short! Despite my reassurances that these grades didn't matter, this event generated a lasting rift in our friendship as if a guillotine had been dropped through it.

The language school experience for Evelyn and me was unique. Despite my three years of high school Latin plus three years of college German, Evelyn matched or exceeded my performance on the final oral exam conducted by Dr. Van Buskirk. Stan Pratt, a U.S. Navy Oceanographer/ Lt. Commander, John, his wife and an U.S. Army Specialist 4 and I constituted a class of 6 students. Under the tutelage of Mrs. Lilian Jorgensen and Mrs. Hanna Franc, we met for 5 hours a day at the FSI. Lillian And Hanna were Danish born housewives, who, as directed, emphasized the daily practice of conversational skills, dialogue and Danish customs. Both were a pleasure with whom to work and both exhibited charm, patience and enviable conversational skills. There was occasional friction, due to impolite interruption of Evelyn by Guillaine, the Commander's wife who generated rudeness and Gallic impatience while Evelyn was speaking. As a group, however, we got along well and completed our training just before Christmas, 1974.

The period in Oxon Hill was a pleasant one. Visits from my brothers, Richie and Ray, as well as the McAdams and Evelyn's Aunt Joan were welcome and happy occasions. There was always a site worth visiting for the young children in the Washington area with benefit to their early exposure to our country's history. We visited

Solomon's along Chesapeake Bay and enjoyed the local crab delicacies. Farther East, we responded to a resort development advertisement touting Virginia's East Shore, just south of the Maryland State line and north of Chincoteague Island where horses still ran wild from a Spanish shipwreck 300 years previous. Foreseeing a possible return to the D.C. area after our Danish tour, we purchased a mosquito infested plot of land in a development attractively named Captain's Cove. Within a year, the developer absconded with a few million dollars in fees, and we sold at a substantial loss about 5 years later.

As we settled into Oxon Hill, Kathy and Liz did well in the local elementary school while little Noreen was dropped off each morning of our language class at the nearby nursery school at Fort Myers, adjacent to Arlington National Cemetery. Each of our daughters did very well in adjusting to their new home and environment of the D.C. Area and made new friends rapidly. One of the more unfortunate memories of Oxon Hill was on returning from a weekend camping trip to discover that our home had been burglarized during our absence. The loss and damage were minimal; mainly my Fisher 600T Stereo Amplifier. Noreen was somewhat traumatized by the experience, fearing that the burglars might return again and steal her favorite dolls.

The New Year of 1975 brought with it, as most years do, its own blend of triumph and disaster. One of the training activities or field trips at the Defense Intelligence School involved a flight and visit to Cape Kennedy and briefings on NASA's mission. It was a pleasant relief from the harsh cold of Washington D.C., and I celebrated too freely, singing Irish songs with one or two classmates in the early hours of the morning at the Patrick AFB BOQ. As a result, I was invited shortly thereafter to visit Colonel Jim Keenan, USAF where, in Evelyn's company, I received a stern warning about the pitfalls of alcohol and attaché duty.

During this period, we paid a courtesy call on Colonel Jorgensen, Royal Danish Air Force and Danish Attaché to the U.S. Everything went well and we were introduced to Captain Leif Fischer, Royal Danish Army and his wife, Erna. Leif had responsibility for Danish military purchases in the U.S. and had extensive world travel experiences with Danish overseas projects and his son, Dan had recently completed RDAF Flight Training in the U.S. Evelyn and I were invited to the Fischer's home for a typical Danish luncheon or "Frokost." This consisted essentially of three separate servings: herring, cheese and meat. With characteristic Scandinavian logic, "the herring had to swim!" Accordingly, it was washed down with Tuborg or Carlsberg beer and chilled, 86 proof Danish aquavit. Brandy or liquor would follow dessert and one would be wisely advised not to drive afterwards. While "Working Lunch" was definitely a misnomer insofar as little or no work was planned or accomplished, the Frokost provided the opportunity for the participants to get to know each other and often lasted long after luncheon hours. Leif and I became long-term friends and corresponded every Christmas thereafter for forty years.

On March 17,1975, Evelyn and I hosted a St Patrick's Day Party for newly acquired friends in the Washington area. Mike Fleming dressed himself in a tan trench coat, fedora hat and a hidden bomb designated for women and children and came as an IRA terrorist. Notable by his absence was Stan Pratt, whose friendship had cooled appreciably and whom I suspected, had complained to Colonel Keenan at Fort Belvoir about my late-night carousing.

Late April 1975 brought the fall of Saigon to the NVA. Of particular note to this American defeat, was the absence of Mike Fleming from his office at Pomponio Plaza. It turned out that Mike had taken "French Leave" or gone AWOL; taking the last Air France flight that was available and flying into Saigon to rescue his Vietnamese family of 5! Somehow Mike ensured that his "second family" made it safely to Clark Air Base in the Philippines, on to Guam and ultimately to the U.S. Upon his return to Pomponio, Mike gave a personal debrief on his mission to Lt. General Sam Wilson, U.S. Army, Director of Attaché Affairs, and was absolved of any AWOL charges by the wealth of information he brought back about the Fall of Saigon. With his nose for danger, risk and raw courage, Mike and I shared a mutual, close friendship for years to come.

By mid-June, we had arranged to move our household goods, shipped our Ford Station Wagon from Bayonne, New Jersey and commenced our journey to Copenhagen. Anticipating the initial experience of proudly traveling with my family on a black, diplomatic passport, I was disconcerted by my mother-in-law's insistence that we carry a packed ham to present to her sister Aunt Kit in Killarney. Diplomatic immunity is one thing, but consciously violating the meat importation laws of a foreign country was something else! The reassurance was that Ellen's nephew, John O'Halloran, Customs Officer at Shannon Airport would head off any import difficulties or problems. As it turned out, we were waved right through. Having landed at Shannon Airport, we were met by Aunt Joan and Jerry and Kit Moynihan. We secured our automobile rental and with three exhausted daughters, experiencing jet lag for the first time, made our way to Aunt Molly O'Callaghan's home in Pallaskenry, southwest of Limerick City and the Shannon River. We enjoyed a hearty lunch and warm hospitality before driving on to Jerry and Kitty's home in Killarney. For the information of younger readers, Molly, Joan, Kit, Ellen and Bart Hayes were all members of the Hayes family from Limerick.

As travelers, the girls; Kathleen 9, Liz 7 and Noreen 4, were exceptionally well-behaved; a habit most appreciated driving Ireland's narrow and view limited country roads. Using Moynihan's as a base, we toured the Rings of Dingle and Kerry. I used the term

"Third World" to describe the auto driving challenges ranging from hairpin turns to sheep and cattle in the roadway. I still recall Aunt Kit's glare indicating her displeasure with my evaluation. Being what it has been from time immemorial, the Irish hospitality was legendary. Jerry and Kit fed us royally and took us on a tour of their family cemetery; a must stop for all Yank tourists. In addition, we were taken to Muckross Abbey, an Anglo-Irish Estate with guided tours inside and Irish Jaunting Car rides on the beautiful grounds. Several days later, we stopped at Jack and Moll Hayes' farmhouse in Limerick where the girls were hosted by pony rides and enjoyed the discovery pleasures of a petting zoo. We arrived next at Garryowen, a suburb of Limerick City and were taken to Knappogue Castle by Paddy and Kitty O'Halloran. Linking arms with Paddy, I'll never forget linking arms with him and joyfully singing the patriotic Irish ballad, *A Nation Once Again*. Particularly moving was the Medieval Dinner at Knappogue with its dramatization of Irish History. The Viking Period coverage concluded with the statement that "there isn't a man or woman alive in Ireland today that isn't related to the Dane"! This could include the O'Dwyers and O'Preys as well as the Dugan and Hayes families. Who knows? However, the kinship feeling was strong, and we were on our way to Denmark.

Driving North from Limerick, we viewed the Cliffs of Moher in Clare and drove through Galway to the Downhill Hotel in Ballina, Mayo, which we used as a base to visit Aunt Madeline Boyd and Maude (Baby) Dugan. Both were widowed but nevertheless extended a warm and gracious hospitality to us. Maude accompanied us on a tour to Achill Island, a scenic, wild and unspoiled sandy spot on Mayo's west coast. Closer to my mother's home, we visited the church at Lacken as well as the Dugan and Lynn ancestor graves at Rathran Abbey. Aunt Madeline was loving and generous of her time and our daughters received previews from her daughter Susan of sights and family members they would revisit in future years. After several days in Mayo, it was time to hit the road for Dublin, a three-hour drive east. Dublin itself is an Irish historian's paradise; the General Post Office; the Four Courts, Trinity University, O'Connell Street, the Book of Kells and the bridges across the Liffey. One unforgettable incident occurred as we strolled through Phoenix Park. A small group of gossoons or young Irish ruffians pelted us with small rocks, one of which impacted and drew blood on the forehead of our totally innocent and vulnerable daughter, Liz. Fortunately, it was just a scrape, and the young culprits ran like the mischievous imps they were. I paid a call on a friend of Joe Taylor's (my father's Best Man) and was invited to do some "pub crawling" with him that evening. It was a pleasant bachelor outing giving me further insight into the character of Dubliners.

Early the next morning, we were on our way to Dublin Airport, our SAS Flight, and the final leg of our trip. We were met at Kastrup Airport, Copenhagen by Fred and Susanna Ross as well as Phil and Jean Vollman. With a week or so of overlap, Fred was my boss and Phil, the Assistant Air Attaché that I had come to replace. We were driven north of Copenhagen to the Marina Hotel, a public resort facility used by the U.S. Embassy for incoming and departing personnel. Situated on the Oresund; the body of water separating Denmark and Sweden, the girls were absolutely delighted with the adjacent beach as I was with the Scandinavian custom of female topless bathing! Our stay at the Marina Hotel was most pleasant. Lasting a week or two until we could move into our new, government-leased quarters at Trongaardsparken 50, 2800 Lyngby, a California-style, single story, 4 bedrooms with an ample recreation room basement. Phil and Jean had described the home in detail, and we were more than pleased with the residence itself and the broad gated patio and lawn areas.

It would be beneficial at this point to describe the Officers who would constitute the Attaché staff of the U.S. Defense Attaché Office (USDAO) Copenhagen. A tri-service group, the Defense Attaché, Senior Officer, "Chairman of the Board" was Captain Sheldon (Lefty) Schwartz, a Naval Aviator, F-4 Carrier pilot and Chief of the Air Group (CAG) on the USS Enterprise. He had conducted air strikes on Haiphong aided by National Geographic magazines maps! Most recently, Lefty had been Naval Assistant to the civilian Secretary of the Navy, Gary Middendorf. His glamorous, kind and considerate wife MJ and he had a 12-year-old son.

The U.S. Army billet was filled by Colonel Blake McIlwain, a taciturn but friendly combat veteran of the First Air Cavalry Division. His wife, Pat, was somewhat younger and they too had a young son.

Major Stanley Pratt, USMC, the Assistant Naval Attaché had a few Purple Hearts in addition to a Bronze Star with a V for valor for his combat tours in Vietnam. His wife, Donna and their three daughters, like us, were arriving to commence three-year tours. Stan was replacing Lt. Colonel George Welsh, USMC and his wife Barbara.

Colonel Fred Ross, USAF and his wife Susanna headed the Air Force billet, and I was his Assistant. They were gracious hosts and he was an open, trustworthy and supporting supervisor, generous in his praise for my work at the office. A former F-106, the Rosses offered us multiple vacation/leave opportunities as their two sons were problem travelers.

Phil and Jean Vollman could not have been more helpful in getting us settled into both the job itself and our new home. Of particular note was the welcome dinner our new next-door neighbors, Orla and Karen Fredung hosted for us introducing us to Kriss and Anna Haldan, who lived across the street. Total sun worshippers, I would go on to meet Karin around the corner of our yard and find us both embarrassed at the accidental occurrence.

Not having diplomatic status per-se but performing

supervisory duties over several enlisted Navy NCO's and two civilian DIA personnel, was Chief Warrant Officer (CWO) Terry Briggs and his spouse was Aloma. They too had young children.

The first few weeks at the office were busy and absorbing new duties. These included introductions to Danish contacts as well as other U.S. Embassy Officers who shared political, economic and cultural interests in Greenland. Thule Air Base in the far north and Sondrestrom at the Arctic Circle were two U.S. Air Force installations which fell under our bailiwick of U.S.-Danish relations. On rare occasions, some of our Air Force personnel enjoying their tours in these northern outposts required the reminder that they were on Danish soil, not Canadian or U.S.! I would replace Phil as Secretary of the Attaché Association and be responsible for planning the activities of that 12-member group. This began with a protocol courtesy visit to the Soviet Embassy and a call on Kapitain Gregor Grigoriev, Soviet Navy and Doyenne or President of the Attaché Association. This was the first of many rare opportunities to meet with Russian, Poles and Chinese military Attaches who maintained residence in Denmark. A subsequent call under the rubric of the Attaché Association Secretary revealed that I was the first American diplomat to enter the premises of the PRC (Peoples' Republic of China) Embassy. On the business of the association. It was intriguing to meet and converse with Mr. Liu and his successor, Mr. Wu. Tea was served and our business was discussed through a very helpful Chinese interpreter.

One of my key duties was to meet and coordinate the refueling stop at Kastrup Airport for the transit of U.S. Ambassador Walter Stoessel and Ambassador Toon, as well as any VIP Americans enroute to Moscow. This gave me the opportunity to shake hands with Deke Slayton, who with other Astronauts was on his way to meet with their Soviet counterparts in Russia. At the time, each of these SAMs (Special Airlift missions required the on load of Soviet Navigators for entry to the Baltic or USSR itself. I recall the exchange of polite nods with these gentlemen but never a conversation with them.

Throughout the late summer and Autumn of 1975, under Fred Ross's tutelage and introduction to the key players in the Ministry of Greenland, the Ministry of Foreign Affairs, and the Danish Defense Intelligence services, I got off to a great start and in actual involvement in politico-military affairs; the reason I had applied and invested time in making this assignment a realty. This was and remains the dream assignment of our Air Force career. I use the pronoun "our" as far as Evelyn was part and parcel; a key ingredient and a full partner in the social and representational aspects of the job itself. In the reception line, her memory functioned perfectly while mine grasped for names and titles. She was a gracious hostess, a charming conversationalist and always a loving, caring mother to our three young daughters. Evelyn qualified in every respect for the highly complementary categorization of attaché wives as unsalaried employees of the U.S. government.

As the Vollmans prepared to depart Denmark, Phil, with George Welsh present, cautioned me to "Trust no one at the Office!" He declined to be more specific, but I believe he was referring to Stan Pratt. I heard what was said; noted but failed to sufficiently heed, as future events would turn out.

On the domestic side, moving into our new residence and putting our language skills to use provided some memorable experiences. Kathleen and Liz began classes in the American School operated by DOD, while Noreen was enrolled in the Danish Bornehave or kindergarten. Within a few months, her fluency would exceed that of the rest of our family. Evelyn, preparing to attend an official function, discovered the water in the shower was blocked. As a result, she called a Vand Mester, (water master) whom she honestly believed would summon a plumber. When a Window Washer showed up, she was totally non-plussed as the Danish word for plumber was "Blikkensager," a term our language school had not given us!

Believing that our social commitments would be far more demanding than they turned out to be, we hired a live-in au pair girl, a comely and English-fluent 17-year-old. Within a month, we discovered that we weren't all that busy and that Inge was legally entitled to entertain her boyfriend in her room on weekends. With no disrespect for Danish customs and a friendly farewell, we terminated Inge's employment shortly thereafter.

Of indispensable assistance to us during this period and throughout our tour was the practical liaison and advice of Jorgen Skoldjager, our Receptionist at the USDAO. While out shopping in our large Ford Station Wagon, Evelyn misjudged the parking distance available and her front fender destroyed a full bar window and shook up some of the drinking patrons. She did receive some well-intended advice from these patrons and gave them our Embassy office number, offering to pay the damages. Jorgen helped us through this process and ultimately the Bar owner's insurance covered the damage.

One of my first duties as Secretary of the Attaché Association was to coordinate the annual Sailboat Race in late October. Boat owners of the Copenhagen Yacht Club would donate their sailboats and on-board presence to a race around a given course in the Oresund. It was a cloudy, chilly race, enjoyed by all and followed by a sumptuous dinner at the So Officers' Foreignigen (Davy Officers' Club) in picturesque Nyhavn.

The host nation Officer from the Ministry of Defense, responsible for all of the assigned attaches' activities was Lt. Colonel G.K. Kristensen, Royal Danish Army. He was capably assisted by Lt. Colonel Emil Veisig, also of the RDA. It was our privilege to have G.K as the guest of honor at our first home-hosted dinner in

November. Our cook Mette Busch and Evelyn took great pains to see that everything went right. Mette was a woman approaching 70, an accomplished, in- demand cook, who decided, based upon her rapport with a client, was willing to prepare a full-scale dinner for 12 to 14 guests. Evelyn and our girls hit it off well with Mette and she announced that she would also be their honorary Grandma (Mor Mor). In accord with Danish custom, G.K. delivered a Thank you For the Food ("Tak for Mad") speech at the conclusion of the dinner that spoke for all the guests and had Evelyn beaming with pride.

One of my first representational duties was to attend the Royal Danish Air Force Open House Air Show at nearby Vaerlose Air Station. I was impressed by the acrobatics of the Red Devils as well as the performance of the Swedish Viggen, a fighter which had the capability to reverse and conceal itself in the hills and mountains of Sweden. This was a family event, enjoyed by Evelyn and our girls. It also provided an introduction to Colonel Bent Amled, RDAF Station Commander and his attractive wife, Birthe. Bent would ultimately rise to the rank of Lt. General and we would exchange Christmas letters for the future 40 years. Like the Amleds, many of our professional contacts became personal friends as well and remained in touch long after our tour had terminated.

Another of the most memorable events of the Fall of 1975 was the family outing we took to nearby Roskilde Cathedral, which contained the tombs of Danish Royalty going back 6 or 7 hundred years. Equally fascinating was the tour of the Viking preserved long ships in the town itself. "Hamlet's Castle" at Helsingor was another historical destination as was the Dyrhave, a royal hunting estate, a block from our home. For the most part, no official functions were planned on weekends, and we enjoyed the family time to tour, relax or rake leaves in our spacious yard. Evelyn commenced a long-term friendship with Tammy Gotchef, (RIP) whose husband Ed was an Embassy Political Officer. Colonel Stan Schneider, his wife Sheila, and their son "Dink" were friendly, as Stan was Chief of the MAAG (Military Allied Assistance Group). Kathy, Liz, and Noreen adjusted well to their new learning environment and Evelyn signed Kathy and Liz up for piano lessons from Bob Hofstadter, an eccentric but competent, pleasant and tolerant instructor.

The oncoming Danish Christmas was a joy to behold; live, lit candles on the Christmas tree; holding hands dancing around it and marching through the house singing Danish Christmas Carols. The warmth and light of the candles offset the Scandinavian "Morktid" or dark time of shortened daylight. Our daughters particularly enjoyed the punch out candy calendars counting the days down to Christmas itself. I made the comment at the time; "Christmas was invented in Denmark!" To top off all these pleasures, Evelyn was the recipient of a fully prepared, all the trimmings goose dinner, given by Peter Heering, a restaurant owner she had met at a dinner party.

At the Embassy, Ambassador Crowe was relieved by Ambassador John Gunther Dean, a career diplomat, whose picture on the cover of Time Magazine, depicted him carrying the U.S. flag out of Phnom Penh, Cambodia. He and his glamorous, French born wife, Martine were energetic role models for the entire Embassy Staff. Their official Residence, Rydhave, had been the headquarters of Dr. Werner Best, the Nazi Plenipotentiary to occupied Denmark during WWII. A bombing mission by the British RAF/SAS missed Rydhave as its target and bombed Rygaards School by mistake. Accordingly, most of the Danish Resistance activity took place in Jutland. Due to the contribution of 30 thousand Danish seamen to the Allied war effort, Denmark was recognized as one of the victorious powers at the conclusion of WWII.

On the negative side and the nadir of our entire tour was my stupidity along with my tendency to over-party and imbibe too freely of alcohol. This transpired during an Office- sponsored fishing trip on the Oresund in late November, hosting our Danish contacts. My penchant for singing Irish songs and becoming inebriated was one thing, but my refusal to accept a ride home by Captain Lefty Schwartz was unforgivable. For two subsequent weeks at office, like Captain Queeg in the Caine Mutiny, he rolled two steel balls in the palm of his hands weighing my fate. He finally called me in and stated bluntly that for the sake of Evelyn and the girls, he decided not to terminate my tour or send me back to the U.S. However, the incident would be reflected in my next effectiveness report, and he would tolerate no repetition of this unacceptable conduct. I expressed my gratitude and promised to cut down drastically on my alcoholic intake. In truth, I can never atone for the humiliation, angst, depression, and disappointment my thoughtless and irresponsible actions had caused Evelyn. Fred Ross offered to send me to a Rehab Facility at Wiesbaden Air Base if I believed treatment was necessary. I declined, stating that I had my drinking abated and under control. Fred assented, complimented me for doing a great job at the office and offered his support. Shortly after, the Lt. Colonel promotion list came out and my name was not on it. As Fred had been directed by Captain Schwartz to have the fishing trip incident reflected in my next efficiency report, the future was indeed bleak. I subsequently took hits in both judgment and military bearing categories. As Fred wrote on my December 1976 effectiveness report; "Were it not for a somewhat misdirected enthusiasm in carrying out his assignments, Major O'Prey would be the model Air Force Officer." The Reviewing Officer, Major General Crittenberger, U.S. Army would add in a Block 2 commentary; "This rating 13/85 reflects Major O'Prey's relative position in the Defense Attaché System against extremely stiff competition. He is a superlative officer who is articulate and perceptive in his intelligence reporting. His aggressive dedication to mission accomplishment marks him as a hard charger who would be a welcome addition to

any staff agency." Under the forced distribution (1,2,3 system), 50%
of the officers under consideration would receive Block 3 ratings;
23% Block 2 and a rare percent,13%, Block 1. Supposedly, this new
system would cure the verbal inflation prevalent in the old system as
the distribution was mandatory and debilitating to most officers
affected by it. It would take 5 years of devoted, conscientious duty
to overcome this setback. Yet the total responsibility, personal
shame and incredible failure to come to grips with alcohol remain
mine alone. I attributed my obstinate refusal to acknowledge a
drinking problem to an overweening pride in my Irish heritage, an
ironclad denial mechanism and resentment at any suggestion that I
should abandon drinking totally. My brothers, Ray and Richie were
encouraging a total break with the substance but characteristically, I
remained "a quart low"!

The Yuletide or Christmas Season in Copenhagen was a
cheering experience during this darkness of light and coldness of
winter. Knud and Kitte Vibe-Hastrup, a retired Danish couple to
whom we had been introduced by the Vollmans, hosted a Christmas
decoration-making party for NATO Attaches; British, German and
Dutch. Knud had been the Chief Executive for Kiwi polish, was a
former member of the Danish Resistance during WWII and had
extensive contacts within Danish military and political circles. His
spouse, Kitte, was a model of warm hospitality and genuine concern
for all her guests and graciously assisted adults and children in

cutting out and assembling ornaments. They made things bright for us during these, the darkest days of our tour. During this period, we met Father Larry Antes, an American Catholic priest, a Missionary Oblate, who celebrated Mass each Sunday at our small parish in Herlev. Due to the shortage of boys, our daughters became one of the first "altar girls." While St. Knud's Church, a modern and imposing Roman Catholic Church was in our neighborhood, we found sermons in Danish less beneficial than those in English delivered by Father Larry or his Assistant, Father Leo. Larry had served on an Indian Reservation in Minnesota, while Leo had served in Greenland.

On January 1, 1976, America's Bicentennial arrived bringing with it many Embassy celebrations and functions. Early in the year, Evelyn hosted a St Patrick's Day dinner party at which corned beef and cabbage was the featured entrée. It was well received by our Danish guests as a delicious, rare treat as the dinner was new to the Danish palette. Fru Mette Busch, our Danish cook and our daughters' honorary "Mor Mor" or grandmother became virtually one of the family and delighted in meeting Grandma O'Dwyer when she visited in July 1976. Among American visitors during this period were Jim and Arlette Aanested, former neighbors from Oxon Hill; Evelyn's cousin, John Hayes, his wife Alice and children, Kathleen, John and Billy visited from Iran. John, employed by AT&T, was building the Shah's telephone network. Other visitors to

Copenhagen were Colonel Jerry Hickman, his red-headed vivacious wife, Ann and their five-year-old daughter, Kelly. Stationed at Ramstein Air Base, Germany as Chief Information Officer for USAFE, he invited us to join them skiing in Austria during their next winter trip to Hans Embacher's Inn in Austria. Located a few miles from Kufstein, Chief Master Sergeant Rudy Schmelz made the arrangements for the party of 12 to 16 skiers. Other visitors of conspicuous note to Copenhagen were Lieutenant Edward V. O'Dwyer, U.S. Army with two of his buddies from Crailsheim, Germany. A high point of their entertainment was a trip to the nearby beaches where Danish topless beauties were displaying their charms.

We became long-lasting friends with Henny (Stella) and Niels Friderichsen, Asger and Merete Jepsen from the Ministry of Greenland, and Jorgen and Inge Taagholdt, an Arctic and Greenland scientist from the Lyngby Technical Institute. These friendships were genuine, long-lasting and treasured memories and ultimately validated by each parties' subsequent visit to us in California.

To recapitulate fully and fairly our celebrated first trip to Rome and the enjoyment of Sister Michaeline O'Dwyer's gracious hospitality would require an entire book! Departing our home in Lyngby at 6 AM in our big Ford LTD station wagon, on April 9, 1976, we traveled by ferry to Puttgarten and then south on E 4 spending the night in an Austrian hotel. The girls were very well behaved enroute but somewhat taken aback by the noise and rowdiness of a busload of American grade school students who had unloaded at our rest stop. Accustomed to the quiet and discipline of their Danish classrooms, they innocently inquired "Mom; is that what Americans are like?"

Enjoying the raw beauty of the Alps and Brenner Pass, we stopped the next evening in Modena, Italy. The size of my car was too great for the garage door which I managed to damage but offered to pay for. Reaching Rome and Marymount International School on Sunday, April 11, the following two weeks were a maze of generous hospitality, fine food, unforgettable sights, comfortable lodgings and spirited social gatherings with Michaeline's clerical associates. The resident nuns, mostly Irish, encouraged our girls to entertain them with their selections from HMS Pinafore. We were all treated like visiting royalty. Rome itself is a sightseer's paradise. Led by the expertise, energy, knowledge and indefatigability of Michaeline and Father Dennis Sheehan, we explored them all; St Peters, St John Lateran, the Coliseum, the Vatican Museum, the Pantheon et alia. Soon to be 5 years old, Noreen, having been warned about telling lies and being punished by the "Mouth of Truth" would go on to warn her sisters, Kathy, and Liz of the penalties they might face! A close and trusted family friend, Father Dennis would subsequently officiate at each of our daughter's marriages. A side trip with him and Michaeline to Assisi was a pleasant and spiritually rewarding experience.

On Easter Sunday, April 18, due to Michaeline's astute planning and clerical contacts, we all enjoyed the privilege of being present for Pope Paul VI celebration of Mass in St Peter's Square. Three days later, we toured Florence, enjoying the Duomo, the art, architecture and scenery of that beautiful city. I recall being captivated by a brass, "Romans vs Barbarians" chess set and purchasing it from a vendor on the nearby Piazza Vecchio.

We could never thank Michaeline and her Roman friends sufficiently for their kindness and hospitality as we departed Florence on Friday, April 23. Driving north on the excellent autostrada, we elected to return via the St Gotthard Pass, actually a tunnel train ride into Switzerland. After paying a visit to Lt. Eddie O'Dwyer in Crailsheim, we continued north on the autobahn and took the ferry from Puttgarden back to Gedser, Denmark. We arrived back home at Trongardsparken about 8PM on Tuesday, April 27.

One of the delights or benefits of Attaché duty was the ability to combine duty with pleasure travel. This was the case on Saturday, June 19 when Evelyn, Noreen and I departed for a tour of Jutland. Kathy and Liz had joined the Danish Girl Scouts, (SpiderPigge) and were at a scout camp when Kathy began to feel homesick. To our relief and delight, Liz was able to comfort and reassure her sister. Accordingly, we could proceed with our travel itinerary. This included a trip to Legoland, Billund and nearby Skrudstup Air Base. We visited Major General Thorsen, Royal Danish Army and his wife for a delicious dinner and gracious hospitality at their home in Southern Jutland. General Thorsen was the commander of BALTAP and AFNORTH, a two hat Nato assignment at that time. He was like a grandfather to Noreen, who very innocently and with genuine curiosity inquired whether he spoke Danish! General Thorsen took us on a walk to view the coastal bonfires of Sanct Hans Aften, a midsummer celebration throughout Denmark, which, presumably "sent the witch back to Germany."

On our return to Copenhagen, we explored Fyn, Viking Runic Stones and toured Odense and the boyhood home of Hans Christian Andersen. Author of *The Little Mermaid,* as well as many Fairy and folk tales, Andersen is revered throughout Denmark for his literary works. This was a most pleasant and rewarding trip for its scenery, great weather and ever deepening insight to Danish culture.

Meanwhile, back at the office, Stan Pratt and I were invited to meet the members of Copenhagen, American Legion Post 1; Danish born citizens who emigrated to the U.S. and had served honorably in WWI or WWII. Throughout the war, 1940 -1941, the occupying German military allowed them, on Memorial Day, to decorate their deceased comrades with American flags as a sign of military respect. The current Legionnaires felt they had been more or less ignored by the Embassy after the initial closeness of VE Day in May 1945 and NATO membership in the fifties. Stan and I were successful in persuading Ambassador Dean to attend a Legionnaire's meeting and invite them to our Embassy on the occasion of the visit of the U.S. National Legion Commander, Robert Charles Smith. I subsequently joined the Danish Post and remain a member to this day of Redlands Post 106. The friendship of the Danish was one of the most practical activities of our representational mission in Denmark.

To the very best of my knowledge, Denmark is the only country in the world which celebrates our July 4ᵗʰ Independence Day. Each year, at Rebild, a community in the hills of Jutland, Danes celebrate the success of their countrymen who emigrated and became successful citizens of the USA. To commemorate this friendship and close relationship, Danes constructed a Log Cabin in Jutland which becomes a focal point of joint commemoration every July 4. During the summer of 1976, I was left at the Office to "mind the store" while the rest of the staff departed to Jutland for the occasion.

In May or June, the Embassy hosted a Congressional visit of approximately 40 members led by Senator Birch Bayh of Indiana. All other work ceased, and no stone was left unturned to insure the comfort, happiness and tastes of the delegation. I distinctly recall

Captain Schwartz's reaction to some inane questions such as "How many Air Forces do we really have; Army, Navy, Air Force, Coast Guard, Marine Corps etc.?" Lefty maintained his cool and polite disposition in the face of this and other similar vacuous queries.

The summer of '76 was highlighted by Grandma O'Dwyer's month-long visit. She was a "hit" with all our Danish friends, particularly, Mette Busch. After nearly a year's absence, we and our girls were delighted to have her warm and loving presence in our home. To celebrate properly, we scheduled an automobile trip to Norway. Driving on to the ferry in Copenhagen and enjoying dinner and a restful night on board, we arrived in Oslo early the next morning. The Viking Ship exhibit and museum were noteworthy. Oslo itself was quiet and sedate compared to Copenhagen. We proceeded on to our hotel lodging at Sognefjord, a village at the base of a 4500-foot waterfall with spectacular scenery all-round. We got a sense of how hardy Norwegians are as we viewed their "hutter," sparse wooden vacation cabins, high in the middle of snow-covered fields at elevations of 5000 to 6000 feet. How one could relax in such a cold and forbidding environment was beyond me; but I am no Norwegian!

After a few days' touring from our comfortable lodgings, we proceeded down the rugged coast at a leisurely pace on a narrow road which we shared with an occasional herd of sheep, goats or cattle. Arriving in Christiansand on Norway's south coast, we embarked on a three-hour ferry ride to Hirtals in Northern Jutland. This was a short drive away from Sjaellands Odde, a spit of land where the North Sea meets the Kattegat; a site characterized by the constant spray of the two bodies of water meeting. Many pictures were taken and Ellen O'Dwyer recovered positively from her aboard-ship confrontation with a well-fed German tourist who had parked herself in Ellen's seat when she vacated it to visit the onboard restroom. A popular book at the time was titled "How to be a good German Tourist;" this woman had obviously neither read nor complied with the advice contained therein!

At our hotel in Hirtals, we rendezvoused with Asger and Merete Jepsen and their 5-year-old son, Jens. Liz and Kathy volunteered to babysit Jens while the adults enjoyed each other's company at dinner. The arrangement was copacetic to all with the solitary exception of Jens, who screamed loudly enough to get the attention of the entire clientele at the Inn! Every time our girls would come close to calming him, he would increase his shouting volume proportionally.

Asger and I became good friends as well as practical, productive colleagues in controlling entry approval or disapproval for third country potential visitors to our Defense Areas in Greenland. I recall with nostalgia the "working lunches" we shared at Tivoli Gardens in Copenhagen. Asger was of great assistance to me during each of the three Greenland Commanders' Conferences hosted by the Danish Government and civilian contractors during the autumn of each year. Our Base Commanders, their wives and their Danish Liaison Officers from Thule and Sondrestrom were brought to Copenhagen to discuss areas of mutual interest; e.g., scientific projects, trade with the Royal Greenland Trade Department, oil drilling requests etc. Danish hospitality was legendary. After each day of working meetings, there would be a full course Dinner and reception for the U.S. delegation which was normally headed by a USAF General Officer, the Commander of ADCOM, (Air Defense Command). Brigadier General Larson, Brigadier General John Paulk and General "Chappie" James were the delegation leaders in 1975, 1976 and 1977 in succession. The Conference itself was the highlight of the Fall Social Season. In a more practical sense, it provided me with valuable experience, contacts and mechanisms to resolve, alleviate or avert several future, potentially disruptive, occurrences. These ranged from an ice floe incident, a Telecommunication strike in Greenland, and a British Air Controllers' Strike in the North Atlantic. Each event was a challenge as well as an opportunity to practice effective diplomacy and exercise timely, accurate and positive judgment. I propose to address each in sequence chronologically as well as the denial of Soviet "Technician" transit of Sondrestrom in 1978.

At this point, it may be beneficial to provide the patient reader with a modicum of background in Danish diplomatic history with respect to her possessions in the North Atlantic Region. From Viking times onward, Denmark claimed and owned Greenland, Iceland, and the Faroe Islands without serious challenge from any other European Power. Greenland, like a gigantic "Ice Bowl," rimmed by granite mountains, contained a permanent ice cap reaching snow- and ice-covered depths from 12 to 14 thousand feet. Its Arctic location made it virtually uninhabitable to all but the Inuit or native Eskimos. The Reverend Hans Egede commenced Lutheran missionary activity in southern Greenland in the late 18th century. Small Danish settlements ensued mainly in the Godhob Area. At the beginning of WWII, May 9, 1940, metropolitan Denmark was occupied, virtually overnight by German Wehrmacht and Naval forces. As its highest terrain, "Himmelberg " was a mere 500 feet and the country virtually flat and indefensible. At the time, the Danish Ambassador to Washington concluded a bi-lateral treaty which gave responsibility for the defense of Greenland to the U.S. British military forces seized Iceland. Prior to our entry to the war on December 8, 1941, occupation duty was performed by the U.S. Marine Corps, whom the Icelanders found more compatible or agreeable than the British. The Icelanders had declared their independence from Denmark on May 9, 1940, the day Denmark was occupied. Throughout the war, Danish military Sled Patrols conducted sovereignty missions along the East Greenlandic Coast which deterred German weather forecasters from establishing forecasting stations. The entire Region became a critical area for the U.S. resupply of war material to Britain during the darkest days of the Blitz and substantial U Boat menace in the North Atlantic. Possession of Iceland and Greenland was absolutely essential to Allied victory in the Battle of the Atlantic and Ultimately, VE Day in Europe.

What is most intriguing in this narrative is the fact that the U.S. was officially neutral from May 9, 1940, until December 8, 1941. A similar circumstance occurred during the Wilson Administration in 1917. Shortly before our declaration of war on April 6, 1917, the Danish government sold the Virgin Islands in the Caribbean to the U.S. A partial Danish motivation at the time was to prevent the Kriegsmarine from establishing a forward naval base at that location. Due to her contribution of merchant seamen, approximately 30 thousand personnel, Denmark was recognized as a victorious ally and joined NATO in the early Fifties.

As the Cold War heated up, the U.S. Air Force, as a separate service founded in 1947, recognized the need for forward bases to counter the long-range bomber and missile threat to North America. As a result, the DEW (Distant Early Warning) Line, a series of radar sites was constructed across Canada and southern Greenland. Sondrestrom Air Base, along the Arctic Circle was built to both support the DEW Line and, when necessary, to project SAC's capability northward. Under the auspices of our Joint Defense

Agreement, Thule Air Base was built to the far north, (within 500 miles of the North Pole) to house the then new, Ballistic Missile Early Warning System (BMEWS). The construction, maintenance and supply of both installations were authorized by the Defense Agreement, a bi-lateral treaty which also provided terms for many products and services provided by Denmark. In addition, the Agreement provided for joint control of accessibility of third country nationals to either installation. Cordial and of long-term benefit to both parties, the annual Greenland Commander's Conference served a most beneficial purpose in sustaining and improving these vital relationships. Among the groups participating were Danish Arctic Contractors (DAC), The Royal Greenland Trade Department (KGH) the Danish Foreign Ministry, Scandinavian Airlines System (SAS), the U.S. Department of State, National Science Foundation (NSF) and the U.S. Air Force.

Colonel Fred Ross was a most appreciated friend and supervisor from whom I learned a lot during the 1976 year of my duties and accomplishments. I thoroughly enjoyed the independent responsibilities of my job and that he and his wife, Susanna, were agreeable to any leave schedule Evelyn and I would propose. Yet, Fred was obliged to render a less than favorable effectiveness report due to my fishing trip episode. Painful as it may be to cite, but accurate, it read as follows:

Were it not for a somewhat misdirected enthusiasm in

carrying out his assignments, Major O'Prey would be the model Air Force Officer." The reviewing officer, operating under the new 1 2 3 Forced distribution system, Brigadier General Crittenberger, U.S. Army at DIA, justified his mid two out of three rating as follows:

"This rating reflects Major O'Prey's relative position in the Defense Attaché System against extremely stiff competition. He is a superlative officer who is articulate and perceptive in his intelligence reporting. His aggressive dedication to mission accomplishment marks him as a hard charger who would be a welcome addition to any staff agency."

Despite my best efforts, the fishing trip episode would continue to defer promotion indefinitely. I really had no alternative but to "suck it up" and accept the reality of being another casualty of the "1 2 3" OER system. Meanwhile, the assignment was the most challenging and productive of a 28-year career. I gave it my best and enjoyed every minute of it. The irony is that the numbers are what really made the difference; not the glowing narrative that embellished them. I'll never know for sure!

As I reflect on our three-year tour in Copenhagen, I would regard 1977-1978 as the most productive and practically useful from the perspective of military-politico affairs alone. Early in the year, I was privileged to join three Danish military officers and my good friend Dr. Jorgen Taagholdt on a tour of Greenland: Thule, Sondrestrom and Station Nord, a small base on the northeast coast.

At the time, the U.S. Navy and the National Science Foundation were conducting an acoustic research project off the coast. Twelve feet of ice covered the surface of 12 thousand feet of ocean depth. Landing in a U.S. Navy RD-4 (C47), we enjoyed the limited hospitality of the four Danish NCOs, who were volunteers manning Station Nord and maintaining its 4000-foot runway. They proudly introduced us to their malamutes or sled dogs, whose lead teams were named Orla and Winnie after the resident Prime Minister and his mistress!

Returning back to the "civilization" of Thule Air Base, we each delighted in the comfort and necessity of a warm shower. Jorgen Taagholdet (absent-minded professor) was frantic in thinking his eyesight had failed until I suggested he remove his glasses in the hot, steamy shower! One of my good friends from Vedbaek, the Danish Defense Headquarters, was in his new position as Danish Liaison Officer at Thule. Commander Erik V. Johansen, RDN, and his wife Alice were honored to serve Queen Margarete and Prince Henrik during a subsequent royal visit. We proceeded south to Sondrestrom and were hosted by the Base Commander, Colonel Millsap, a " Red River Rat " and confirmed party animal prior to returning to Copenhagen via SAS.

The practical knowledge of Greenland that I acquired on this trip was invaluable and highly useful in two future events; a GTO strike and the transit of Peruvian Air Force transports through our

Defense Areas. Each summer, fuel oil was resupplied to Thule Air Base by ship/tanker. During a routine voyage, the U.S. Navy ship Potomac struck a "growler" or mini-iceberg in Melville Bat off the West Coast Baffin Strait. No injuries were involved but 40,000 gallons of bunker oil were spilled into this pristine ocean area. To further complicate matters, the Greenland Technical Organization (GTO) was on strike which severely limited telephone communications with Denmark.

In a direct conversation with the Commandant of the U.S. Coast Guard, I was assured that a C-5 loaded with clean up gear, nets, chemicals etc. had been dispatched and would arrive shortly at Thule. In a proactive manner, I passed this welcome information on to both the Ministry of Greenland and the Danish Ministry of Defense. I also offered the services of the U.S. Air Forces' Communications facilities to pass up-dated information on the clean-up progress to the Danish Authorities in Copenhagen. The oil spill problem was ultimately resolved to the satisfaction of all parties involved. I was complimented for my timely and effective initiative.

In June 1977 Ev and I said farewell to Fred and Susanna Ross and welcomed my new boss Colonel Robert and his wife Lynn Piper. Bob Piper was a former F-105 pilot in Vietnam and our relationship was characterized by immediate friendship, mutual respect, and most supportive understanding. He let me know early on that he was the "New Guy" and would appreciate any advice I might render him. Bob had a good and ironic sense of humor. After meeting Colonel Yuri Sacharov, Bob jokingly told Yuri that they both could retire comfortably if Yuri could deliver a new fighter aircraft, the "Foxbat"!

In the Fall of 1977, my experience as a MAC Navigator was most beneficial in understanding the operational implications of a British Aircraft Controllers' strike over the Shanwick Flight Information Region (FIR) of the North Atlantic. Upon being informed of U.S. Air Force violations of Danish airspace in the area, I immediately requested a waiver from the Ministry of Defense for the duration of the strike. As the disruption of normal air traffic flow took place during NATO's annual Reforger Exercise, it was essential to maintain the flow of troops and cargo to our European NATO Allies. Again, timely and effective action on my part resolved the potential problem before it could recur. I was in the position of advising Pentagon officials to keep the airflow going while I worked on the problem.

The absolute highlight of my three-year tour occurred in a military-politico affairs context in January 1978 during the height of the "Cold War. One of my pleasant duties in Copenhagen was to escort visiting Junior USAF Officers on R & R tours of either the Carlsberg or Tuborg breweries. It was said by the Danes that a prolonged strike at either or both facilities could bring down a government! On one such tour, I made the acquaintance of a young

USAF Captain named Mark. He was serving his one-year tour at Sondrestrom, Greenland as Base Operations Officer. I received a communication from Mark to the effect that Peruvian Air Force AN-26 transports with Soviet technicians on board had been transiting the airfield without either Danish or USAF approval. Subsequent investigation revealed that President Jimmy Carter had canceled sales of military equipment to Peru based upon that country's suppression of human rights. As an alternative, the Peruvian Air Force had purchased 12 to 15 Antonov 26 transports from the Soviets and were training Peruvian aircrews for subsequent flight delivery to Peru. In itself, this was no problem. The "fly in the ointment" was the presence and transit of Soviet technicians on board the Peruvian flights. Mark requested embassy guidance on how to handle the situation. My advice was to make sure the Soviets remained on the SAS side of the base while I looked into the situation.

Through the Peruvian Embassy, I established contact with the Peruvian Mission Commander, Lt. Colonel Luis Triante, Peruvian Air Force. After a pleasant lunch at a nearby restaurant, he informed me that he had enjoyed an Exchange Officer's tour in Washington D.C. and was personally grateful to the U.S. military for the successful surgery his wife had experienced at Walter Reed Medical Center. More to the point was his assurance to me that the Soviet technicians were neither needed nor essential to his onward flight progress.

Equipped with this information, I found myself that very evening at a Diplomatic Reception at the Peruvian Embassy. Standing amid conversation between a high-ranking Danish Foreign Ministry official and the Peruvian Ambassador, the Minister stated that his government was highly upset that no advance request or notification had been received and that the Soviet technicians were trespassing Danish as well as Greenlandic sovereignty. Both parties turned to me and asked what the U.S. Air Force would do about the situation. My response was immediate and on the spot. Assured by the Mission Commander that they were neither essential nor necessary for the safety of his flights, the technicians should return to their home country, the Soviet Union, as soon as practical. The Ambassador and Foreign Minister were both in pleasant agreement with this solution and appreciated my decisiveness.

In retrospect, I was honored to be in the decision-making chain of a potential international argument and thankful for the commonsense outcome. The Soviets flew back to the USSR shortly thereafter and Captain Robert Frankenfield, USN, DATT passed on to me Ambassador Dean's compliments for a job well done. In my own estimation, "This was my finest hour!"

From the perspective of 40 years after the fact, my "finest hour" may well have occurred in the Spring semester of 1976 when, providentially, I received a call from Kathleen's school to the effect that she had broken her finger after taking a tumble in her gym class. Her pinky finger was 90 degrees displaced and had to be reset by a doctor. I winced at the needle injection which numbed her hand but could not bring myself to witness the resetting of the finger itself. Kathy was a good and brave patient and totally recovered within a few weeks. I felt grateful that, in Evelyn's absence, I could be present and supportive during Kathleen's emergency.

During the winter of 1975-76, Elizabeth had a serious bout with flu and required a doctor's visit to her at our home. The physician who treated her was a veteran of the Danish Resistance during WWII. He was an Underwater Demolition Team Member and his photo hung in the Danish Resistance Museum with a newspaper article about his attempt to dynamite a German destroyer. Liz did recover from her bout with the flu but was taken aback somewhat by the doctor's suggestion that she might have her large-sized ears cut back!

I have no recollection of Noreen experiencing any illness or injury. All three daughters attended Rygaards School, an English Catholic elementary school during our last year in Copenhagen, 1977-78. Academically, they all did well. Liz was challenged in the classroom by her teacher, Mrs. Glick, who contended that North and South America were actually but one continent! Liz stuck to her guns in claiming otherwise. She received a comment on her report card stating that, on occasion, her classroom behavior was "obstreperous." This generated a visit from Evelyn and the offensive word was ultimately removed. Ironically, Liz and Mrs. Glick formed a post tour friendship and enjoyed a reunion years later after she graduated from Stanford. As a compliment to the British/Danish education system, I would estimate that each of our daughters was approximately two years ahead of their respective American contemporaries when we returned to California.

As Secretary of the Attaché Association, my most challenging and unsuccessful diplomatic moment was attempting to persuade, Mr. Wu, Dean or Doyenne of our group to act friendly and extend a handshake to the visiting and accredited Israeli Defense Attaché, Colonel Ziv Reuter. The Danish Ministry of Defense was conducting a social gathering prior to a tour of Sjaelland. Despite encouragement from myself and Lt. Colonel Heinrich Wall, German Defense Attaché, Mr. Wu was adamant; insofar as his country, the People's Republic of China did not recognize the state of Israel, he could not formally or informally shake hands with Colonel Reuter. When the appropriate rounds of introduction took place, Wu reached in his pocket, turned aside and blew his nose! Zvi Reuter's subsequent and private comment to me about the situation is best left unsaid! The point here is that the rest of our Association members agreed that differences between our countries were no reason we could not socialize in a friendly manner among ourselves.

Combining business with pleasure, the summer of 1977

brought with it a business trip to Wiesbaden, Germany followed by a ten-day family motor tour of Northern France, Belgium and the Netherlands. We drove west to Trier, originally a Roman settlement and from there to Verdun and the "Sacre Voi," forts and Ossuary. Our return route encompassed Paris and the landing beaches of Normandy, where I had the privilege of signing the guest register on behalf of my Uncle Joe Clancy who arrived there in June 1944 with the 82nd Airborne Division. We drove along the coast to Honfleur, Dunkirk, Picardy, Flanders, Brugge, Belgium, Leyden, Amsterdam and back to Copenhagen. Touring the Louvre, despite Evelyn's strongest encouragement, Noreen and Kathy grew "museumed out" and even the Mona Lisa could not retain their interest. I made a major error in trusting Evelyn's college French and ordered "Hirn de Agneau" believing it to be a lamb entrée. I was truly shocked and bereft of appetite when "Hirn" turned out to be brains. Given the variety of cities and sights visited, this trip was a most rewarding geographic and cultural experience.

On January 23, 1978, as a family we took the ferry from Esbjerg to Harwich, UK and drove on to Lakenheath where I took my annual flying physical. I passed the physical, but was diagnosed with suspected glaucoma, which has been successfully treated since then with eye drops. The opportunity to tour Ipswich and East Anglia and learn more of English history was appreciated by all as was the return ferry trip back to Denmark. Shortly thereafter, Liz and Evelyn, under the auspices of the Embassy Wives Club, traveled as tourists to Moscow and Leningrad. They were in the company of Kai and Janet Harders, a couple we knew from church. Their experiences with Soviet customs officials make for a tale in itself. Thirty years later in 2008, Evelyn would observe that a cathedral had been built on the site where a swimming pool had existed in 1978. Due to her attentive behavior on previous trips and the limit of one child per adult traveler, Liz began to experience and enjoy her life-long passion for travel and adventure.

Perhaps the most memorable of our various travels was our second Easter visit to Rome from March 17 to 31, 1978. Once again, we took the ferry from Rodby to Puttgarden; drove south on the now familiar autobahn, E 4 and spent the evening in Mitterwald, Bavaria. Driving through the Brenner Pass and down the Italian Autostrada, we were greeted that evening by Michaeline at the Marymount High School in Rome. Unexcelled as a hostess, tour guide, restaurateur and shopper, she led us to Castle St Angelo, the Villa Borgese, Spanish Steps, Baths of Caracalla and Vatican Museum. The company and mirth of Father Dennis Sheehan was much appreciated as we all enjoyed dining at the Tivoli Restaurant, south of Rome. The specter of Noreen's pretty smile covered with spaghetti and sauce amused all of us, but even more so, Dennis' confirmed fastidious bachelor cousin, Joe who joined us for the repast.

On Thursday, March 23, Evelyn and Michaeline went shopping for shoes in Rome. Having purchased seven pairs and locked them in the automobile's trunk, they spent about an hour on other shopping. Returning to Marymount and proceeding to unpack, they discovered to their great chagrin that the entire purchase of footwear had been stolen from the car trunk during their absence. The theft and circumstances of the theft remain an unsolved mystery to this day.

On Good Friday, March 24, we departed for Sorrento and witnessed the most somber and moving penitential service I have ever seen. Clad in total black, a large and mournful candle lit procession bore crucifixes and statues of the Blessed Mother through the Piazza to observe the Passion of Jesus Christ.

Checking into the Hotel Vesuvio in Sorrento, we drove down the Amalfi Coast and toured Salerno, the temples at Paestum and Pompeii on Saturday. Easter Sunday arrived and with it a ferry trip to Capri. Michaeline had thoughtfully secured dinner reservations at one of her favorite restaurants where the proprietor gave her the warmest of welcomes. After a pleasant dining experience, a sudden storm came up causing waves that negated a return ferry trip. Our only option was the operating hydrofoil. Thanks to Dennis' fleetness of foot and timely purchase of five tickets, we were able to return to our hotel in Sorrento. Fully booked, hotel space was unavailable in Capri, and it would have meant a cold and rainy night on the pier! With characteristic Italian efficiency, Michaeline was informed the next morning in Sorrento, that if she wanted a refund for her unused ferry tickets, she would have to return to Capri for that transaction! I noted that the Italian temperament differs significantly from that of their more efficient and rational German and Scandinavian neighbors to the north. Returning home, we toured Pisa, Lake Como and Heidelberg. The only discordant note was running out of gas near Puttgarden and being assisted by a friendly German motorist in obtaining a refill.

Evelyn was invited in April to join me on an SAS flight to Sondrestrom Air Base in Greenland by Mogens Lund, an SAS Manager. We were treated to a visit to Dye 2, a Radar site on the Ice Cap. Flying from Sondrestrom in a Twin Otter aircraft equipped with skis, we both enjoyed the visit with the five civilians who manned the site. To the best of my knowledge, Evelyn is the only Air Force wife to have enjoyed this adventurous and unique experience. In early May, she had been an American Girl Scout Troop Leader (Troops on Foreign Soil) for about two years. The scouts met in our basement playroom and led by Evelyn, were treated to a Camp Out at a Danish facility in North Sjaelland.

In mid-April, I drove to Aalborg RDAF Base in Jutland to coordinate airdrome parking arrangements for Air Force Two, the Presidential VC-135 which flew our Secretary of Defense to the NATO Planning Group meeting. I enjoyed meeting and assisting the USAF Special Airlift Crew as well as a reunion with Captain Leif Fischer, RDA our amiable Danish host in Oxon Hill. The RDAF at Aalborg did a flawless reception plan for all the Distinguished Visitors. I enjoyed the company of Steve Buckley, a young Foreign Service Officer on the return trip to Copenhagen.

As our three-year tour in Denmark drew to its inevitable close, I note that my calendar for May through July 12, 1978, indicates approximately 30 separate dinner or social commitments. Each was a cherished and memorable event; some more so than others. A contemporary and vivacious couple of similar age, Major Flemming Harboe Schmidt, RDA and his attractive spouse Gisela were charming and gracious dinner hosts. To his Danish Army counterparts, Flemming's nickname was "Smukke" (Pretty Boy) Schmidt. This was due to the fact that he had at one time posed for a Danish Army recruiting poster; a dubious title, but one which Flemming bore with customary good grace.

To be the only Americans in attendance at Fru Busch's 75th Birthday Party was a signal honor and testimony to her closeness to our family. I have frequently commented and observed that most of our professional contacts, in short order, became good personal friends. Henny (Stella) and Niels Friderichsen were both good neighbors in Lyngby and became frequent visitors at our home as we were at theirs. On one biblical occasion, their dog, Puki, signed our guest book with his paw! Asger and Merete Jepsen and Jorgen and Inge Taagholt were also close friends, who like the Friderichsens, would subsequently visit us in California.

During this busy period, we received visits from Jean Vollman as well as my brother, Ray and his family. Ed and Nadja O'Dwyer, as newlyweds, took the opportunity to visit and all were welcomed warmly.

I considered it an honor to be invited to Danish social functions and particularly appreciated the friendship of G K Kristensen, Head of the First Office (Attaché Liaison), who was promoted overnight from Colonel to Lt. General by the Minister of Defense. Lt. General Bente Amled (RDAF) and his wife, Birthe would go on to correspond with us over the next thirty years.

Professionally, I owe much gratitude to Colonel Robert Piper, USAF for his support and thoughtfulness. In early 1980 I was privileged to be promoted to Lt. Colonel. Robert hosted a promotion party in absentia and sent me a tape which bore congratulatory messages from all those mutual friends in attendance, Kay Kristenen's sincerity was matched with regret that the promotion had not come earlier while we were in Copenhagen.

Many details required our attention as we prepared for our new assignment to the 14th Military Airlift Squadron at Norton Air Force Base in San Bernardino, California. I commented at the time that if one was obliged to leave Denmark, Southern California was not the worst pace to go. Visits from our Danish friends would bear this out. Our last week or so was spent at the Marina Hotel, where we had arrived three years previously. We bid farewell to all on July 12, 1978, and boarded Pan Am Flight 73 direct to JFK.

Arriving at JFK at 1645 on July 12, we were met by a most hospitable Kathleen McAdam and driven in her station wagon to our "home away from home", 810 Springfield Avenue, Cranford, New Jersey 07016 As we had not seen each other in three years, our reunion was joyous and memorable; particularly among the young cousins. Having traversed the country twice, I was anxious to repeat, this time in an RV (Recreational Vehicle) and vary our routing to explore new sites. In two subsequent days of shopping along Route 22, I discovered a used vehicle suitable to our purpose, purchased from a used car dealer, on July 14, the 1976 GMC had a V-8 engine, an overhead sleeping compartment and could sleep seven passengers in some kind of comfort. It also had a refrigerator, gas stove and enclosed toilet with shower capability. Picked up on July 18, we drove to Great Adventure and Bradley Beach on "shakedown" trips. Having promised young Michael McAdam an overnight camping experience, we drove almost the length of the Jersey Shore without finding a suitable KOA or other camping facility. Obliged to return to Cranford, Michael was more than a little disappointed to discover he had been sleeping in his own driveway!

July 17 and 18 provided memorable opportunities to visit and reunite with Ray and Pat O'Prey in Palisades, New York and with Richie and Mary O'Prey in Stony Point, New York. Again, the visits were opportunities for the cousins in their rapidly growing families to delight in a most hospitable reunion.

Despite the fact that my newly acquired RV flunked its emission exhaust test and needed a replacement taillight bulb, we stuck to our planned departure date on Monday, 24 July and with Grandma O'Dwyer on board, departed Cranford around noon amid tearful good-byes and promises to visit us in California after we got settled.

We drove 260 miles south to Captain's Cove, a planned recreational community on Virginia's East Shore near Chincoteague Island. Anticipating a possible Pentagon assignment after attaché duty, we had purchased a lot there in June 1975. Meanwhile, the developer had absconded with a few million dollars in funds and we were left with a financial lemon. In retrospect, this was just as well since we were harassed by multiple mosquito attacks that evening when we camped. More consoling was the reality that we were heading to California and not D.C.

On Tuesday, July 25, we drove 264 miles west to visit Ed and Tammy, friends from Copenhagen, in Vienna, Virginia, and John and Pat O'Dwyer in McLean, Virginia. The following day brought a visit to the National Air and Aerospace Museum near Dulles Airport. After two days' rest and a good night's sleep, we hit the road west: 451 miles to Cedar Point Park and a KOA campsite at Port Clinton, Ohio. On July 28, we hit the road early and drove 441 miles to John and Fran Damman's home in Madison, Wisconsin. Again, we enjoyed a most hospitable welcome; toured the Wisconsin Dells and acquired Aunt Joan as an additional passenger. She and her sister Ellen were most welcome as they were attentive to the girls and would provide me with a healthy liquid libation after a long, hot day's drive. Motoring west along the Interstate, we visited Mount Rushmore and introduced Kathy, Liz, and Noreen to four of our most revered presidents; Washington, Jefferson, Lincoln and Teddy Roosevelt. Proceeding along Interstate 90 through South Dakota, we stopped at Wall Drugs for the obligatory free water and drove on to attend a Rodeo in Cody, Wyoming. Our next notable destination was the magnificent Yellowstone National Park. We saw the buffalo roam and thoroughly enjoyed the scenery and wildlife.

One of the prize photos in my slide collection is that of Ellen and Joan in their PJ's overlapped with blankets to stave off the morning chill. Exiting Yellowstone, we then viewed the magnificence of the Grand Tetons and enjoyed a raft excursion down the Snake River. Transiting Jackson Hole, Wyoming, we failed to locate a single Mormon soul who could direct us to any nearby Catholic church for Sunday Mass on 6 August. A long but pleasant drive from Wyoming through Salt Lake brought us to Winnemucca, Nevada. By sheer coincidence, August 6 coincided with Kathy's 12th birthday. Her celebration was sparse and minimal; two Twinkies to share with her sisters! Evelyn recalls me celebrating by delivering a splash of whiskey to Aunt Joan while she was occupied doing laundry at the RV Park Laundromat. By this time in our journey, each of us had experienced our limit of desert driving. The last and welcome of these long days, from Winnemucca to Donner Lake, California brought cheers from all passengers and the pleasure of a cooling dip in its crystal waters.

I believe that we spent the next evening at our old base, Travis in Fairfield. From there, we proceeded down a familiar I-80 dropping Joan and Ellen at San Francisco International Airport for their flight back East. Their company, spirit of adventure, patience and cheerfulness was most appreciated on every segment of our safely completed, coast to coast odyssey. While I readily concede that this narrative can become repetitive and trivial, I write it as fond memory entertaining the hope that a yet to be born descendant may enjoy it. I cherish the memories of our travels and happy family motoring across the U.S. in 1978; an 18-day trip in total at 10 to 14 miles per gallon in a used but serviceable RV.

Driving south from SFO, we enjoyed a visit with Bob and Nancy Matus at their home in Merced. With characteristic thoughtfulness and care, Nancy prepared a birthday cake for our rapidly growing and most appreciative 12-year-old, Kathleen. Bob was back in Wing Standardization (KC-135) after completing his three-year tour as an AFROTC Professor at San Francisco State. After a pleasant visit, we departed Merced and arrived at Norton AFB in San Bernardino on August 11. We checked in to the Transient Lodging Facility (TLQ) a well-appointed and spacious motel-like unit; a welcome reprieve from the cramped quarters of the RV. Located adjacent to the Officers' Club and its inviting swimming pool, the girls were delighted with their new surroundings and their ability to make new friends at the pool.

Returning to a full-time flying assignment at squadron level was not difficult after spending three years in the rarefied atmosphere of Attaché duty as an accredited diplomat. What was initially challenging was relearning the updated characteristics of the beloved C-141 transport. The C-141 B model, with its three Stretched pallet positions and a brand-new Inertial Navigation System were major changes from what I had left four years previous. It didn't take me long to realize that, properly programmed, the INS did a far more accurate job of tracking the aircraft's position than any human navigator or pilot. It became the navigator's task to monitor and update the system as required for trans-oceanic flights and to provide last minute, updated information for its airdrop calculations. In summary, returning to the cockpit was like revisiting a familiar area of operations, the Pacific littoral, without the incentive of an on-going war. On opposite sides of the globe, I participated in airlift missions ranging from Diego Garcia in the

Indian Ocean to North Yemen in the Middle East.

My immediate supervisor was Lt. Colonel Roger Palmberg, a fair, sociable, soon to retire officer, who made our entry into the 14th Military Airlift Squadron an easy and pleasant task. In the Autumn of 1978, the 14th was commanded by Lt. Colonel Chris Warack, an affable Air Force Academy graduate who served on a voluntary basis as a swimming coach at Redlands High School. Colonel Duane Cassidy, a charismatic leader, assisted by his charming wife, Rosalie would go on to earn four stars and become Commander-in- Chief (CINC), Military Airlift Command. Despite my promotion failures, I continued to seek higher level job responsibilities. "Flying the Line" was enjoyable but led nowhere. The duties could be performed by a Second Lieutenant through a Lt. Colonel. My personal opinion was that at the squadron level, there should be room for only two field grade officers; the commander and his operations officer. Most of the other field graders I had met were content to fly their missions and had no aspirations whatsoever for any Wing Staff Position. As I had now completed 20 years for retirement eligibility as a Major, I readily accepted Lt. Colonel Herb Bevilheimer's offer to get me a position working as Assistant Wing Mobility Officer for Lt. Colonel Tom Mahach, a logistics planning genius, a fair and pleasant supervisor and definite "hard Charger. Together, Tom and I would design and implement an effective Mobility Plan for the Wing's forthcoming

Operational Readiness Inspection (ORI). Future events would demonstrate and validate the wisdom of this job selection and partnership.

Our efforts were crowned with success when the Wing passed the ORI in May 1979 and our Wing Mobility Control Center (WMCC) achieved an outstanding rating. Our Wing Commander, Colonel Cassidy summoned me to his office and asked how I would feel about becoming his Wing Information Officer. My response was that I was honored, thankful and delighted at the prospect. However, I felt obliged to inform him that I faced the likely possibility of a final Passover to Lt. Colonel on the next promotion board. As this was a highly visible position with the local community, it could be risky and potentially embarrassing to him and to the Wing itself. He thanked me for my interest, time, and honest response. I have every reason to believe that he was impressed with my candor and, while that position never materialized, a more prestigious one was hovering in the near future.

On the domestic side, our search for a new home had been a novel family venture. Having decided to purchase our first home, and armed with the recommendations of Carl and Jan Swenlin, old friends from Travis AFB, we met our realtor, Sharon Dawson. Sharon was the wife at that time of Dick Dawson, a Major and fellow Navigator in the 14th. After several days of searching, our daughters and I decided that the view of the pool from the kitchen window at

118 Anita Court was irresistible. Evelyn liked the home too but was apprehensive about the danger of a backyard pool. I was apprehensive over how to cover mortgage payments on a retired Major's pension! We reassured Evelyn that we would observe water safety, and she could monitor our compliance from the kitchen window.

One of the benefits of having Sharon Dawson as our realtor and mediator was her introduction of us to the previous homeowners, Chuck, and Carolyn Shoemaker. Once the ice was broken, we became very good friends and exchanged mutual home visits. In addition, our families enjoyed outings to Camp Pendleton's Beach at Delmar and the sociability of attending the Redlands Bowl together. Chuck, a Notre Dame graduate and USMC veteran provided most appreciated assistance with sprinkler systems, lawns, flower beds and routine pool maintenance. Being a total neophyte to home ownership, his practical and abiding advice was always appreciated.

Through Chuck and Carolyn. and Carl and Jan Swenlin, we were introduced to contemporary couples who became long-term friends; among them Miles and Debby Miller and David and Ann McMahon, fellow New Yorkers, and transplants to California. Our near neighbors, Larry and Ellen Barrett and Larry and Helen Hurley rendered a plethora of practical assistance with pool and lawn maintenance. Helen was School Secretary at Kimberly Elementary where Liz (10) and Noreen (7) entered the sixth and second grades, respectively. Kathleen (12) entered Moore Junior High as a seventh grader. Each of the girls accommodated rapidly to their new academic environment in California, testing tooth braces and developing an interest in going to the town movie theater.

An amusing incident occurred at the time with Noreen. She informed her schoolteachers that she was called "Bernardette" as she could not find bicycle plates with her given name "Noreen." Cautioned by her father that her name change was ill, she resumed her baptized name with trepidation. In conversation with her teacher, Mrs. Webb, Evelyn was told that she thought it strange that Noreen did well in spelling; could even spell San Bernardino but could not spell her own name!

One of the major highlights of the summer of 1979 were the performances of Evelyn, Kathy, Liz, and Noreen in the Redlands Bowl production of *Fiddler on the Roof*. In addition to acting and being a "stage-mother," Evelyn achieved a 96th percentile grade on the National Teachers' Exam in Mathematics. This resulted in being hired to teach at Moore Middle School, conveniently attended at the time by Kathy and Liz. She brought not just brilliance, but discipline to the classroom and earned the dubious sobriquet, "The Detention Queen."

As 1979 came to an end, we enjoyed the closeness of our five- member family and the coziness of our new and fire-place equipped home. Christmas Season was celebrated in Danish style; live candles on the tree; dancing around it and through the house and decorating with Danish plates, Nissemaender and Julemaender. It had been an eventful year and who could predict what the future might bring! Apprehensive over mandatory retirement and what direction a second career might take, I found the words of Rudyard Kipling relevant to my uncertain situation:

> *"If you can meet with triumph and disaster and*
> *treat those two imposters just the same..."*

The common thread weaving through my narrative of triumph and disaster was the influence of alcohol through either of these extremes. Whether celebrating a promotion or the lucrative assignment to Copenhagen or consoling myself for failure, my obstinate, stubborn, and incredible refusal to acknowledge a problem would pay its own price. However, that story remains for the next decade, The Eighties.

Wedding Day, June 30, 1962.

Honeymoon in the Bahamas.

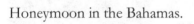

Saying goodbye to Liz and Kathy before tour of Vietnam, 1969.

In front of the Presidential Palace in Saigon, 1970.

Bernard with Vietnamese orphans in Saigon.

Enjoying R&R in Hawaii with Ev.

Military Ball, 1971.

Noreen's arrival at Travis AFB, August, 1971.

Official family photo from 1973, taken before Bernard's military
attaché assignment to Denmark.

Arriving in
Denmark,
1975.

Bernard in
Copenhagen,
1976.

Evelyn with Fru Mette Busch.

In Rome visiting
Michaeline, 1977.

Skiing in Austria, 1977.

In Greenland,
1977.

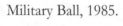
Military Ball, 1985.

Retiring as Lt. Colonel, at Norton Air Base, September, 1987.

Kathy's wedding, 1993.

Liz's wedding, 1994.

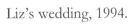

Noreen's wedding, 1999.

The Trumans: Steve, Meaghan, Jack, James, and Kathy

The Walkers: Rob, Liz, Colin, Kiera, and Aidan

The Ashtons: Noreen, Andrew, Grace, and Annie

Celebrating Evelyn's 70th birthday in Hawaii with the family.

Celebrating Evelyn's 80th birthday in San Diego with the grandkids.

50th wedding anniversary
at Redlands Country
Club, June, 2012.

Family at Kelly and Alex Montalvo's wedding,

2016.Cruise in 2019.

60th wedding anniversary celebration in Newport Beach, June, 2022

CHAPTER SIX

THE EIGHTIES

There was something ominous about the Eighties. One way or another, it promised change and new directions in my life and our family's future. The new decade began with a family ski trip to nearby Big Bear Lake, hauling all the clothing and equipment up the mountain in our faithful RV. We joined a couple from Redlands, Carl and Judy Hastings and their son Robby and daughter, Laura. Sharing rental costs at a condominium. They were good skiers as were our girls. I had progressed to initial intermediate status mastering parallel skiing and turns. This, however, did me no good whatsoever when a "hot dog" skier sped non-stop right over the front of my skis, knocking me over with a left ski boot which failed to release. I sustained a severely broken ankle which could be healed only two months in a thigh to toe cast. Dr. Coolbaugh, the orthopedic surgeon, told me that multiple, small fractures would join together but none was large enough to hold a pin. The blessing, not exactly in disguise, was Evelyn's tender loving care at home during the early weeks of my recovery.

Placed on convalescent leave by the Flight Surgeon's

Office, in early February I was most pleasantly surprised to receive a personal phone call from Colonel Don Hargrove, Deputy Commander for Operations, 63rd MAW. He notified me that I had been promoted to Lt. Colonel by the recent permanent Board and could pin the silver leaves on immediately. I thanked him profusely for his thoughtfulness and asked him humorously whether pinning them on my pajamas would suffice for the time being!

My relief and incredible feeling of ultimate vindication was joyous. The promotion would provide seven more years of active-duty service prior to a legally mandated retirement date of 1 October 1987. The more crucial aspect of this would be the ability to fully support my family through their educational needs of the future. If I were to select a single senior officer whose advice sustained me throughout the pre-promotion period of uncertainty, it would be Colonel Bob Baldwin (RIP), the non-rated, Chief of Personnel in the 63rd Air Base Group. Congratulating me on my successful promotion, he said it was now time to "pay the piper" and "get to work." At the time, Bob was acting Deputy Base Commander, serving Colonel Reginald Shaleski, Base Commander, who was soon scheduled to be relieved by Colonel Marilyn Coffinger.

Marilyn was a "fast burner" i.e., an officer who had received several "below the zone" promotions in her highly successful career. She arrived at Norton AFB after serving as Deputy Base

Commander at Elmendorf AFB, Alaska. At this point in her career, she had the distinction of being the first female to command a major military installation in the "lower 48". Of all the officers to whom I was assigned, none was as diligent, thorough, hard-working, and totally dedicated to their job as Marilyn. She became a celebrity in her own right; being interviewed in her office by Tom Brokaw for a TV broadcast. She set a hard-working example, on and off the job. Accordingly, I was not at all surprised when, during my last weeks of convalescent leave, she had me writing speeches for her from my home.

A more revealing aspect of Marilyn's leadership style occurred when Colonel Robert H. Custer arrived from his assignment at Kunsan, South Korea to fill the slot of Deputy Base Commander. A tall, thin, and amiable fighter pilot, Bob's arrival was preceded by an inch thick packet of commendations from the Mormon Church and the U.S. Secretary of Defense on down. During a period of unrest in South Korea, he sheltered American missionaries on Kunsan Air Base and distinguished himself by his timely and effective actions. I admired his style, bearing and accomplishments and looked forward very much to working with him.

On his very first day on the job, Marilyn sent the two of us across the street to inspect the Visiting Officers' Quarters where the Inspection team from MAC Headquarters would be billeted. We returned about a half hour later to report that all looked well. "Did you flush every toilet bowl?" "Did you turn on each shower and faucet?" These were Marilyn's questions to which our response was not every bowl, faucet, or shower but that we conducted spot checks. "Well, go back and check each one" she ordered. I felt embarrassed for Bob as he was a "full" Colonel and presumably beyond such petty details. At any rate, we carried out her more precise orders and ultimately the Wing passed the Facilities Inspection, and we were exempt for another year. "Whatever it takes!" was Marilyn's style and neither of us was inclined to argue or demur.

The job or position I was entering, depending upon my ability to walk on crutches, was Base Executive Officer in 63rd Air Base Group, an organization of approximately 1200 people, civilian and military. Under the Wing Commander structure, there were four major subordinates; the Base Commander, the Deputy Commander for Operations (DO), Deputy Commander for Maintenance (DCM) and Resource Manager (RM). The Norton AFB Clinic was commanded separately by a Medical Officer; a Colonel/Flight Surgeon.

One can liken the Base Commander's responsibilities to that of a City Manager; three subordinate squadrons; Headquarters, Security Police and Civil Engineering. In addition, mission staff agencies; Personnel, Data Automation, Judge Advocate,

Administration, Chaplain and Morale Welfare and Recreation provided base-wide support to an installation population of 12 thousand people, military and civilian. With three or four resident tenant General Officers; the Air Force Inspection and Safety Center (AFISC), Ballistic Missile Office (BMO) et alia, there were constant demands for one thing or another on an installation with antiquated WWII era plant and facilities. Priorities, judgment, and action were required to satisfy the varying demands of approximately 40 tenant agencies in addition to those of our parent MAC Airlift Wing.

The Base Executive position came with a reserved parking spot at Wing Headquarters and the prestige of the Base Commander's Office. I developed cordial, positive, and productive relations with each of our subordinate units Margie Berry and Mim Pestrella, two office secretaries to the Base Commander and Deputy Base Commander were of tremendous assistance to me during this process as they handled my clerical needs as well. Two of my initial duties were to prepare an agenda for weekly staff meetings and review the financial status of each of our units at a monthly financial working group.

This truly was a "whole new world," vastly more complicated and challenging than flying the line as a Navigator. I was gratified to use much of the management lore I had acquired in the MBA Program years earlier at Westover. The variety of tasks I tackled as Base Executive, I felt, would prepare me well for post Air

Force employment. I was delighted with the prestige and managerial challenges of the position itself and the opportunity to direct a base-wide project, the annual Commander's Facilities Inspection. I was privileged to represent the Base Commander in the local community serving on the Military Affairs Committee of both the San Bernardino and Redlands Chambers of Commerce. At the office, there was always some action to be taken; some policy to review and message traffic/paperwork to process with or without recommendation.

An additional task for the following five years was to maintain flying proficiency as a Navigator. Actually, flying overwater missions was a welcome relief from office duties which normally stacked up during a week or 10 day flying absence. Previous policies had provided excusal from flying duties with flight pay continued for certain positions; but not for mine, which, on paper, did not officially exist!

By late March or early April of 1980, it surprised no one to see Colonel Duane Cassidy's name on the Brigadier list. At a reception to honor him, he told me eye to eye that he was happier to learn of my promotion than he was of his own to BG. I responded to the effect that I didn't believe a word he said but thanked him profusely for his complement. Duane Cassidy would go on to earn four stars as a General and become Commander of Military Airlift Command; his successor at the 63rd MAW, Claudius

E. Watts III would go on to earn three stars, retire and become Commander of the Citadel, a military college in Charleston, South Carolina.

In the early Eighties, the San Bernardino Chamber of Commerce and American Legion Post 14 sponsored a Military Appreciation Parade honoring the U.S. Army, Navy, and Air Force on Armed Forces Day. As luck would have it, it was the Air Force's turn to provide a marching squadron along with High School and other units, down E Street in San Bernardino and terminating on the Orange Show grounds. American Legion Post 14, directed by Mike Gaughn and Colonel Tom Chandler, U.S. Army Reserve, hosted several highly hospitable planning sessions at their Post in San Bernardino. I thoroughly enjoyed their hospitality as well as the opportunity to meet counterparts in the U.S. Navy and U.S. Marine Corps Reserve. I was in a position at Norton AFB to assist them in supporting some of their unit's activities on the base. The Parade went off well and I felt privileged to ride along with Colonel Al Casey, Ballistic Missile Office Commander in the Parade itself. He went on to earn three stars as a Lt. General and to retire in Redlands.

At the Office itself, one of my unwritten and unspecified duties, yet one in which I excelled was that of handling, what I referred to as "heavy Breather" telephone calls. The Base Commander's Office was a constant target of inquiry; What time does the BX open? etc. Most of these questions were handled efficiently and courteously by either Margie or Mim. Others, mainly complainers insisted on speaking to the Base Commander herself. At that point, I would get on the phone; respectfully hear the caller out and refer that person to the proper agency of the office for resolution of their problem. In most cases, this worked. If, however, the Boss needed to be involved, I would promise and deliver a call back. An example of the more serious problem was when the antiquated air conditioning system broke down; when could it be expected to come back online etc. In some instances, civilian employees threatened to walk off their jobs due to extreme heat. The possible spoilage of BX or Commissary consumables made these situations critical. The Base Commander was required to deal directly with the problem, remaining at the mercy of the Base Civil Engineer for power restoration or air conditioning repair. In most instances, however, I could save her valuable time and attention by responding positively and effectively to the problems at hand.

I recall two notable but somewhat humorous exceptions. A young man called the office stating to me and the secretaries that "he had information of interest to the highest levels of the U.S. Government!" I advised him that if this were true, we should not be discussing it over the phone and that he should visit me at the office ASAP. He agreed and I subsequently listened to his tale of "They" zapping him in the middle of the Mojave Desert and how he was suspicious that NSA had performed the deed. He provided me with his phone number in Redlands. When I called it, his surprised father exclaimed "He's Where?" referring to the Base Commander's office. The father retrieved his mentally confused son and that was the end of that episode.

A more humorous event occurred when a woman called to inform the Base Commander that the candy sales lady at the Base Theater was having an affair with the ticket salesman and the Base Commander should put an end to the liaison immediately. I agreed with the caller, that if true, this was immoral, but under the Privacy Act, not the business or jurisdiction of the Base Commander. She agreed and that was the end of that incident.

Even more dramatic was the afternoon when our very capable and professional Commissary Manager, Mr. Bill Davis gave a rare call to the office and asked that I come to the Commissary for an unforeseen and provocative situation. Upon arrival, I was informed by Bill that a female patron had been pushing a basket, topless or near topless, causing consternation and confusion throughout the store. Regrettably, she had departed prior to my arrival, but had been wearing a wide fishnet top rather than a blouse. At Bill's request, I promised to research what legal consequences could be taken if and when she chose to revisit the Commissary. Coordinating with the Base Legal Office (JAG), we discovered that the Department of Defense (DOD) policy with respect to clothing attire was that a top garment and a bottom garment was all that was required. Further, it specifically forbids Installation Commanders from supplementing or adding further restrictions to the policy itself! An interesting world and outcome, but nevertheless an example of how wide-reaching and varied my duties could be!

With respect to leisure and recreation, our trusty RV occupied my and the family's attention. In the summer, we enjoyed a visit from the McAdams. After touring Kings Canyon and Sequoia National Parks, Aunt Kathleen needed a break from the chattering, bickering and claustrophobia of the RV itself. When she rented a motel unit at our resident campground, all five children deserted Evelyn, me, and the RV for her more spacious, air-conditioned quarters! A nearer and more popular destination was the primitive camping facility at Del Mar Beach, Camp Pendleton. We made friends with two of the resident MWR Marine employees, Carl, and Johann, who provided us with freshly caught fish and good company.

We had the benefit of meeting 2nd Lieutenant Bill (Sonny) Liston, USMC and his spouse, Kaia. Bill was a native of Cahirciveen, County Kerry; played and sang Clancy Brothers and Irish Rebel songs on his guitar. Bill was always entertaining and welcome at our campsite as we were later at his home. Although he promised Noreen that he would "wait for her," the age difference won out and we were privileged to attend his and Kaia's wedding several years later. The magic of RV camping at Pendleton was that around a campfire at night, and fortified with a jar of whiskey, one could tell or hear war stories from fellow campers in an atmosphere of camaraderie and nostalgia.

With a campsite conveniently located next to a placid saltwater lagoon, I was encouraged to drive up to Big Bear Lake in response to a promotional give-away regarding a time-share there. I had no intention whatsoever of purchasing one, but our attendance would reward us with an inflatable rubber raft which would add to our camping pleasures at Del Mar Beach. To my extreme dismay, Evelyn signed up for the Condo rental against my expressed wishes! Halfway down the mountain, I was able to persuade her to cancel the purchase. Her stated intention was to "cure me" of responding to "free offers." We did enjoy paddling the "Rubber Ducky" around the Camp Pendleton lagoon together.

As blossoming teenagers and confirmed sun worshipers, it was about this time that Kathy and Liz requested that when I came to the beach, I "walk on by" and not join them on the blanket. I suspect that their motive was to attract the attention of beach-going Marines of whom there were many. As part of his driving safety program, the USMC Commanding General would sponsor on-base recreational events, boxing matches, beauty contests for varying age categories, unit picnics etc. Well-attended and popular, these events had the effect of encouraging young troops to stay on, celebrate and avoid the dangers of driving and drinking off base. A mere 80 miles from roasting Redlands, we spent many relaxing family days at Del Mar Beach, enjoying the cold Pacific and broad, sandy shore. I invested about $90 in purchasing "Boogie Boards" for Kathy, Liz, and Noreen. Consequently, I was quite upset to learn that they had been stolen while the girls were showering in the Ladies' bath house. Win a few and lose a few!

The RV generally served us well. We did sustain a transmission breakdown, the repair of which necessitated an unplanned overnight at the garage station in nearby Oceanside. Today, I treasure the memories of the sunshine and the beach as the risks of skin cancer and old age itself preclude spending an hour or two sunbathing or ocean dipping.

In the Spring of 1980, old friends from Denmark, Commander Erik (EV) and Allice Johansen visited us from Thule, Greenland where Erik had been assigned as Danish Liaison Officer. He and Allice had the privilege of hosting Prince Henrik Queen Margarete in their Quarters at Thule. Unfortunately, the weather in Southern California failed to cooperate with their visit. As EV stated with characteristic Danish irony; "My former friend; I come all the way from frozen Thule to visit you and all you can give me is constant rain!" Later in June, Niels and Henny (Stella) Friderichsen arrived with their three daughters; Frederika, Pauline and Julianna and we enjoyed a marvelous reunion. A humorous incident occurred while standing online at Universal Studios.

Pauline was making entries in her diary. When I noticed that a young man was looking over her shoulder, I remarked on what a coincidence it was that she should meet a fellow Dane at random in Southern California. Her reaction was more abrupt and to the point; "He should mind his own business!"

Upon visiting Dr. Heinrich, an orthodontist in Redlands, it was decided by him that Kathleen and Liz required dental braces to straighten out their alleged overbites. I opined to him that their teeth looked perfectly well to me and that possibly the braces were not required. His response was to the effect that I could always get a second opinion. Needless to say, "Tin Grins" placed by Dr Heinrich became the order of the day and the young ladies wore them well!

1982 was the year of our most memorable St Patrick's Day Party. With lots of Jameson and Bushmills to go around, one of my aviator friends, Ron Eckels arrived as a bagpiper and serenaded the party of 50 to 60 celebrants on our poolside patio. Lt. Colonel Bob Larson, the Base JAG, brought his pet goat, dyed in green as "Paddy McGinty's" goat. Our pet dog, Reggie, thinking he was female companionship, reacted ardently to the hilarity of all spectators. We've had more than a few St Patrick's Day Parties, but that of 1982 remains the most memorable!

As we explore together the early Eighties, I owe the patient reader a periodic update on the family members with whom I share these precious memories. I am assisted in this process by a collection of annual family Christmas letters. Today, these are priceless, often sentimental reminders of the "Good old days" and the blessings I received as a husband and a father. In 1982, Noreen joined the braces club at the age of eleven. These did not interfere with her soccer team play or her ballet and jazz classes. Nor did they repel boyfriends or her interest in male classmates. After an arbitration hearing on Evelyn's dismissal from Moore Middle school, the arbitrator ruled totally in her favor. She received not only tenure but restoration as a full-time math teacher at Redlands High School, a more favored academic environment than the Middle School or Junior High. One of her first students was our daughter, Kathleen, starting a tradition that each of her sisters would follow in requesting Mom as a math teacher. Evelyn herself would go on to accumulate 24 highly successful years at RHS, retiring in 2002.

At this point, Kathy stood a statuesque and head-turning six feet tall, proud of her straight A s in 11th grade High School and also of her acquisition of a California driver's license on her very first attempt. Kathleen played varsity basketball, was on the Speech team and began to research colleges of her choice.

Liz entered the 10th Grade after garnering academic honors in Junior High and lent her talent and contagious good humor to the Redlands Bowl production of *Carousel*. Between jazz and ballet dancing, voice lessons and choir practice at school, Liz donated her volunteer services as a candy striper at Redlands Community Hospital. She attended her first formal in a stunning gown and held the attention of a steady beau throughout High School.

The family highlight of Summer in 1982 was a trip to Waikiki via space-available flight from Norton AFB. We enjoyed the facilities at Fort Derussy while staying at nearby hotels and enjoying the Waikiki Market.

As 1982 drew to a close, we took a pre-Christmas RV excursion to visit Ed and Nadja O'Dwyer in Colorado Springs where Ed was stationed at Fort Carson. The hospitality was warm, and the alcohol and war-sites flowed onward. The area was hit by a massive and windy snowstorm. In order not to lose each other or the person leading the group, we had to hold on to a rope outdoors to maintain direction Ed entertained a convivial group of young Army Officers and their wives. I enjoyed the novelty of transiting Raton Pass in New Mexico on our route over to and from Colorado Springs.

As 1983 dawned, I had little or no idea of what a momentous year it would be. As alluded to often in this narrative, I frequently enjoyed a few drinks. The word "few" is misleading as it never was my habit or practice to limit my intake to few. Quite to the contrary, I delighted in the effect of inebriation and was inordinately proud of my capacity for bourbon, a particularly

American potage. What I do recall and could never deny was the fact that it took more and more of the substance, alcohol to reach the same effect. In addition, I had the poor judgment to over imbibe on the wrong occasions and in the wrong company. I heartily resented any observation that when I drank, my speech became slurred. My denial mechanism was overwhelming, and, to my warped way of thinking, my "capacity" precluded any realistic acknowledgement of a problem.

I began to feel morose with respect to post retirement job prospects and alcohol fueled this penchant for self- pity. Never one to leave the Officers' Club early, I got in a confrontation, while drunk, with a young Captain who was filming patrons at "my bar." To make a long story short, this incident was brought to the attention of my boss, Colonel Robert H. Custer, who, in August 1982, succeeded Marilyn as Base Commander. Bob called me into his office, shut the door and in a classic intervention manner, informed me that my job performance had fallen off and that it was time to go back to the squadron and "slow down." Puzzling and shocking as this was, the actual telling blow fell, when, with a tear in his eyes, he suggested that I take a look at what my drinking was doing to my family! In the early eighties atmosphere of "It's OK not to drink," I was obviously well ahead of the pack, and as such, a prime candidate for rehabilitation. No one needed to tell me that if this rehab failed, my Air Force career would be over. At the

Annual Bob Hope Charity Golf Tournament, 11 and 12 June 1983, I had over-indulged to the point of embarrassing Evelyn and being a classic "horse's ass". When the firing occurred on Monday, June 12, I was devastated and asked for time off. This was readily granted, and I choked up with actual tears on my way home to Redlands. On the next day, I was visited by Lt. Colonel Jay Burkey and Lt. Colonel Miles Miller, two personal friends with whom I shared my story. Jay, Squadron Navigator in the 14th Squadron, my putative supervisor, had experienced tragedy and alcoholism in his own family. If I chose to come and fly my missions, that would be fine. On the other hand, if I admitted I had a problem with alcohol, this might be the proper opportunity to do something about it. The choice was mine.

I admitted to these two friends and brother officers that, for the umpteenth time, alcohol had negatively affected my Air Force Career. I could no longer deny that as a fact or hard evidence that I definitely had a problem with alcohol. With their encouragement, I agreed to meet with Mr. Gearge Murray, the Base Alcohol and Drug Abuse Counselor. Having met George frequently at the office, his assessment and blunt statement was to the point; "Bernie; those that think they have a problem with alcohol, usually do." George then informed me that he had already arranged a billet for me at the Naval Hospital Alcoholic Treatment Facility at Long Beach. Having the wedding of Evelyn's cousin, Joan Damman scheduled for the coming Saturday, June 18, I gave George my word as an officer that I would not drink before, during or after that occasion if I could enter "Dry Dock" on Monday, June 20, 1983. He accepted and I complied with this promise which, in my estimation, was the equivalent of a vow.

I responded positively to the 44 days of treatment at Long Beach Naval Hospital, the most beneficial segment of which was its introduction to Alcoholics Anonymous. For me, this was a radical change of direction in my life, and I remain profoundly grateful to Evelyn for being willing to join me there for her support and willingness to join me for two weeks. By the grace of God and her unwavering support, I recently celebrated 34 years of sobriety. I thank the U.S. Air Force for its patience and the allowance of four more critical years of active service until mandatory retirement in October 1987. I apologized to Bob Custer for "letting him down" on the job. His response was "You didn't let me down; I didn't want to see you kill yourself!" In itself this statement alone wiped away any shame or regret for being obliged to seek treatment and generated a spirit of enduring gratitude to Bob Custer for initiating the action he took.

After 44 days of treatment at "Dry Dock" in Long Beach Naval Hospital, the program ended the first week of August 1983. I was delighted to return to Del Mar Beach at Camp Pendleton for a few days of reflection and relaxation. Reentry to the 63rd Military

Airlift Wing ran smoothly and without any recrimination or embarrassment and resumption of previous peer friendships. Attached for flying to the 14th MAS, I got my flying status restored on an overwater flight with Lt. Col Rick Lindeman, Squadron Commander. When summer rolled into September, Lt. Colonels Miles Miller, Ed Sagmeister, and I were detailed as Loaned Executives to the Arrowhead United Way, reporting to Mr. Ray Stevens, its civilian Director. Our task along with seven or eight other volunteers was to deliver appeals to several civilian and governmental corporations seeking their financial support for our communities' needs. For an eight-week period, we reported in civilian attire, coat, and tie, and visited our respective clients with a prepared appeal. Relieved temporarily of all Air Force duties, this was the ideal mechanism for transition to civilian life. On the less than positive side, my particular clientele was the U.S. Post Office in the San Bernardino Metropolitan area. Politically, the United Way had supported "right to work" legislation to which many postal workers were opposed. In my appeals for contributions, I took no position on this issue, but emphasized the need for charitable support of our local agencies. This was a fascinating and most worthwhile experience in which I achieved moderate success.

In December 1983, I was offered a desk at Wing Headquarters with Lt. Colonels Kent Morey and Mike Kobald in Combat Tactics. As Special Assistant to the Deputy Commander for Operations (DO), I then reported to Colonel Dill Haugen and was assigned varying ad hoc duties. Among these were Commander's Facilities Inspection and Summary Court Officer for Staff Sergeant Scott Hertell. Sgt. Hertell had been killed in a motorcycle accident on his way down highway 330 from Running Springs. If variety was the spice of life, I was being served a good dose of it! Yet, my positive approach to these duties was successful and essential to my recovery.

As Base Commander, Colonel Bob Custer retired in April 1984 and was succeeded by Colonel Bill Hillyer, a former C-130 pilot in Vietnam. I was grateful to both these officers when they offered me my former job as Base Executive Officer in April 1984. Our new Wing Commander was Colonel Tom Eggers, an Air Force Academy graduate with a commendable background in Special Operations. Returning to my former job, I felt most appreciative and welcome without any stigma, by the new leadership and my peers. My staff officer experience was put to practical benefit by assignment to the Wing Exercise Evaluation Team for ORI preparation. By 1986, Colonel Bill Hillyer retired, and Colonel David (SK) Voigt succeeded him as Base Commander along with a new Wing Commander, Colonel Marv Erwin. I enjoyed and respected David Voigt and only disappointed him once. He requested that I prepare a "frocking" ceremony for our newly promoted Base Chaplain. The big problem here was that, to the very best of my knowledge, only the U.S. Navy "frocked" newly promoted officers, i.e., they could pin on their new rank insignia prior to their effective promotion date. One of the innovative and more imaginative personnel officers provided SK the required verbiage for the ceremony and it took place without incident.

I was honored by Colonel Voigt when he sponsored a retirement Luncheon for 60 to 70 guests and was later presented with an Air Force Meritorious Service Medal at a formal parade and retirement ceremony. I was particularly moved by the presentation of the U.S. flag which flew over Norton AFB by the enlisted men and women of the 63rd Air Base Group and the shadow box of decorations painstakingly built by my replacement, Major Jerry Odette. These events closed out an Air Force career, 28 years of triumph and disaster; for the most part positive, memorable, and replete with life- long friendships. I was justifiably and immensely proud of Evelyn when, at the retirement ceremony, she received a Certificate of Appreciation from the United States Air Force for her invaluable contributions as an Air Force wife. In a humbling and deeply thankful manner, without her love, support, and loyalty I could not have accomplished the success we achieved.

As an approaching 50-year-old, I found employment prospects as a "generalist" bleak to dismal to non-existent. Nobody was knocking on my door and the resume was not producing job interviews. On the positive side, Bob Garrene, a barrel-chested,

Irish American, former Los Angeles Police Officer got me an offer to teach *Introduction to Supervision* part-time at San Bernardino Valley College. I accepted readily and eagerly as teaching was a pleasure and the Air Force had provided me with both practical experience in briefings as well as its own management challenges. I was very relieved to have employment, even though it was part-time; three hours a week. At the same time, I was enrolled in the teacher credentialing program at Cal State San Bernardino with the objective of achieving a credential in Social Studies. It turned out most beneficial that I could cross-feed techniques I was learning at Cal State with my classroom lectures and program at Valley College.

I found that teaching adults was a psychologically rewarding experience as I discovered a profound respect for students who worked all day and were prepared for a three -hour course that night. It was a pleasure to assist serious students on their way up their respective career ladders and to share their job site experiences with me and their classmates. In return, I learned from them; their experiences, opinions and reactions to the cases represented in the textbook. I later added an additional three-hour course in Public Administration to my repertoire and found it dry as dust and a greater challenge to teach. In the subsequent nine years teaching at SBVC (1987-1996), I enjoyed pleasant and productive relationships with Jan Green and Queen Hamilton, the two subsequent Chairpersons of the Business Department. When Queen was promoted to Dean of the College, her replacement opted to bring in a new part-time instructor to replace me. In the Community College System, there were no guarantees of job or tenure and that was that!

I completed the credential program at Cal State in 1989 and acquired a Substitute teaching credential during the same period. Student teaching was accomplished at Clement Middle School and Redlands High School. The experience left me with a distinct preference for High School. In either locale, I discovered that classroom presence was but the tip of the iceberg; grading tests, essays and lesson planning demanded a substantial amount of time, and I was not at all positive that I was devoted to spending it!

Reentry to the world of academics was a learning experience. Possessed of a life-long interest in History, I wrongly anticipated that high school students would bring a similar disposition to the study of the subject. While many did so, the disruptive few earned my wrath for their disinterest, distractive behavior, and waste of classroom time. On the more positive side, I found the creation of stimulating lessons, videos and outlines a challenge to my personal ingenuity and paucity of creative instincts. I learned much from veteran teachers; Dave Nollar, Tom Atchley, Paul Butler, and Sue Wallace in particular.

In April 1989, having completed the teaching credential and having an additional year or so of unused GI Bill benefits at my disposal, I decided to pursue an MA in History at the University of California Riverside (UCR). While I found the courses stimulating and in a depth to which I was not accustomed, I discovered the difference in being the dilettante that I am and the character of the true scholar willing to spend hours of research activity in the library. My personal motive had been to acquire an MA in History which might lead to a full-time teaching position in that subject at the Community College level. At the same time, I noted that such openings were rare to non-existent. Employed by virtue of my MBA at San Bernardino Valley College and kept reasonably busy as a High School Substitute in Redlands, I saw no point in further pursuit of the MA in History at UCR. However, the academic experience itself was deeply appreciated. Professors Tobey, Wall, Ravitch and Ransom were particularly stimulating with their courses on the History of Science, Modern European History and Economic History. Of note with other academics was the attitude of snobbish superiority they exuded with respect to the academic status of their presumed intellectual inferiors in the Cal State system! I would submit that Professors Bob Blackey and Kent Schofield at Cal State would equal or exceed the abilities of the snobbish elitists at UCR on any day of the week.!

By December 1990, I concluded graduate history studies with no regrets. As I expressed at the time, "History is too much fun to be consigned to library footnotes or the interpretations of irrelevant, arcane and obscure scholars." That being said, I do entertain a respect for those scholars willing to dedicate their time, discipline and energy to necessary in-depth research in pursuit of a PhD or other narrow subject of expertise.

On the domestic front, the Eighties represented a decade of positive growth and multiple blessings for our family. It is my fondest hope that each member will pen her memoirs for future generations. In the meantime, I would submit this paltry sketch of their accomplishments during the period of their teens. Kathy attended Redlands High School after three years at Moore Junior High from September 1978 to June 1980.

Tall, blond, and athletically inclined, she played varsity basketball and was an achieving academic role model for her younger sisters. In September 1982, Evelyn plunged back into the busy world of a high school math teacher and was rewarded by receiving tenure as well as Kathy as a student. Kathy gave us the scare of her young life (16) when she sustained a compound fracture of her left tibia bone while skiing with the family at Mammoth Mountain. She was hospitalized there and sustained further complications with fat cells in her circulatory system after her leg was set and casted. After an evening in an oxygen tent, her blood count returned to normal, and she faced five months on crutches with a leg cast. In June,1983 her grades earned her membership in the RHS Daisy Chain, a group of thirty female students at RHS.

Our pride knew no bounds as she entered the march into the Redlands Bowl on a walking cast! Graduating from RHS in June 1984, Kathleen addressed her fellow graduates at the Baccalaureate Ceremony with a speech titled "Hello; I Must Be Going"; an epic which I was privileged to edit for her.

Having won a California State Scholarship as well as an Officers' Wives' Club stipend, Kathleen entered the college of her choice, UCLA in September 1984. Her highly successful pattern of academic success culminated in her selection to the Mortarboard Society in 1988. After joining Pi Phi Sorority and serving as its president, Kathy's social life was active and productive. I had the privilege of being invited to share Dad's Day with her in 1985. I proudly watched her perform the duties of Keg master, tending the beer keg which provided liquid refreshment enroute to the Rose Bowl. Graduating with honors in June 1988, Kathleen achieved 91st percentile on the Law School Admission Test and was awarded her law degree after three years, 1988 to 1991 at Hastings Law School in San Francisco. In the Fall of 1989, we were introduced to Steve Truman, her tall and most amicable future husband. That story remains for inclusion in the Nineties.

After three years at Moore Middle School, Liz entered RHS in September 1982. Continuing to excel academically, Liz exhibited an abiding interest in drama, music, and musicals. At her suggestion, if not insistence, we purchased a family piano, which she faithfully practiced on and then some! Her acting talents were displayed in the Redlands Bowl production of Carousel in the summer of 1982. Between jazz, ballet dancing, voice lessons and choir practice at school, Liz managed to donate her services as a candy striper at Redlands Community Hospital. Ever the stage-mother, Evelyn joined Liz in the respective upper-class roles of Mrs. and Miss Upton in the production of *Auntie Mame* in the summer of 1984. To give credit where it is due, Evelyn's role demonstrated shapely legs as well as a latent acting talent and her tendency to remain ageless through aerobic dancing and disciplined, if faddish dieting.

Liz's crowning achievement in acting won her selection by her drama coach, Dave Chenowith to play the lead role of Maria in the RHS senior year production of *Sound of Music*. Liz was selected by the American Legion Post to attend Girls' State, a week-long study seminar on government hosted in Sacramento.

One of my rare opportunities to become a hero in Liz's eyes occurred when she was informed by a seedy telephone promoter that she had "won" a trip to Hawaii. As this would highly excite any teenager, she was asked to provide a credit card number for the "other" expenses. Together, Liz and I confronted the perpetrator at his boiler room operation in Redlands and retrieved the reservation Liz had made under false or extremely misleading premises.

Following her graduation from RHS in June 1986, Liz

pursued her language and travel interests by attending the University of Salamanca, Spain in the summer. At the conclusion of her studies, Liz sustained a gastro-intestinal infection which had her hospitalized in Spain. With no memory of the onset, we were spared much anxiety when our 17-year-old traveler telephoned to advise us that the worst was over, and she was "on the mend".

Liz's high grades and extra- curricular activities at RHS provided a number of options for her college selection. She and Evelyn were back east in Georgetown, when, with their permission, I opened a package from Stanford University advising us that she had been accepted into the Stanford Class of 1989. Our joy and pride knew no bounds! Liz attributed her success to the letter which she had composed and forwarded with her application. In September 1985, the family made a dramatic entrance to Roble Hall, Liz's new dormitory residence where she breathed a sigh of relief after the RV was unloaded and removed from public visibility in the parking lot.

Pursuing her major in American Studies and starring in several University musical productions as well as conducting campus tours for the Travel Office, Liz graduated in June 1989 and began teaching ESL (English as a Second Language) at Junior High School in East Palo Alto. Liz went on to secure a position as a travel leader and subsequently, Director of the Stanford Alumni Travel Office. Her accomplishments remain a source of pride to all of us in her family.

I cringe at the memory of her graduation when I stubbornly refused to put out my smoky cigarette at Liz's request in my car. Actually, my three daughters had been pleading with me to quit for a number of years, but the addiction was entrenched. My selfishness and obstinacy resulted in a painful scene and memory which endures to this day.

On a similar note, the demise of our pet dog, Reggie during the summer of 1987 was a story in itself in which I reluctantly supported Evelyn's decision to no longer put up with his canine love antics with neighboring dogs!

Hardly daunted and never intimidated by her older sisters' stellar academic performance, Noreen followed their path attending Moore Junior High from 1983 to 1985; RHS from 1986 to 1989 and UCLA from 1989 to 1993. Celebrating her 14th birthday on a cruise of the Mexican Riviera with Evelyn and me, her good looks and sophistication turned heads whenever she passed by. At RHS, Noreen exceeded her sisters' accomplishment by achieving Five on the AP U.S. History Exam. As I commented in a Christmas letter in 1984, "As a leading scorer for her soccer team, and connoisseur of contemporary rock music, Noreen lives in a louder world than her noise-sensitive father can normally tolerate. She exhibits a definite penchant for funky clothes, privacy and an unmistakable enthusiasm for school dances and boys." As her sisters had before her, Noreen passed her Driver's Exam on her first effort. I distinctly recall the tears in my eyes generated by the purchase of her first automobile and the realization that in September of 1989 our family nest would be empty. She entered UCLA and was accepted into Alpha Delta Phi sorority. I subsequently received an invitation to join her for Dad's Day at the football stadium. Upon graduation in June 1993, Noreen secured a position with Oracle Corporation which was based in San Francisco and offered her enviable travel opportunities. While my memory continues to recall their names, I can express my continued friendship with each of my daughters' high school and college sweethearts.

Kathleen and her beau, Ken Sumalo, a varsity football player, were highly respectful and impeccably polite. When he and Kathleen were followed as a "Prom Special" for the *Redlands Daily Facts* in June 1984, my picture taking their picture became part of our family legacy. Evelyn still shudders when she recalls my wet bathing suit and protruding tummy.

Liz kept pretty steady company with Keith Carlson, a true gentleman and model Christian. Liz was invited to sing at his church, and we were good friends with his parents.

For her last two years of high school, Noreen dated David Hewlett, an Air Force Colonel's son. David was well-mannered and tended to be on the quiet side. For reasons still unknown, David decided to disappear out of Noreen's window one evening, generating a police search requested by our neighbor Walter Mook, who had heard an intruder in our backyard. All ended well when David showed up at our front door without further incident. While a Junior at UCLA, Noreen's beau was an amiable Naval ROTC cadet, Todd Abrahamson. Probing his knowledge of geography one afternoon in Redlands, I asked Todd whether he could locate Holland on a map of Europe. His response was a startling no; as long as he could program his airborne computer with the coordinates, the computer would do the job! To validate this assertion, Todd went on to become Commander of the U.S. Navy's Blue Angels several years later. I remain highly impressed and wary of any tendency on my part to rush to judgment!

While at Stanford, Liz invited a classmate of Indian origin to visit and dine with us. Prior to his arrival, Evelyn had sternly admonished us not to bring up any ethnic or racial commentaries during our conversations. It was hilarious, when, on a neutral topic, Evelyn herself blurted out "Don't be such an Indian giver!"

As the Eighties came to a close, my concern over the economic realities of seeing three daughters through college began to subside. Evelyn's salary and my retirement seemed to be adequate for our situation. We had and have a lot to be thankful for; Kathleen in Law School at Hastings; Liz teaching Junior High School in Palo Alto and Noreen entering her freshman year at UCLA. I am wary of getting too involved in our daughters' stories as the risk of misrepresentation is high and I would hope to see each of them take up pen or pencil and elucidate their memories for the sake of posterity. I had entered my fifth decade and Evelyn had successful thyroid surgery in 1987. Our travel plans had commenced to Denmark and Spain and together, we anticipated continued travel and good health for the approaching Nineties.

CHAPTER SEVEN

THE NINETIES

Hardly anticipated at the time, the key events of the Nineties would be the weddings of each of our daughters to their respective fiancées and the subsequent change in our status to becoming new grandparents. 1990 was the first year of empty nest syndrome, which was by no means unpleasant; less bickering, no more Liz singing songs from *Phantom of the Opera* in the shower etc. Kathleen and Liz had established apartment outposts in San Francisco, while Noreen became a resident in her sorority house (Pi Phi) adjacent to the UCLA campus. As occurred with Kathy at Alpha Delta Pi, Noreen hosted me for an enjoyable Dad's Day at a UCLA football game.

To her credit, accompanied by Sandy Minkler and Sue Hearn, her colleagues at RHS, Evelyn anticipated completion of her master's Program in Math Education at CSUSB. In my graduate study situation at UC Riverside, it was time to decide upon and commence work on a thesis. Yet, there were few to zero history teacher positions available in the Community College System. The rationale for pursuing an MA in History became questionable and ultimately not worth the time and effort. My MBA, acquired at Westover AFB in 1969, sufficed for the enjoyable, part-time task of teaching Introduction to Supervision, and, upon occasion, Public Administration. In addition, I taught an occasional course in Management at the Whitehead Center at the University of Redlands.

Aside from my immediate family, there are few people whose memory I revere more than that of my mother-in-law, Ellen O'Dwyer. Always welcome in her home for tea, dinner or breakfast, her smile was contagious and her TLC heartfelt and genuine. She kept our lines of communication open when Evelyn and I were on the verge of going our separate ways due to arguments or petty misunderstandings. In June of 1990, the entire O'Dwyer and Hayes family came together to celebrate Ellen's 80th birthday at Friendly's Restaurant in Cranford, New Jersey. It was a memorable occasion and we, once again, enjoyed the benefits of Aunt Kathleen's warm hospitality.

A brief glance at a desk calendar reveals the date of Friday, 16 February 2018 and is, in itself a chastisement for my penchant for procrastination which has retarded the progress of this narrative since its inception. Having celebrated my 80th birthday in reasonably good health, my shortness of breath is a consequence of 40 years of smoking and an obstinate refusal at that time to heed the loving pleas of Evelyn and our three daughters to cease the vile habit. It took until 1995 to finally give it up. I have adopted the practice of a daily (weather and schedule permitting) quarter mile walk and find the habit somewhat beneficial. Two other health issues, eyesight and kidney function require annual checkups, both scheduled for the coming weeks. I retain a spirit of positive optimism, strongly encouraged by Evelyn. This is balanced by the reality that this life is a temporary journey and I have far more to be thankful for than I have to regret. Enough of these musings and a return to the Nineties narrative!

1991 was an auspicious year for education and travel. It began when I commenced a long-term substitute assignment for Tom Atchley, a highly respected Social Studies teacher at Redlands High School. At its conclusion, one of the advanced placement students remarked to the effect, "When Mr. O'Prey entered the class, it was as if Mr. Atchley had never left!" A more generous, cherished or deeply appreciated comment could not have been made.

When the summer of 1991 had arrived and Operation Desert Storm was a huge success, Evelyn and I flew to Frankfurt, Germany, rented an automobile and initially enjoyed the hospitality of Ed and Nadja O'Dwyer. At the time, they were based at Kaiserslautern Kaserne, a major U.S. Army installation in the area. As the Berlin Wall had been torn down in November 1989, we were delighted to drive through Prague, Vienna, and Berlin. In Prague, we stayed in the unique accommodation of the "Boatel," a barge on the river converted into staterooms for tourists. The Czech menu provided no translation for the numerous menu items but did advise, in English, that any entre one ordered would be delicious. They were absolutely right! A stop in Munich brought a visit to Hitler's retreat in the Alps as well as an enjoyable reunion with Paul and Nancy Reinman, my former co-pilot, and good friends from the old days at McGuire AFB. Vienna and Salzberg were predictably delightful.to visit. Like Munich and Berchtesgaden, they were replete with scenery, history, the cultural arts, and challenges to my college German.

Berlin was a most impressive city and a visible reminder of the repressive nature of The Wall and the Cold War itself. The gratitude of Berliners themselves to the U.S. Air Force for the Airlift in 1948 was expressed by our freedom to ride their buses or subways at no cost. Touring "Checkpoint Charlie," we were fortunate to share the company and memories of a Canadian Army Forces Major who had vivid recollection of being there at the height of the Cold War.

Driving west through Leipzig enroute to Frankfurt, the stark differences between East and West Germany became even more apparent on the autobahn. The number of luxury western automobiles; Mercedes Benz, Audi and BMW were clearly in a superior class compared to the smoky, underpowered Trabi and the Soviet imported Lada machines.

After three weeks of touring, it was a definite relief and pleasure to again enjoy the hospitality of Ed and Nadja. They were the much-appreciated local experts on the Gutenberg Museum, local street Fairs and recommended restaurants. This was a highly memorable and ambitious trip as we thoroughly enjoyed the itinerary and their generous hospitality.

The academic heroes on the home front were Evelyn and Kathy. Ev completed her master's degree in Math Education after publishing her ponderous thesis in CAI (Computer Assisted Instruction) in the High School Math Class classroom. Evelyn had successful gall bladder removal in October 1991 and enjoyed six weeks of convalescence; particularly after the medical attendant duties were turned over to her mom! While Evelyn was recovering at the Redlands Community Hospital, I took my three daughters to breakfast at a local luncheonette. Our waitress, in good humor, rendered an accurate assumption describing me in the group as a "thorn among the roses"! No one else could compete with Grandma's tender loving care, gardening skills or culinary abilities. I was beneficiary of her largesse when, returning from a routine and unspectacular golf round, I discovered that grandma had resurfaced our driveway during my absence!

Kathy completed her final courses at Hastings Law School

and accepted an Associates position in Los Angeles with Latham-Watkins, a prestigious west coast law firm. Liz converted her teaching credential into working full-time as an ESL Junior High Teacher in San Francisco She put her singing talents to good use working part time in the piano bars of "The City." With a year and a half remaining at UCLA, Noreen sought an internship at Pete Wilson's Office in Washington D.C. as an adjunct to her Political Science/Latin American studies.

As is the case with each of our household improvements, Evelyn's initiative generated a 400 square foot extension or room addition to our home. We vacated our front bedroom moving to the rear bedroom with its added convenience of an opaque, glass-bricked adjacent bathroom and shower.

In response to an invitation from Kathleen McAdam and to celebrate our 30th Wedding Anniversary, we joined her and our convivial Cranford friends on a cruise from Montreal to New York City via the St Lawrence, Gaspe Peninsula, Nova Scotia and Newport, Rhode Island. Arriving in New York harbor on July 3, we anchored and enjoyed a spectacular review of the Tall Ships which dwarfed the replicas of the Nina, Pinta and Santa Maria. Not only did we observe the 500th anniversary of Columbus' discovery but had a memorable voyage meeting some real fine and genuine friends, mainly from Bayonne, New Jersey.

I have a dim recollection of being introduced to Steve

Truman at Noreen's sorority Presents, a social function at UCLA. His height, manners, friendliness, courtesy, and love for Kathleen were obvious qualities. To this very date, his advice is gratefully sought in resolving any of my numerous computer application problems. The major event of 1993 was their marriage in Phoenix, Arizona on September 4,1993. Officiating at the marriage was Monsignor Dennis Sheehan, a good family friend from our days in Rome. The wedding took place at St Mary's Basilica, a Cathedral in Phoenix. As a warmup to the wedding itself, was our golf outing at the Wigwam Resort, a posh golfing hotel west of Phoenix. As I commented in my Christmas letter at the time; "It couldn't have gone better if I had planned it myself!" The Truman family extended their warm and cordial hospitality to all the visiting wedding guests, making for a most memorable experience for all. Kathy was a beautiful bride; Steve handsome but too numb to say anything other than "I do." As he knelt at the altar, no one could miss the statement "HELP" chalked on the soles of his shoes. Evelyn was in all her resplendent glory as mother of the bride, relishing each second of this joyous occasion. The reception went flawlessly as did the post reception happenings back at our suite.

Having been introduced to our family previously, Rob Walker, Liz's fiancée, was in attendance. Peter Hancock, Noreen's U.S. Marine Corps beau at the time was on a deployment to the Western Pacific Rob Walker was a friendly fixture ever since. I was impressed by his business acumen, sense of humor, wit, and golf prowess. My mother in law's incisive observation that Rob had "thin lips" remains a mystery comment in our family legend to this day.

Earlier, in June 1993, Noreen graduated from UCLA with a major in Political Science/International Relations. One of her beaus at the time was a sharp, pleasant, polite, and courteous Naval ROTC Cadet, Todd Abrahamson. During a visit to Redlands, I took the opportunity to question him with respect to his future plans. Todd asserted that he planned to become a naval aviator; specifically, a carrier pilot. I complimented him on his ambition and, attempting to plumb his knowledge of geography, asked him if he could locate Holland on a map of Europe. His surprise response was to the effect that he could not, but his GPI (Ground Position Indicator) would do this for him! We were truly in the computer age. Todd validated his hopes and abilities by becoming, a few years later, Commander of the U.S. Navy Blue Angels, their crack aerial demonstration team.

1994 was certainly a year of reunion for Evelyn and me from both a travel and family perspective. Having acquired a Mileage Plus Credit Card some years ago, Evelyn put it to intelligent and productive use in her monthly shopping endeavors. The result was that she accumulated enough credits for round-trip airline tickets to the British Isles. In June, we took off for a glorious month of touring Ireland, England, Wales, and Scotland. In eight fascinating days we drove a complete circuit of the Emerald Isle, a feat accomplished only by the understanding, patience, and legendary hospitality of relatives in Killarney and Mayo as well as our bed and breakfast hosts in Dublin. A major highlight was the long overdue reunion we enjoyed with relatives and "suspected" relatives in Castlewellan and Newcastle, County Down. The suspected relatives; Jim and Marian Cowan, had been touring San Francisco earlier in the year. Finding our daughter Liz's name in the telephone book, they called her and inquired whether there existed any family connection. Liz passed our phone number on to them and I enjoyed the privilege of an hour's conversation comparing mutual relatives in County Down. Close, but never certain, we promised to visit them during our planned tour in July.

Driving through Banbridge town, five kilometers west of Castlewellan on July 12 (Orangeman's') Day in Ulster, we discovered later that Banbridge was 90% Protestant while our destination was heavily Roman Catholic. As this period was experiencing the "Troubles" or major sectarian violence at the time, we cautiously made room reservations at the Down Patrick Motor Inn, some 10 to 15 miles north of Castlewellan. The Cowans had scheduled a "Craic," or party, in our honor, and we delighted in meeting their large family as well as Martine (nee O'Prey) Fulcher, my actual second cousin and several O'Prey aunts; Maureen O'Prey and Peggy Mc Carton. The Cowans had formed a family band which entertained our joyful assembly until the wee hours. More adventure followed on our return to the Downpatrick Motor Inn, when, in pitched darkness, our car was flagged down at a roadblock by the Ulster Volunteer Force (UVF), a Unionist, anti-IRA military group. I exited our vehicle as ordered and was questioned by a camo-uniform, AR-15-armed guard. Informed us that cars with Dublin plates were very suspicious, particularly at 3 AM, we were relieved to return safely to our hotel.

In subsequent daylight, Marian and Martine helped us tour my great grandparents' graves in Kilcoo as well as the Church where my grandparents married on November 3, 1907. In addition, Martine took us on a cautious drive through sectarian Belfast, 30 miles to the north, where the conflict raged without remorse. As a counterpoint to this visit, we flew to London where ironically, we were hosted as guests of Squadron Leader Peter Russell, RAF at his Squadron's formal Mess Dinner. Due to the violence taking place in Ulster, Peter and his RAF companions were restricted from visiting Northern Ireland in toto.

Having survived a near disaster driving down O'Connell Street on the wrong side of the road, it was a relief to board a Globus tour bus in London and be guided for 15 days of viewing castles, cathedrals, towns and villages in England, Wales, and Scotland. Our English friends, Peter and Daphne Russell-Smith were most hospitable, and we enjoyed a variety of memorable activities ranging from the RAF Ball to a round of golf and tour of Leeds Castle. Our visit to Cambridge University and punting on the Cam River was an imaginative highlight provided by their daughter Kate, a vivacious and informative student at the time.

Evelyn reverted into her "mother-of-the-bride" role in August 1994. We got a preview of wedding protocols when my nephew, Kevin O'Prey, Raymond's son and his bride, Maren Proulx exchanged vows on September 4 in Carmel. A family reunion was most appreciated, even with the antics of "the groper" as a disconcerting side-show. A scant three weeks later on September 24, the Stanford University Chapel provided a dignified and monumental ambiance to our daughter Liz's wedding to Rob Scott Walker of Cupertino, CA. With the indispensable assistance of Rob's parents, Jim and Linda and a convention of deaf-mute softball players at the Santa Clara Marriott, the reception was memorable, humorous, and poignant. The signature memory of the lively wedding reception is that of our resplendent bride, Liz sitting on her husband Rob's lap doing a Marilyn Monroe impersonation singing Making Whoopee.

As 1994 drew to a close, we found Steve and Kathleen Truman living in Redondo Beach and Liz and Rob Walker residing in Fremont, CA in the East Bay. Noreen was renting an apartment in San Francisco where she had secured employment with Oracle

Corporation and was dating a young U.S. Marine, Pete Hancock. Aunt Mary; Sister Michaeline O'Dwyer, working at the Jesuit School of Theology at Berkeley was an appreciated neighbor and hostess, renowned for her knowledge of recommended wineries in the Napa Valley. It was a blessing to have all three daughters in California and within a day's drive from Redlands. Evelyn continued full-time Math teaching at Redlands High School; played Bridge and was very involved with AAUW activities during this period. My part time Community college teaching and high handicap golf game remained a comfortable lifestyle for me. Of far greater significance was my success in abandoning my heavy smoking habit (two packs a day) during this period on the advice of Dr. Sheldon in Redlands. He put it bluntly; if I wished to cash in early, smoking was doing the job for me. If I wanted to see grandchildren; then quit immediately. The Good Lord's intervention enabled me to take the latter course!

1995 was a year of promise and travel to several destinations. February brought a family ski weekend at the Walker family condominium in Bear Valley, CA. When the water and electricity were interrupted by a storm, we were treated to an unrehearsed and unprogrammed exercise in Arctic living! Prepared to cancel our plans, Rob was surprised to learn that we had every intention of staying put! It turned out to be a pleasant venture, hauling water from the basement and enjoying the restoration of electricity.

Summer brought a return visit to Ireland and a three-week driving tour of the Republic and Ulster. Ellen O'Dwyer, returning to the town of her birth and family cemetery, stated that had we stopped nowhere else, the trip, in her estimation, would be a great success. Once again, the families in Limerick, Down, Sligo and Mayo provided genuine and warm hospitality to the three of us. Our trip was saddened by the death of Kitty O'Halloran, Evelyn's cousin. Her funeral gave us the experience of witnessing Irish grief and mourning.

In early September, Kathy and Steve gave us the very welcome news that a grandchild was due to arrive in April 1996. Later, on September 23, we celebrated Helen and Joe Clancy's Golden Wedding Anniversary at a party hosted by Richie and Mary O'Prey at their home in Stony Point, New York. Similarly, we enjoyed the accustomed hospitality of Kathleen McAdam and were delighted to view Phantom of the Opera then running on Broadway. We were privileged with a backstage visit with Brad Little, the star of the production and a native of Redlands. In addition to Phantom, young Kelly Slachman, Evelyn's niece, escorted and treated me to *Commandant From Connemara*, a bloody, horrific spoof play on the theme of IRA terrorism; a topical subject at the time. Kelly's interest in Irish history is both consoling and most encouraging. She, of all family members, displays the most understanding of the heritage of our families, the O'Preys and O'Dwyers.

As the Eighties was the decade for academic achievement for our daughters, the decade of the Nineties was one of love and marriage, travel, and initial home ownership. The most vital and beloved, however, was the commencement of grandchildren's arrivals. Meghan Hayes Truman arrived predictably, safely, and beautifully on April 30, 1996, where her father Steve dutifully recorded her emergence into the world via video camera. Her parents had taken up residence in Redondo Beach, Ca. A blessed spin-off of this event was my successful determination to abandon my 40-year-plus habit of smoking. Had I not, you would not be reading this reflection!

Liz continued to teach high school in San Francisco and performed part-time singing gigs in wine bars in the city. An eventful year for Liz, 1996 witnessed her career change from classroom teaching to join the Stanford University Alumni Study and Travel Office as a tour planner and trip leader. Liz would go on to become Director of the Office and be in a key position to rescue her mother and I from a perilous medical situation in Belize a few years later.

Noreen climbed the corporate ladder at Oracle Corporation. Her ascent would, in due course, be interrupted when she met Andrew Ashton and joined his travel team of Oracle consultants. As an Internal Auditor, she traveled to nine countries in Europe, Asia, and South America. In December 1998, celebrating their engagement they spent Christmas 1998 at his parents' home in Killarney Heights, Sydney, Australia.

Kathleen returned to Latham and Watkins Corp after her maternity leave and began to realize that the "Glass Ceiling" was a reality which she was not willing to accept. She would go on to form a most successful partnership with Todd Elliott and enjoy a lucrative practice together in a well-appointed office in downtown Los Angeles

1996 was not without its sadness and family loss. My uncle, Joseph Francis Clancy, husband of Hellen Clancy and father of Ellen, Joe and Daniel passed away in September. Evelyn and I were privileged to provide some comfort to the family as Joe, an 82nd Airborne Veteran of Normandy, Holland and the Bulge left a legacy of patriotism, service, and love to all in his family. I was privileged to deliver a graveside eulogy at the VA cemetery in mid Florida.

Having entertained a lifelong curiosity with respect to my paternal grandfather, Patrick O'Prey and the conditions he experienced as a copper miner, Evelyn and I selected Butte, Montana as a travel destination in the early summer of 1997. We drove north to Park City and Salt Lake, Utah; Butte and Helena, Montana, Glacier National Park and Hells Canyon, Utah. I was privileged to sign the guest book in Butte, discovering records of

Patrick and my grand uncle Jack in the city museum. Butte enjoyed a boom in copper production, labor peace and record mine owner profits prior to and during WWI. The main street of Butte displayed the original Ancient Order of Hibernians Hall, the Miner's Union (IWW) Hall and several Irish bars. Across the street from these facilities stands a house of prostitution, the ladies of which provided letter writing and sewing services as well as physical delights to their clients. The open pit mine in Butte is the world's largest. The mining operation itself shut down in 1985. Of ancillary note is the fact that Butte claims the largest population of Irish American per capita of any city in the U.S. At the turn of the 19th century, Butte was the largest city between Chicago and San Francisco, boasting the first five or six story Otis Elevator west of the Mississippi.

Despite these attractions, Patrick returned to County Down in February 1921. His daughter, my closest aunt, Helen arrived on January 5, 1922. Patrick returned to New York City in 1923 and died of silicosis, miner's lung disease in August 1931.

The contemporary attitude of the natives in Montana can be captured by a brief and friendly conversation we enjoyed in a downtown bar: "Are you visiting from California and enjoying yourselves?" "Most definitely yes!" Then don't tell anyone about Montana after you get back!"

Later, in August 1997, Evelyn went off with Liz on their long-anticipated cruise of the Aegean with the Stanford Alumni

Travel Office. Liz and Rob purchased an upgraded home in Redwood City and hosted a housewarming dinner following our annual Thanksgiving gathering at Joan and Frank Slachman's home in Sacramento. Evelyn's sister, Mary left the Jesuit School of Theology at Berkeley (JSTB) posting she had enjoyed in northern California for a new assignment at Marymount in Tarrytown, New York. Noreen made plans to become the family expatriate acquiring Irish citizenship which provided her with a working visa for a year in Australia. In addition, she presented Evelyn and me with two round trip tickets to visit her in Sydney in March 1998. In a minor miracle of packing expertise, Steve Truman managed to box my old green desk, while one of Noreen's good friends brought it back, as baggage with her to Sydney!

In late February 1998, Evelyn's mom, Helen O'Dwyer died in the arms of her daughters in Cranford, New Jersey at the age of 88. We gathered together in Pearl River, New York to celebrate her priceless legacy of faith and unconditional love. Her funeral mass was celebrated by Monsignor Dennis Sheehan. Her burial took place at Gate of Heaven where her remains joined those of her husband, Jack O'Dwyer and their son Michael O'Dwyer. A follow-on reception and celebration of her life took place at a nearby Irish restaurant, The Flight of the Earls, which Helen had pre-selected in Hawthorne, New York. Joy and remembrance characterized the contributions and recollections of the many attendees, friends, and family, who were invited to share their recollections of her long and loving life.

Evelyn and I enjoyed the 14-hour flight to Sydney to visit Andrew and Noreen as well as touring that beautiful city as well as Melbourne. It was also a genuine pleasure to meet and be hosted by Andrew's parents Bill and Vivienne Ashton at their home in Killarney Heights, a community north of Sydney. I am particularly grateful for being hosted for rounds of golf at both Bill and Andrew's home courses while Evelyn and Vivienne explored shopping venues in the area. Andrew and Noreen announced their engagement and set a wedding date for late August 1999 in San Francisco.

Meaghan Truman's younger brother, John Caroll Truman arrived, healthy and on-schedule on May 19, 1998, and Evelyn's baby-sitting gigs became more frequent and varied in distance. After such a commitment in Nogales, Arizona in July, Ev and I drove north to Santa Fe and Taos, New Mexico. The pueblos, rugged scenery and Western Art were fascinating and added significantly to our appreciation of the American West.

Consoling myself with daily, if inept golf, Evelyn, once again joined Liz and the Stanford Travel Group for a cruise of the Stockholm Archipelago and the Baltic. Copenhagen was on the itinerary and provided the most welcome opportunity for them to tour Lyngby's Danish homes and reunite with close friends from our three-year tour, Niels and Stella Friderichsen and Asger and Merete Jepsen. A similar reunion took place in San Francisco in November 1998. Joining Andrew to accomplish wedding reception site selection, we went to meet Liz at the airport. Having just returned from a three-week tour of Saudi Arabia, Yemen, and Kuwait, our one and only Liz arrived at SFO completely decked out in a black chador, a traditional woman's garment she had worn during her tour! Our surprise at seeing Liz so attired was matched only by the arrival of Noreen herself, the next morning from Australia. Liz and Rob had very graciously planned a celebration dinner party for Andrew's visit; Noreen's presence was the icing on the cake.

The New Year of 1999 began its inevitable approach to the Millennium with Jack and Meaghan bringing more love and challenge to Evelyn's baby-sitting talents. Exhibiting a precocious form of masculinity, Jack managed to squirt his grandma during a routine diaper change. March 1999 brought the ominous news that our son-in-law, Rob Walker was experiencing a life-threatening bout with pneumonia and hairy cell leukemia. His response to chemotherapy and an anti-cancer "cocktail" designed at the Stanford University Medical School was positive. His long- term recovery is miraculous and testimony to the family power of prayer.

A surprise 60th birthday party for Evelyn came off without a glitch at the Odd Fellows Palette in Redlands. Well attended and well catered a month before her actual birthday on May 9, the event was a well-deserved tribute to Evelyn; her love, positivity, and consistent display of concern for others. Total astonishment was achieved and, thanks to her relatives and friends' willingness to travel from afar, the day after turned into a mini family reunion.

The annual mother/daughter bonding trip for 1999 brought a two-week African Safari to Kenya and Tanzania. Evelyn returned with 20 rolls of African wildlife film and many tales of their adventures.

The major event of the year, Noreen and Andrew's wedding took place on August 28 at St Ignatius Jesuit Church in San Francisco. Bill and Vivienne hosted a rehearsal dinner for all at the San Francisco Yacht Club. The reception itself took place at the Top of the Mark with band dancing and dinner in the Ballroom of the Mark Hopkins Hotel. The painstaking planning of the bride; the mother of the bride; the conviviality of the Ashton family and the blending of Yank and Australian party makers ensured a pleasant, unique and unforgettable experience for all. Prominent in my particular memory was the Best Man's toast to the Bride and Groom and my brother-in-law, Edward O'Dwyer's encouragement to all to vacate the Church or otherwise, the Australians would beat us to the reception bar! Joan and Frank Slachman provided a lively post reception venue at their Top of the Mark Suite. Revelry of all kept things lively until 3 or 4 AM with Irish singing, dancing and the dazzling piano playing by one of the most beautiful and well-endowed female guests.

In addition to our immediate family's happenings, my brother, Richie and his wife, Mary celebrated the wedding of their son, Brendan to Christine Irene Jolly on October 4, 1998. The wedding took place at St Athanasius Church in Harriman, New York with a follow- on reception at the West Point Officers' Club. We were privileged to attend and enjoy the festivities as I was honored to read the epistle at the Nuptial Mass.

New Year's Eve found us at Kathleen's home in Cranford, New Jersey, where we attended a New Year's Party with her Cranford close friends. The Millennium arrived cold, clear and bright with no inkling whatsoever about the world-changing events it would bring with it.

CHAPTER EIGHT

THE MILLENIUM

We watched the new century begin from Cranford, New Jersey where the sun rose brilliantly, innocently and on-schedule on January 1, 2000. The sunrise had been preceded by a dinner party for about 15 people hosted by Kathleen McAdam's closest friends, Sally Kinsella and her sister, Kathleen. Their conviviality and Kathleen's warm hospitality had made her home at 810 Springfield Avenue, our "Home away from Home" for many years during our visits back East. No cousins grew up closer than our three daughters and her daughter Mary Jo and younger brother, Michael.

A subsequent visit to New York's Carnegie Hall for a performance of Handel's Messiah with Kathleen and her older sister, Mary made for a festive and memorable holiday. Our sole casualty of the season was the Y2K2 Crisis with the Apple IIGS which did not recognize 2000 anything! Evelyn and I still had a lot to learn about computers; their problems and their "fixes." In this respect, Liz, Kathy and Noreen had married men of great technical skills, who were always ready and willing to resolve our problems.

Personally, I had come a long way from making Elizabeth a "Coleco Scholar" upon her entrance to Stanford, where I received a $250.00 rebate for my purchase of their cassette tape driven machine.

In February, we once again joined the Stanford University Travel Group for a fabulous 15-day cruise around both the North and South Islands of New Zealand. The cruise toured every major city in the country as well as the magnificent mountains and fjords. Touring the small Stewart Island of New Zealand's south coast and being briefed by a local guide with respect to their self- sufficiency, I inquired whether they ever intermarried with people from the mainland. The guide's response was terse but appropriate to my insipid question; "Of course we do from time to time but have not experienced to-date the birth of any three headed babies!"

Upon completion of the cruise, we flew from Auckland to Sydney, Australia, enjoying the gracious and informal hospitality of Bill and Vivienne Ashton and the delicious "shrimp on the barbie" at their home in Killarney Heights, NSW. Constantly on the move, in late May we flew to Ireland enjoying visits with Evelyn's Aunt Kit Moynihan in Killarney and my aunt, Madeline Boyd in May, as well as our numerous cousins in Mayo, Sligo and County Down. Scenic wise, this was our first trip to the wilds of Donegal with its spectacular wild heather hills and ocean vistas.

Returning to Redlands on June 5, Evelyn had 13 days to assemble her hiking gear and paraphernalia for her annual trip with

Liz. This excursion caused them to walk and ride the Pilgrimage Route through Northern Spain from the Pyrenees to Santiago de Compostela. Myth and history merged with the legend of St James appearing armed on horseback and helping to drive the Moors out of Spain during the Reconquista.

Our frequent trips to Ireland were rewarded in late July and early August by reciprocal visits to Redlands by Susan and Aidan Tighe from Mayo and Jimmy and Marian Cowan from Castlewellan, County Down. Their experience of the Redlands summer heat was alleviated to some extent by dips in our backyard pool and visits to the mountains at Big Bear Lake.

We, the Trumans, Walkers and Ashtons joined together for a family celebration at Lake Tahoe over the Christmas and New Year holidays. Our thanksgiving prayers were focused mainly on Rob Walker's recovery from his bout with Leukemia. God has been good to us while we all too frequently fail to acknowledge His love and assistance.

Maintaining a golf handicap in the mid-twenties has been a challenging but questionably useless habit! The fact is that the game itself is highly addictive, the social benefits welcome and pleasant and the achievement of a lower handicap simply beyond my reach. Nevertheless, given the benign climate of Southern California, it would be sinful not to participate!

We had the delightful experience of welcoming two brand

new grandsons into the family during the summer of 2001. James Patrick Truman arrived on July12 and his cousin, Aidan William Walker on September 16. In Aidan's situation, his mom, Liz, was most relieved that Aidan had not chosen to present himself on the ominous date of September 11, 2001. With respect to the other grandchildren, Meaghan was described as a glamorous, if not overly aggressive soccer player with her dad, Steve as coach and her mom, Kathy as chief cheerleader and refreshment provider. Jack was described as gregarious, but not tolerant of dissent from his four-year-old contemporaries. Both enjoyed their grandmother's love and affection, while younger brother, James Patrick was content to sit on my knee, smile, drink his bottle, play baby games and never take offense when his diaper maintenance needs reverted to those, more qualified than I to administer them.

Holding my xenophobia in abeyance, Evelyn and I thoroughly enjoyed a three - week tour of China in April and early May. The people were friendly and the scenery breathtaking. Our five- day cruise on the Yangtze River was particularly notable as, in a few years' time, the towns in the valley would be underwater when the new dam would raise the water level by 700 meters. The Beijing Opera was a unique experience as was the rickshaw tour of the Hutong, a working- class district of the city. Considering the antiquity of Chinese culture and the total diversity of customs and language, we enjoyed the experience of an absolutely exotic land.

One ancillary benefit was that the language barrier precluded any political discussion or argument!

Evelyn's 40th College Reunion for the Marymount Class of 1961 brought us back East in June. I gratefully noted that Evelyn was holding her own in the glamor and non-aging department. Al and Joan Diaz were very gracious hosts taking us to visit the Pequod Indian Museum, near their home in Connecticut. Richie and Mary O'Prey hosted us equally well at their retirement home in Mashpee on Cape Cod as we enjoyed touring Cape Cod after a 35-year absence. Enjoying the traditional and warm hospitality of Kathleen McAdam in Cranford, New Jersey, she and Evelyn planned their upcoming "Ladies Only" trip to Paris, a nine -day sojourn for the O'Dwyer sisters and two nieces. C'est la vie; more time for me at the golf course and evenings at the Redlands Bowl!

The spectacular horror of 9-11-2001 found me waking at 0730 local, PDT and casually flicking on the bedroom TV. I was immediately captivated by the gruesome spectacle of the hijacked airliners crashing into the World Trade Center, the Pentagon building and the countryside of Pennsylvania. Evelyn was at school teaching her high school math class. I had the immediate realization that I was witnessing the beginning of a new age; for our country and for the world. Given the location and scope of the attacks, I cried initially and involuntarily. Unlike Pearl Harbor, which I was too young to fully understand, I had a front row seat on this conflict and expected an immediate declaration of war; nuclear or conventional. That was "my home," NYC, the "Big Apple that was attacked and someone would pay dearly for it! I recognized that we had entered a new age and stage of terror. Airlines now could not only be hijacked but could also be employed as "weapons of mass destruction" given the number of civilians killed at the World Trade Center.

I had been looking forward to flying back East again for my 50th Incarnation School Reunion. Sister Elizabeth, my first- grade teacher would be there as well as good friends from the Class of 1951. In the aftermath of 911, confident that we would shortly be at war in the Middle East, I abandoned this travel plan. This initial expectation of decreased travel failed to materialize. If anything, our travel plans increased while security measures relating to air travel became legitimately and increasingly more onerous. Evelyn would consistently hush me to silence in these inspection lines as I muttered "The Legacy of Islam!" to no one in particular.

Having completed 27 years of teaching Math, Evelyn retired from Redlands High School in June 2002. I remain forever in her debt as her employment enabled us to fund the college expenses of our three daughters: two at UCLA and one at Stanford. Detecting an imbalance in our respective activities; too much golf for me and too little mutual social commitment for her, Evelyn volunteered my services as Program Chairman for the Retired Officers' Association

Chapter in San Bernardino. Subsequently renamed MOAA, the Military Officers' Association of America, I went on to proudly serve three years as President from 2003 to 2006. We made many new friends and looked forward eagerly each month to dinner with wives at a local hotel or restaurant. To this very date, we cherish MOAA for being our primary social outlet for patriotism, the common bond of military service and unique good fellowship.

In March 2002 we flew to Belize, (formerly British Honduras), toured the Mayan Ruins in Tikal, Guatemala and were looking forward to our first transit of the Panama Canal enroute to Costa Rica. On March 17, our cruise was abruptly cut short by a pulmonary edema episode Evelyn experienced while snorkeling on the reef in Roatan, Honduras. Hospitalized for two days in a local, third world hospital, the intervention of our daughter, Liz and Dr. Frank Slachman generated an air ambulance, Learjet, directly to San Bernardino International Airport/ formerly Norton AFB. Subsequently checked and released from Redlands Community Hospital, we were most grateful for her recovery and for the clean bill of health received from her own physician. While my relief after this scary episode knew no bounds, Evelyn's courage and calmness was exemplary. Providence itself provided the proximity of two male physicians when she first experienced her lack or shortness of breath in the water. I remain skeptical and apprehensive about traveling long distances from home while Evelyn doesn't blink at the challenges of reaching far-away travel destinations.

On April 14, 2002, Cape Cod provided the site for the wedding of my niece, Maureen, Richie's daughter to Nick Daily and an appropriate occasion for an O'Prey family reunion. When the rites were said and done, the reception was a predictable success. On her way back to Logan Airport in Boston, our daughter, Liz, intrepid travel director, discovered she had booked her return travel destination for the wrong day. She did manage to rectify the arrangement and managed to return to California on time.

A few days later, Evelyn and I flew to Amsterdam for the Tulip Festival and a two- week river boat cruise down the Rhein, the Mail, the European Canal, and the Danube River to Budapest. The novelty of river travel combined with short tour bus jaunts made this a most preferable mode of sightseeing.

The wedding of Evelyn's niece, Mary Jo McAdam, to Kevin Fuller on July 5, 2002, brought us back East for a star- spangled weekend. The elegant Hoboken ceremony, bagpiper presence and the ambiance of the Liberty Island reception evoked nostalgia for New York with the fantastic view of lower Manhattan and the profound memories of 911.

Our next destination, with Aunt Kathleen accompanying us was East Stroudsburg, Pennsylvania for a reunion of the "Cabrini Gang;" guys and girls from the old Washington Heights neighborhood. Well-planned by Hank DeEsposito, it brought together many of us who hadn't seen each other in over 50 years.

A few weeks later, we flew to Chicago for the wedding of Chris O'Dwyer, Evelyn's nephew, who married Sarah Brooks in Napierville, Illinois. Ev, Kathleen, and I took the opportunity to tour the impressive sights of Chicago.

In this year of constant travel, our most adventurous trip took place in October 2002. We spent 11 days touring Vietnam via cruise ship, bus, and sampan. Danang, Hue, Nha Trang, Ho Chi Minh City and the Mekong Delta were all points of interest as well as the cultural history of the Vietnamese people. The realization of their tenacity and perseverance was overwhelming! The war today is a distant memory with the Vietnamese who are more interested in attracting tourists and capitalizing on the beauty and tropical climate of their country. We flew on to Siem Reap, Cambodia, and from the luxury of a 5-star hotel, toured the fabled ruins of Angkor Wat.

As a codex to this busy year of travel, after a five- day respite in Redlands, we took the long flight to Sydney, again enjoying the Ashton hospitality and joined Andrew and Noreen for a tour of Tasmania. The unspoiled beauty of Freycinet and Cradle Mountain/Lake St Clair National Parks were as spectacular as the tour of the Victorian Prison near Hobart was grim. As an aside, we noted the intense interest of Andrew and all the Australians visible in the football match which was being played against New Zealand!

The New Year of 2003 brought little change to my regimen of high school substitute teaching, Rotary attendance, and marginal golf performance. With respect to our weekly foursome at the General Olds Golf Course in Riverside, I bore a weekly example of the definition of insanity; i.e., doing things the same way and expecting better results! From a more positive perspective, the ancient and noble game of golf provided sociability and the continual opportunity to exercise the virtue of humility.

In her own retired state, Evelyn showed no signs of slowing down. Constantly in demand as a grandmother, she had served for a number of years as a bookstore volunteer and accepted the position of President of Friends of the Smiley Library. Her active involvement with AAUW continued in fundraising, theater events, bridge, and sponsorship of their annual Math/Science Fair for female 8th Grade students.

In mid-April we flew to Iquitos, Peru via Lima and, aboard the riverboat, La Amatista, cruised the upper Amazon River. We fished for piranha, sailed in dugout canoes and, from our motorized flat boats observed an incredible diversity of flora and fauna. It was absorbing to visit this primitive environment and witness the native settlements along the river. A long-desired dream was realized when we toured Machu Picchu and Cuzco, the middle age capital of the Inca Empire. We flew home on May 2 having experienced the Andean spectacle of snow-capped mountains, the cosmopolitan atmosphere of Lima and the friendly smiles of the indigenous peoples.

A relaxing summer brought visits from the Trumans and a cooling, refreshing trip with them to Sequoia National Park and a dip in a frigid mountain stream. Driving to Redwood City on September 12, we visited the Walkers and were present at the Stanford University Hospital to greet the arrival of Colin Robert Walker, healthy and on-schedule on Tuesday, September 16. As a coincidence, the date was the same birth date as Colin's older brother, Aidan. After congratulating Liz and Rob, we flew the next day to Sydney, Australia. Noreen and Andrew presented us with our sixth grandchild, Anne Hayes Ashton, who arrived at the Mater Misericordiae Hospital in North Sydney on Sunday 28 September. It was a genuine pleasure to share the joy of the occasion with Bill and Vivienne Ashton, first-time grandparents.

Departing Australia on October 2, favorable winds and good connections got us to Carmel, California for the rehearsal dinner of Evelyn's nephew Mike McAdam and Cindy Garabedian. They were joined in Holy Matrimony at the Carmel Mission on Saturday, October4. The occasion provided a great reunion opportunity for the O'Dwyer families against a mission atmosphere as unique as it was beautiful. A casual drive down California Route 1, a world class scenic route through Big Sur ultimately brought us home to Redlands on October 5.

Five days later, we flew back East; enjoyed the high- rise hospitality of Mary Jo and Kevin Fuller in Hoboken and drove up to Mystic Seaport, Connecticut. The wedding of my niece, Katherine O'Prey to Kaih Fuller provided the background for a most welcome O'Prey/Clancy/Burke family reunion. The Autumn Aura of New England, seaside atmosphere and excellent venue brought the ancillary benefit of the first reunion of the three senior O'Preys in too many years. Similarly, Evelyn and I enjoyed the company of our three daughters, their husbands, six grandchildren, the Slachmans and McAdams gathered together for Thanksgiving Dinner at Lake Tahoe in November 2003.

If I were to count the days in the past year of 2004 that Evelyn has traveled, the total would come to approximately two months! Her year began with a fascinating tour of Egypt and the Nile with a side trip to Jordan. Veteran traveler that she is, she was thoughtful enough to send me a picture of herself in a belly dance outfit. She looked great and could give Cleopatra a run for her money. I was invited to join her, but reluctance to get in the middle of an unprogrammed Mideast war, substitute teaching and playing golf four days a week were somewhat prosaic, but less expensive and less risky pastimes.

March brought a trip to Maui and Lanai, a relaxing week of whale watching and the opportunity to reunite with my brother Ray and his wife Tak. Not exactly the most atmospheric place to celebrate St Patrick's Day, the volcanic, tropical scenery and warm hospitality compensated with a profusion of green. Shortly afterwards, we were off to Sydney and the resort city of Noosa, joining Andrew, Noreen, and Annie for Annie's baptism. The ability of Andrew to hold the return flight due to unforeseen heavy traffic was nothing short of miraculous. The hospitality of the Ashton's, both younger and older, was legendary as was that of their good friends, Harry, and Jacqui Stone.

On the home front, Meaghan Truman celebrated her First Communion in May. She and Jack were involved in soccer and basketball and doing well in school. Steve and Kathy have generously devoted their time to coaching and the never- ending details of being a soccer mom. James, at three, charms visitors with his conversation and lovely personality. To the North, their cousin Aidan Walker attended Stanford's Bing Nursery School and displayed a strong interest in trains and planes. His younger brother, Colin shadows him and is fascinated by Aidan's activities. Annie and Noreen Ashton were with us for a good part of the summer, and we took grand parental pride in watching Annie take her first steps.

In the late summer, we were dismayed to learn that Aidan was diagnosed with a developmental disorder in the autism spectrum, but mildly so. Professional treatment, behavior modification et.al. could be employed to alleviate many of the disorders. To her great credit, Liz devoted her full-time effort, ingenuity, and resources to get Aidan the care he required. She and Rob received total support, constant prayers and admiration for their courage and positive outlook during this difficult, troubling, and uncertain period.

Thanksgiving took a different twist this year as Evelyn was traveling through India on a two-week tour with her college buddy Jeanne Shevlin. The rest of the family enjoyed the traditional meal with Frank and Joan Slachman in Sacramento. During the busy holiday season, we took the time to shop and buy a 2005 Honda Accord as a replacement for Evelyn's 1995 Mazda.

As president of the Orange Empire Military Officers' Club, Evelyn and I had the duty and pleasure of hosting the Club's Annual Christmas Dinner Dance at the local Elks' Club. The dinner went well, and I continued to enjoy the comradeship and support of my fellow veterans and good friends.

As the years accumulate and lead up to the present, I become more aware of how this epic can easily turn into a compendium of family drivel, grandparent boasting and repetitious, dull travelog. It is my hope that this assembly of facts may stimulate favorable memories in the minds of future readers. The only provision I ask is that you remember to thank The Almighty for the blessings He has bestowed on all of us and pray that these continue in the interests of familial love and good health.

The year 2005 brought with it continued growth and increase in the number of grandchildren. As was the case with each of her cousins, we were privileged to be present for the healthy arrival of Keira Elizabeth Walker on July 21. As a nine-year old, Meaghan Truman began playing volleyball at a height equal to that of Grandma Evelyn. After more than ten years at Latham & Watkins, her mom, Kathleen made a major career change, leaving to become a partner at a smaller firm practicing environmental law.

For the first time in five years, we had our whole family together for Christmas. A special treat was to listen to Annie Ashton loudly and often belt out her theme song "Tomorrow" as a two- year-old actress. Aidan and Colin exhibited an abiding interest in model trains and airplanes. I particularly enjoyed escorting them on several occasions to a local airport museum with an impressive, interactive collection of various aircraft. Another highlight was to travel to Oakland; board an actual railroad train and enjoy the hour plus trip to the California Railroad Museum in Sacramento. Aidan's progress with his treatment programs has been positive and testimony to the love, patience and determination of his parents Liz and Rob.

In addition to two trips to Sydney, several flights north to San Carlos and equal visits to Redondo Beach, Evelyn managed to squeeze 10 delightful days in NYC with her teacher colleagues from Redlands High School and Riverside. Minus my nagging presence, she claimed it was her best 10 shopping and touring days in New York ever! I was compensated by a subsequent visit with her to Fort Worth, Texas and a reunion with Bob and Nancy Matus, our old Air Force friends from our days at McGuire AFB. We learned a lot about Longhorn cattle, the Czech community of West, Texas, the proud traditions of Texas A&M and Nancy's success at running a pecan plantation.

The highlight of the late summer was the wedding of my niece, Tricia, to Paul Hasenfus at Hyde Park, New York over Labor Day Weekend. It was a delight to see Aunt Helen Clancy and my brothers, Richie, and Ray as well as a plethora of seldom seen East Coast relatives. The venue was excellent insofar as it provided an opportunity to visit FDR and Eleanor Roosevelt's homes and absorb the history and famous visitors who had been there. The beautiful view of the stately Hudson River was a reminder of its pristine nature during the period of Dutch Patroon ownership.

After the wedding, Evelyn and I drove to Gettysburg, Antietam, Charlottesville, Monticello, and Appomattox Court House. The trip combined a visit to Ed and Nadja O'Dwyer in Doylestown, Pennsylvania as well as John O'Dwyer's home in Crozet, Virginia. A reunion with these branches of the family was a pleasure as was the accumulation of historical American historical lore at each visited site. I find there is always something new to learn with respect to history itself. Whether it be a battlefield or a mansion such as Mount Vernon, multiple visits add aspects previously undiscovered or perhaps not previously considered.

Accompanied by Aunt Kathleen, October brought with it a visit to Australia. Noreen had broken her ankle a few days prior to our arrival, giving us plenty of exercise running after Annie as well as learning to negotiate Sydney's hilly and hectic terrain on the "wrong side." The itinerary took in the sights of Adelaide, Kangaroo Island and Ayres Rock and wine tasting for the ladies in the Hunter and Barossa Valleys. Always appreciated for their patience and tolerance for my marginal golf game, the rounds with Andrew, Bill Ashton, and Andrew's mates Mal and Blackers provided excellent company and hospitality.

The year 2006 brought with it two great blessings to our immediate family. In January we were informed of the successful chemo treatment outcome for our son-in-law Rob Walker. In addition, the proliferation of grandchildren came to an end with the arrival of our 8th grandchild, Grace Lindsay Ashton in Sydney, Australia on August 4th.

It occurred to me that grandkid maintenance is virtually a full-time job performed mostly by Evelyn. During 2006, I calculated that she spent well over 50 days this past year being present when needed for Meaghan, Jack, and James Truman; Aidan, Colin and Kiera Walker or Annie and Grace Ashton. Our daughters continue to bicker over which of them receives the most attention. The certainty, however, is that Grandma is there when needed. Being a grandpa is so much easier provided I don't even try to keep up with Evelyn in the travel department. Our mutual travels, planned sufficiently in advance, are still our major hobby.

In March we participated with great satisfaction in an Elderhostel trip to Patagonia. This was a "whole new world" experience. The scenery of the Andes was striking and our highly competent tour guide, Carlos, gave us an appreciation of the European heritage of Chile and Argentina. Meeting German carpenters in their craft costumes in Valdivia and being asked to read the Doxology at a 19th century Welsh Colony in Argentina were only two instances of this cultural phenomena. Taking tango lessons in Buenos Aires, visiting Eva Peron's grave and touring the Opera House were more localized experiences.

June brought a three-week jaunt back to New York City to celebrate my fraternity, Alpha Sigma Beta's centennial anniversary. Singing the "old songs" and swapping memories of the college years was a cherished pastime of all. At a casual lawn reception, Brother Tom Scanlon, FSC made the not unrealistic observation that half of the class that he saw at the Reunion were members of AA and the other half belonged there! In addition, we took in two Broadway shows and my cousin Kerry Clancy's college graduation party in Long Beach. We enjoyed the excellent hospitality of Jeanne Shevlin, Evelyn's college buddy and bridesmaid, who introduced us to the

Museums and Sculpture galleries of Brooklyn. The spiritual finale of the trip was to join in the celebration of Micheline O'Dwyer's 50th Anniversary of profession as an RSHM nun. The planned dinner in Sea Girt, New Jersey was decimated in attendance by several when they developed the "California Crud," a digestive disorder blamed on our young granddaughter, Kiera Walker.

Moving on to October 2006, we joined Kathleen McAdam and her good friend, Sally Kinsella for an 11-day trip to France. Three days in Paris followed by a week cruising down the Rhone River was a pleasant, historically fascinating, and highly relaxing pastime. Of particular note was the Resistance Museum in Lyon and the cultural erudition of our most knowledgeable tour director.

In the autumn of 2006, Andrew Ashton's new company had him and his family moved from Sydney Australia and Singapore providing us with a destination priority for 2007 as well as a geographic closeness to my brother, Ray and his family and spouse Tak.

2007 was a year of miracles as far as having experienced numerous years of alcohol intake which ended in 1983, and an estimated 40 years of heavy smoking, I reached my 70th birthday! An appropriate recognition was displayed at the annual Thanksgiving Dinner at Joan and Frank Slachman's estate in Sacramento. The privilege of having six of eight (Walker and Truman) grandchildren and their stateside parents together at an annual Thanksgiving Dinner has been a great success since the mid-eighties. We owe so much to the continual gracious and generous hospitality of Joan and Frank in providing a caring and comfortable venue for this classic American Feast.

Confronting the "Glass Ceiling" at Lathrop and Watkins, Kathleen formed her own law firm and opened a well-appointed office with her partner, Todd Elliot in downtown Los Angeles. It's hard to believe Meaghan is now 11, almost 5' 10" towering over her grandma; Jack is 9 and James 6. Steve remains an unflappable Soccer and Basketball coach with their teams. They purchased a cabin in Angelus Oaks, a mountain community near Big Bear Lake and are in the process of "fixing it up."

Rob and Liz Walker remained excellent and imaginative hosts, both at their home in San Carlos and at the Walker Retreat in Bear Valley. I marvel at the logistics involved in birthday celebrations; the setting up of a Train "Jumpee," supervising games and feeding two distinct groups of guests; Aidan's 6-year-old set and Colin's 4-year-olds. While both brothers celebrated the same birthdate, September 16, foxy little Kiera mixed easily with both groups. Aidan now skis and rides a two-wheeler; Colin provides "sugar" for grandma and Kiera charms all!

It was a delight to greet Noreen, Annie (4) and Grace (1/12) in late June at LAX. Unfortunately, Gracie's first week in Redlands required three trips to the Urgent Care Unit to treat a stubborn virus caught enroute from Singapore. All eight grandchildren were well enough to celebrate the 4th of July at a Beach House in Carlsbad. Hosting a baby shower for Mary Jo McAdam Fuller became a sporting proposition as the Singapore virus made its way through Evelyn, Kathy and Liz. Joan Slachman and Kathleen McAdam flew down safely and without contagion! Annie, Grace, Noreen and I subsequently enjoyed a day in the mountains and a delightful Cinderella carriage ride at the Redlands Market Night.

One major excursion for 2007 was an April Elderhostel Cruise from Charleston, South Carolina to Jacksonville, Florida along the Intercoastal Waterway, Maureen and Nick Fuller's hospitality in Charleston was exceptional. The cruise itself was a perfect combination of magnolias, forts, mansions and Civil War lore. The on-board, nautical themed entertainment was as memorable and enriching as the cities and towns we visited. The in-depth exposure to the culture of the South as well as that of the "peculiar institution" was most enlightening and mind-broadening.

October 2007 brought our eagerly anticipated trip to Singapore and Thailand. Noreen and Andrew's 17th floor apartment, spacious swimming pool and cordial hospitality were very much appreciated as was the opportunity to take Annie and Grace to the Bird Park and Annie to the Night Safari. We subsequently flew to Bangkok and took a two Overseas Adventure Tour of Thailand. We made and thoroughly enjoyed all the obligatory stops, passing up the numerous opportunities to purchase cobra meat from roadside vendors. Arriving in Chiang Mai we were treated to a reunion with my brother Ray and a delicious dinner feast prepared by his wife, Tok. I remain puzzled to this day of why Ray insisted that I try on my father's police uniform coat but was pleased to see him take pictures! Ray was particularly solicitous and most instrumental in helping me bargain on the street bazaar for a "knock-off" Breitling Navitimer Watch.

Evelyn celebrated her High School Class of 1967 Reunion, keeping her youthful good looks, playing Bridge, running an AAUW sponsored Math-Science Conference for 8th grade schoolgirls and serving on the Board of our local Smiley Library.

By any conceivable standard, 2008 was a banner year for domestic and international travel. We responded enthusiastically to Michael Dammann's superbly well- organized Hayes Family reunion In April, meeting cousins we hadn't seen in a good while. We were definitely among the oldest in attendance! The privilege of touring Gettysburg Battlefield with Jack and James Truman was a cherished delight even if they were more interested in climbing on cannons than they were in my droning historic asides!

In mid-May, Evelyn and I departed for a one-week bus tour of the Baltic Republics followed by a two- week cruise down the Volga from St Petersburg to Moscow. For scenery, historic sightseeing and exposure to a different cultural perspective, this trip was highly educational, informative, and entertaining. Evelyn had been in Moscow and St Petersburg thirty years previously and noted many remarkable changes in historical sights, particularly Gums Department Store and the restoration of Churches and Cathedrals.

In September, we departed for Athens, the Aegean Sea, Crete, Turkey, and the Black Sea as far east as the Crimea. A particular highlight for me was a tour of Gallipoli while Evelyn took in the nine level remains of Troy. We traveled on the MS Minerva, a ship originally built in Odessa for the Soviet Navy as a submarine tender and intelligence platform. Converted to a luxury liner, 30 Elderhostel participants joined about 150 equally "seasoned" British tourists. Playing Trivial Pursuit was a cultural challenge to both sides, especially responding to sports and team questions. The guides and on-board lectures were absorbing, highly professional and replete with British humor and understatement. The stops in Romania, Odessa and Yalta presented great touring and educational perspectives as did our final two days in Istanbul.

Summer in Redlands was predictably hot but evenings at the Redlands Bowl or Theater Festival a pleasant and entertaining relief. Annie, Grace, and Noreen visited in July enjoying respite from the humidity of Singapore as well as the cooler temperatures of Bear Valley with the Walkers and the nearby hospitality of the Trumans at their newly acquired cabin in Running Springs, a leisurely drive up into the local mountains near Big Bear Lake. All the Grandkids enjoyed dips in our pool and the familial company of their cousins.

Autumn brought with it forest fires to Malibu, about 100 miles to the west of Redlands. It was most reassuring to receive emails from our European correspondents stating their concern for our safety. That their concern and communication across the many miles is testimony to our long-term friendships.

While Evelyn delighted in the election of Barack Obama, the Spirit of Christmas and residual patriotism obliged me to wish him and his in-coming administration well.

With the passage of time, predictable patterns of activity emerge. Foremost of these is celebrating Thanksgiving with the Slachmans in Sacramento. A revered family tradition, this normally embraces 20 to 25 guests sitting down together for this most hallowed of American holidays. I marvel that, at the age of 72, I enjoy the blessings of good health and eight beautiful grandkids.

With respect to diverse activities, I enjoy Rotary, golfing several days a week and salving my flexible conscience by substitute high school teaching on a regular but totally volunteer basis. My "domain" also includes minor tasks; Christmas letter writing, checkbook balancing, income tax preparation and daily garbage disposal. By comparison, Evelyn is a dynamo of activity belonging to several Bridge groups; active with AAUW and their annual Math/Science Conference as well as Docent duties with the nearby

Kimberly Crest Mansion and treasurer of the Heritage Foundation; a group which conducts historical tours of Redlands. In her spare time, she also does volunteer work at our Smiley Library Bookstore.

We are both at an age where funerals and memorial services occur with a frequency previously experienced by weddings and christenings. The saddest event in our family this year was the death of my sister-in-law, Mary Burke O'Prey in June. We were able to be back with my brother Richie and his bereaved family for the funeral. May she rest in Peace and the Good Lord comfort her family.

On a happier note, Manhattan College sponsored a 50th Jubilee Reunion for those of us in the legendary Class of 1959. What a pleasure it was to socialize with ASB fraternity brothers and enjoy the privilege of a visit with Brother Luke Salm (RIP) our revered and brilliant Professor of Theology. The President of the College, Brother Tom Scanlon (RIP) made the private, but not inappropriate comment to us that half of the Alumni he met were members of AA and the other half belonged in the organization!

Planner of the Year Award for 2009 goes to Evelyn for her July orchestration of her belated 70th Birthday Party at Turtle Bay in Oahu. Trumans, Walkers and Ashtons, Aunt Kathleen and all eight grandchildren were joyous and enthusiastic participants in the celebrations. After several toasts at the birthday dinner, Andrew announced that his company, Polycom had just promoted him to

Global Financial Officer. With the promotion came a short-notice family move from Singapore to Danville, California. Since Danville is in the San Francisco Bay Area, nothing could have delighted us more! We will celebrate Christmas at their new home and enjoy a reunion with Bill and Vivienne Ashton who will be visiting from Sydney.

As we anticipate the new Decade of 2010, we are most grateful for the health and welfare of our large family and the many blessings we have received over the years. International travel continues as the main pastime of Evelyn and me. She has been most persuasive as far as taking advantage of our continued good health while I bristle at the inconvenience of the airline industry's security measures in the aftermath of 911. Once we get to a destination, I can relax and enjoy the adventure. In the deployment and redeployment phases, I've been chastised for muttering annoyingly "Legacy of Islam" etc. to the consternation of Evelyn that I might be overheard! I thank Evelyn for both her patience, imagination in destiny selection and packing us both appropriately.

We flew to Rome in May and after two days near the Trevi Fountain, boarded our cruise ship for a circumnavigation of Sicily and the Adriatic. Each port of call; Palermo, Syracuse, Split, Dubrovnik, and Venice presented new vistas of the Greek, Roman, Byzantine, Arab and Norman historical heritage of this Mediterranean littoral.

July brought a flight to Anchorage; a railroad trip to Denali (Mount Whitney) and the enjoyment of breath-taking scenery in the company of Evelyn's sisters, Kathleen and Mary. A discordant element of the trip was the train halting near Elmendorf AFB for a moment of silence in honor of the C-117 Aircrew who had crashed nearby while practicing for an airshow. Moving and appropriate, this generated a prayer of thanks and gratitude for my 6500 hours of safe flying time. Our return trip was via the Denali Princess; a cruise from Whittier, Alaska to Vancouver, British Columbia. The ladies spent an additional three days in Victoria including Butchart Gardens and high tea at the Empress Hotel. I opted for an early return to Redlands and golf.

August provided an excellent opportunity to visit good friends, Brian and Eileen Major in Bermuda, North Carolina; a tour of the Biltmore Estate in Asheville and a drive down the Blue Ridge Parkway to my fraternity brother, John Gearity's home in Sapphire. The final treat was to travel the width of North Carolina to Emerald Isle on the Atlantic coast. We were very pleased to participate in the 60th birthday celebration for Ed O'Dwyer; an event superbly planned and executed by his wife Nadja. Evelyn has yet to say no to a travel invitation. When her sister, Kathleen had a roommate who canceled on her cruise in October, Evelyn was delighted to "fill in" and subsequently enjoyed another Mediterranean Cruise, Venice to Barcelona. She's been praising Gaudi architecture ever since and chalked up over 70 travel days away from home for the year of 2010.

The news of my Aunt Helen Clancy's sudden death in Brattleboro, Vermont on November 28 was a shock and a source of great sadness to the O'Prey/Clancy family. Helen was a source of love; a model of patience and good humor as well as a most caring Grand Aunt to our daughters throughout my Air Force career. May she rest forever in the Peace and Comfort of the Lord.

CHAPTER NINE

THE TEENS

As a compliment to the patient reader and a profound sense of gratitude for the encouragement of my brother Richie, we enter a new Decade. Personally, lacking the imagination for a more creative title, Richie's suggestion was the "Penultimate Decade" with its implicit trust in making it to our nineties. As unlikely as this may be, I chose the "Teens." This imaginative title suggests more years as well as the possibility of a second childhood in returning to the memories of our youth.

With my ugly swelling nose caused by a reaction to a skin cancer treatment, Evelyn, Kathleen McAdam, and I enjoyed a scenic bus trip through Costa Rica in March 2011. Significantly, Costa Rica is the only country in Central America without a standing military force; a fact which adds to its attraction as a popular tourist destination. Keeping the tradition of reunion with her sisters, Evelyn joined Mary, Meaghan and Kathleen Truman in Rome and Capri in April. Evelyn was particularly impressed by a tour of the Skavi, a necropolis under St Peter's Basilica bearing the purported remains of the Saint himself.

Evelyn made it to NYC for her 50th Marymount College Reunion in June. We were privileged to assist her brother John in celebrating his 70th birthday in Washington D.C. in August with the numerous members of the O'Dwyer family. An additional highlight was our visit with Tami and Ed Gotchef, friends from our Embassy Days in Copenhagen. We are grateful to all for the tours of Manassas, the Tolerance Museum, the 911 Pentagon memorial and the other more recent monuments erected since we were there in 1978.

Fulfilling a constant and life-long wish, our motor trip of Ireland in July with the Truman family eclipsed all other destinations! We experienced a very shaky start at Newark Airport when after racing through two terminals to catch our scheduled flight, the entrance door was shut in our face! This obliged us to reschedule our flight through Belfast rather than our original destination, Dublin. Upon landing in Northern Ireland, Kathy and Steve took a bus to Dublin to pick up their rental van, a large SUV. We rendezvoused with Marian Cowan in Castlewellan, County Down. I cherished the blessed opportunity to introduce Meaghan, Jack and James Truman to their many cousins in Castlewellan, County Sligo and County Mayo. Prior to these pleasant experiences, I had the misfortune to sustain an attack of vertigo, probably the result of the revised flight travel and subsequent uncertainties. After spending our first evening at Cowans, with the room spinning, the tender, loving care of Marian Cowan and Martine Fulcher restored me to good health within 24 hours. Of memorable note was the house visit made by one of Martine's Doctor friends, who reassured me that the malady was not serious and would shortly pass. He refused my offer of payment and my gratitude for his house call knows no bounds!

We went on to enjoy the unique Irish hospitality of the Cowans, Fulchers and O'Preys in County Down; Mary and Brendan Boyd in Sligo and Susan Tighe and Mary Golden in Mayo. Watching the youngsters ignore the drizzle; play football and socialize with their Irish cousins was a particular pleasure. To be entertained by a Cowan family Craik revived many old memories. To visit my aunt Madeline and to watch four generations of the Duggan family assemble in Mayo and to relive our celebrated visit of 1948 was an unforgettable blessing.

Steve and Kathleen Truman did an excellent job driving and navigating the subsequent roads to Clare, the Bourne, Cliffs of Moher, Killarney, Glendalough, and Dublin. I was proud and content to provide supervision service to the Truman kids while Kathy, Steve and Evelyn did some minor pub-crawling along the Liffey. Significantly, the taste in "Rebel" music had subsided somewhat due to the Good Friday Agreement of 1998 as Evelyn noted when she asked a balladeer to sing Sean South of Garryowen.

In early December, we boarded HMS Queen Victoria for a

15 -day cruise; Fort Lauderdale, Aruba, Panama Canal, Costa Rica, Nicaragua, Guatemala, Mexico, and San Pedro (LA). Unaccustomed to large ship cruising, we enjoyed the ports of call, mainly Aruba, but reluctantly recall the three hours required to disembark at the Port of Los Angeles.

Christmas of 2011 was warm, memorable, and hospitable in Northern California in San Carlos with the Walker family and in Danville with the Ashtons and five grandchildren. The Trumans evened out the score, stopping in Redlands on their return from their customary visit with Steve's relatives in Phoenix, Arizona.

The major family travel event of 2012 was the African Safari which took Evelyn, Jack, Steve Truman and Kathleen McAdam to South Africa, Botswana, and Zambia. I defer to a future memoir of Evelyn's creation to adequately address the many photographs, movies, and adventure tales which they experienced. I elected to remain on the Redlands home front, hopelessly attempting to remediate my atrocious golf game. Evelyn is clearly and indisputably the family adventurer. I concede that a lion can outrun me and prudently avoid any such contest!

In an appropriate but low-key manner, Evelyn and I renewed our marriage vows at Holy Name of Jesus (formally Sacred Heart) Church on June 30, 2012, our 50th Wedding Anniversary. Subsequently, on July 13 we had the whole family and close friends in attendance for a patio barbecue at our home. Things got a lot more formal the next evening when our daughters hosted a sit-down dinner celebration at the Redlands Country Club. We are particularly indebted to our family members and guests who traveled from far and near to share the memories of this once in a lifetime occasion. We owe thanks to all for their hard work and planning for this successful event. However, our primary joy and gratitude goes to our daughters for their company, thoughtfulness, love, and generosity.

As a reprieve from formality, we spent the following week with our grandkids, their moms, Trish, Katie, Lily and Paul Hasenfus, Mary Jo and Molly Fuller, as well as Aunts Kathleen and Mary at Del Mar Beach, Camp Pendleton at a rented villa in Oceanside. The company of our eastern relatives, like my brother Richie was most welcome and hopefully, a harbinger of more to come on behalf of the younger generations.

By mid-August, Evelyn and I were ready for a change of venue. This came in the form of a trip to England and a cruise around the totality of the British Isles. At its northernmost port, we were overwhelmed by the age and breadth of Scottish History, particularly with the 5000-year-old excavations in the Orkneys and the visit to Scapa Flow, where the German Imperial Fleet was scuttled at the end of the First World War. While touring Edinburgh Castle, it was a pleasure to meet Neal and Carol Emper and Nick and Amber Costa, four retired military friends from Redlands. To attend the Edinburgh Tattoo and thrill to the skirl of the massed pipers was an additional highlight as well as our visit to Colchester Castle, originally a Roman Temple. A fitting coda to our trip was several days in London; touring Buckingham Palace, the Churchill War Room and enjoying a delightful lunch with our respective cousins, Jennifer O'Prey and Christine Hayes Cresswell.

The enjoyment of genuine and appreciated Southern Hospitality was ours in October at the wedding of Evelyn's nephew, Chris O'Dwyer and his bride Jenny in Savannah, Georgia. A subsequent drive north to Charleston provided a visiting opportunity with Nick and Maureen Daily and their two lively and lovable sons, Declan and Seumas. Their names would reflect the vitality of their grandfather, Richie, and our esteemed Irish heritage.

As the New Year of 2013 arrived, I conceded to Evelyn the uncontested title of family traveler. In the company of her sister Kathleen and her friends she enjoyed museum visits, Broadway Plays and the cultural highlights of the New York Metropolitan area. In March and April, they resumed their annual "pilgrimage" to Rome and Northern Italy in the company of their sister, Mary, aka Michaeline.

In July, accompanied by our daughter, Kathleen, her son James and her grandson Aidan Walker, Evelyn toured the Galapagos Islands. They returned with many tales of adventure, resolving to repeat the experience at a future date with Noreen and her daughters Annie and Grace. In all, Evelyn intends to invite each grandchild on a similar adventure/learning experience. Please note that I get invited too but find the daily golf schedule and civic delights of Redlands preferable to long flights to exotic destinations.

As we are both committed patrons of Rhodes Scholar, we enjoyed their cruise from Portsmouth, UK to Portugal, Spain, Sardinia, Tunisia, Lipari, Pompeii, Ostia, Antica, Rome and Orvieto. We enjoyed the company of Evelyn's sister Mary on the cruise and afterwards for a five-day stay in Rome. It was an ironic delight to play Trivial Pursuit aboard the cruise ship with Oxford professors who thought that being a Rhodes Scholar implied high IQ or Mensa category intelligence. We all enjoyed a good laugh when we got to know each other and realized that no unfair threat to their intelligence existed! The four ship's lecturers were outstanding speakers; experts in their respective fields. Of particular note was meeting and having dinner with Rear Admiral and Mrs. John Lippiett, CB MBE. Retired from the Royal Navy, he was the current Chief Executive of the Mary Rose Trust. This trust surfaced the flagship of King Henry VII from the English Channel where it had sunk in 1545. This cruise's programs blended archaeology, history, art, religion, and maritime conflict in the Mediterranean. It remains in my memory as the most stellar of our many travel experiences. On the more humorous side, a street vendor in Carthage made the offer to exchange thirty camels for Evelyn's hand in marriage!

Once again, enjoying Kathleen's hospitality in October, we attended Kerry Clancy's wedding to Tim Varian in Long Beach, Long Island, and the following reception in Queens. It was a long overdue reunion with the O'Prey / Clancy side of the family. Clearly, we represented the "older generation" and were not particularly enthused over the blaring volume of the disco music. At least, the breaks provided the opportunity to converse with my cousins, Jim and Ellen Clancy.

A coincidence of family marriages brought my cousin Brendan Boyd and his lovely wife Mary to Jersey City. With my brother, Richie, we recounted the "good old days" in Mayo and Sligo. We subsequently toured Lower Manhattan; the 911 Memorial and the monument to the victims of the Irish Famine (An Gort Mor). We lunched at Fraunces' Tavern and marveled at the changes there since our last visit.

On the home front in Redlands, I continued to accept part-time jobs as a substitute teacher and enjoyed the interaction with high school students and using the modest income to defray green fee expenses. I was reminded of my age when I worked as a sub for one of Noreen's old boyfriends! Maintaining an astronomical golf index, Military Officers' Club Monthly Dinners remain popular pastimes. Reading and listening to historical epics and transporting Evelyn to her airport flights are steady if unspectacular activities.

Evelyn herself is vastly more occupied. She enjoys riding the train to Los Angeles with her lady friends to enjoy the LA Symphony as well as the various art museums. She remains active with the Heritage Foundation, AAUW, California Cuisine, Kimberly Crest Docents as well as several Bridge groups. As we gathered at Joan and Frank Slachman's home for Thanksgiving Dinner, our pride knew no bounds   when we learned that Meaghan Truman, our 17-year-old granddaughter had been accepted by Yale University based upon her academic record and athletic performance on the volleyball court.

As I review my annual Christmas letter of 2014, it occurs to me that I owe the tolerant and patient reader of "Decades", the admission that its text is not derived from my spotty memory, but from a collection of Christmas letters dating back to 1973. Accordingly, and for the potential benefit of our grandchildren, I take the liberty of providing a somewhat lengthy recap of their respective activities five years ago.

Aidan Walker had his acting debut as a police officer in a summer production of the musical "Annie" while Kiera played a spirited orphan. Across the Bay in Danville, his cousin Annie Ashton did a highly praised performance in the title role of the same musical. Displaying her Australian athletic heritage, Grace Ashton went to the county finals as a breaststroke swimmer. Colin Walker inherited the athletic ability of his father, Rob in baseball and other sports. Meaghan Truman graduated from high school; attends Yale University and is playing volleyball with the varsity after a side-lining, temporary foot injury. Her brother, Jack excels in volleyball where his height of 6' 9" challenges that of his dad, Steve. He has received an offer of 70% tuition et alia from UC Santa Barbara. James Truman is a participant in the academic decathlon and the grandson we turn to most frequently for solutions to computer/internet dilemmas. His savvy and cheerful willingness to help those of us less technologically gifted (grandparents) has been noteworthy as his competitive spirit on the volleyball courts.

During a visit to Truman's in Redondo Beach, Evelyn's 2005 Honda accord was stolen overnight from its parking space across the street from their home. Our insurance company, USAA, did a fantastic service, providing a rental car and subsequently a generous settlement enabling Evelyn to select and purchase a new Honda CRV. This SUV is equipped with more "bells and whistles" than I have ever seen and is a comfort and pleasure to drive.

Our major overseas trip for 2014 was to cruise the Normandy Coast for the 70th Anniversary of D Day. After touring the Mary Rose Museum and HMS Victory, we embarked once again on the Minerva, our chosen cruise ship. Touring WWII cemeteries in Ypres as well as the Allied British and American invasion beaches, we remain awed and inspired by the spirit and sacrifice of our "Greatest Generation." On its way back to Portsmouth, our cruise rounded the Brest Peninsula, toured several cities in Northern France and provided welcome sights in the Scilly Isles, Cornwall, and the Channel Coast. A British couple, Allen and Josie Boag most generously offered us a ride back to London where we enjoyed the hospitality of my cousin, Jennifer O'Prey and her roommate, Claire.

The New Year of 2015 had hardly arrived when Evelyn and I departed for an often- deliberated cruise from Santiago, Chile around Cape Horn to the Falklands, Buenos Aires and a side trip to Iguazu Falls, Argentina. The Falls were a magnificent spectacle. However, I was obliged to acknowledge my step-climbing limitations, panting heavily while Evelyn went non-stop! The world seemingly got smaller when, by sheer coincidence, we met Bruce and Barbara Bowers, friends from Redlands while debarking at a port in Chile. In April, Evelyn joined her sister, Kathleen for a cruise of Japan's Coast and the Korean Port of Pusan.

Evelyn and I once again were delighted to enjoy her sister Mary's fabulous hospitality in Rome in October. We cruised the Mediterranean and Spain and rode the Bullet Train from Seville to Madrid. Earlier, in July, we cruised the Great Lakes from Toronto to Chicago. This was truly "a whole new world" as we learned the history of ore transportation during WWII and the French/English/ American conflicts in the region during the 17th, 18[th,] and 19th centuries.

Our grandchildren are growing rapidly and enjoying their various hobbies and activities; Meaghan (19) playing volleyball at Yale; Jack (17) has a scholarship to UC Santa Barbara for volleyball; James (14) just started at Loyola High School; Aidan enjoys play acting and will play Jafar in January; Colin (12) plays soccer, basketball and baseball; Annie (12) loves horseback riding; Kiera (10) is a soccer player and Grace (9) is a competitive breast stroker.

Thanksgiving 2015 was noteworthy for several reasons. 27 family members participated, and the locale was Donner Lake, California. Traditionally hosted by Joan and Frank Slachman at a beautiful home with a full lake and mountain view, they were assisted as co-hosts by Noreen and Andrew Ashton at their recently purchased and nearby cabin. The turkey dinner was great; the kids were not too noisy and the presence of Alex Montalvo and Jordan Viduna a most welcome harbinger of a new generation of family members. We had a lot to be Thankful for; good health, a fresh snowfall, six degrees temperatures and subsequent clear skies.

February 2016 brought Evelyn's quasi successful right knee surgery; a recovery procedure which precluded any overseas travel for the rest of the year. Kathy, Liz, and Noreen ministered lovingly to their mom during her first two weeks of post-operative recovery. Their care was very much appreciated. As the year progressed, we were reduced to watching the ludicrous spectacle of the 2016 Presidential campaign. We ultimately and characteristically split our vote. In my humble belief, God continues to bless America and the Republic will survive based upon our constitutional balance of powers. I took the initiative to reassure our overseas friends and allies that our close relationships will endure personally and politically despite rhetoric to the contrary. We share a common belief in freedom and liberty which unify our separate national interests.

In April, we were privileged to attend Mary's 60th year of profession as an RSHM nun and enjoyed a visit with Kathleen in Cranford, N.J. while she was undergoing radiation treatment for uterine cancer. After an eight- month struggle, she now enjoys a clean bill of health. The ladies of the O'Dwyer/Hayes family enjoyed a mini reunion at the Jersey Shore while I enjoyed a visit with my brother Richie. He conducted a fascinating tour of old homes in the Nyack /Tarrytown area and arranged the pleasure of Aunt Pat's company at an Irish restaurant in Nyack.

The major family social event of 2016, the "Wedding of the Century" brought all of us to Santa Barbara on September24 to witness the wedding of Kelly Slachman, Evelyn's niece, to Alex Montalvo. The vows were exchanged at Our Lady of Sorrows Church with a classic reception following at the Bacara Resort in Santa Barbara. Frank Slachman, the distinguished and eloquent father of the bride, rendered a speech distinguished for his pungent wit, sense of humor and 30-minute approximate length. He undoubtedly set a record for longevity, while he came close to "getting the hook" from his radiant wife, Joan!

Throughout 2017, Evelyn and I enjoyed monthly dinner meetings with other retired officers and their spouses or significant others. Ev's AAUW Chapter hosts a monthly self-prepared social dinner, calling it "California Cuisine." Ev belongs to several Bridge groups, one of which I partner with her once a month. It's still a toss-up whether my bridge game or golf game is most inept! Her community service instinct is served by participation in "Meals on Wheels" as well as running Heritage Tours for fourth grade students. We both enjoy our local playhouse theater. Our daughter, Liz, presented us tickets to "Hamilton" which we enjoyed during its run in Los Angeles.

In February, Evelyn and I traveled to Cuba on a bus tour sponsored by Road Scholar. We viewed the sights; vintage automobiles, Hemingway's home, and a trip from Havana to Camaguey. Overall, the trip was a pleasant venue and learning experience. During a tour of Che Guevara's Museum in Santa Clara, I experienced the misfortune of tripping in the same spot where Fidel Castro had stumbled and fell a few years back. Nothing was broken and the immediate first aid and TLC from Evelyn very much appreciated. I have tended to watch sidewalk cracks more closely ever since.

Rhodes Scholar was again our tour selection as we traveled

on their Loire River Cruise from Nantes and St Nazaire upstream to Chartres and Paris. It took me several tour stops to find a tour guide knowledgeable or willing to discuss the Revolt in the Vendee! Delightful weather, many chateaus and cathedrals, as well as fascinating history characterized each stop on our itinerary. Celebrating our last weekend in Paris, we were gratefully guided and thoroughly walked about by Michaeline O'Dwyer, Evelyn's sister, the most energetic, knowledgeable, and proficient tour leader in the business! Her hospitality and that of the resident RSHM was legendary. We could not say the same for the cab driver who dropped us off at the wrong terminal at the international airport! Rushing to catch a plane may well do me in on one of these trips.

Our three daughters and Evelyn's younger sister, Joan conspired to make Thanksgiving 2017 an indelible and cherished memory. In the company of 25 family members, we gathered at The Estate, a luxury ranch resort in La Quinta. On separate evenings, we celebrate Michal McAdam's 50th and my 80th birthdays. A genuine surprise to me was the bagpiper; a fully attired, kilted and recently retired U.S. Marine. Thanks to Meaghan's thoughtful recording, we listened to Irish music favorites from the "good old days." All in attendance; O'Preys, Truman's Ashtons, Walkers, Slachmans, McAdams and Montalvos participated and earned well-deserved praise for organizing and executing three days of eating and celebrating. My particular thanks were extended to Rob Walker for booking a prime tee time for eight golfers and to Frank, Joan and Kelly for comping my undistinguished round!

As we entered the New Year of 2018, a description of our respective household tasks would be appropriate and helpful to the reader's understanding of the sources for this biography. The dates, times and incidents are based upon Christmas letters composed by me at the end of each year. These have been of great assistance to my fading memory but do tend to get repetitive. During each Christmas season, I have the task of dispatching cards; e-mails and sundry greetings as well as the stringing of roof lights and the assembly of our mini tree. For her part, Evelyn keeps our social calendar, does all the shopping, decorating, and baking. In addition, she acts as a dependable and cautious safety observer that requires me and a ladder.

With respect to substitute teaching, I had the privilege of experiencing AP Classes where students discuss and present fascinating oral and visual briefings on U.S. and European historical personalities. Virtually all presentations are recorded on a thumb drive and graded by the regular teacher. I am most delighted to relax and enjoy practicing my favorite hobby, History. Evelyn remains an avid and sophisticated Bridge player in several groups as well as a book club member, AAUW participant and volunteer for Meals on Wheels. She also runs Smiley Heritage tours for young students.

In March 2018, we flew to New Orleans and enjoyed four

days touring that beautiful city and tasting its unique Cajon food specialties. Boarding our paddle wheel cruise ship, we sailed north up the Mississippi River with our first stop at Baton Rouge, where we visited several Ante-bellum mansions. A visit to Vicksburg, the town itself and the sites which dramatically illustrate the siege and Union victory were as impressive as they appeared in 1974 when we stopped there on our way to Washington.

Constantly on the move, mostly due to Evelyn's initiative, May brought a visit to Kathleen McAdam and an enjoyable Italian dinner with her, Sally and Kathy, two mutual friends. It was a similar pleasure to enjoy a luncheon with my brother Richie and Patricia O'Prey on the banks of the Hudson River in Nyack. June brought Evelyn's long-awaited and highly anticipated return trip to the Galapagos Islands; this time with Liz, Kiera, and Colin Walker. August occasioned a trip to the Ashtons in Danville and the Walkers in San Carlos, California. Always a pleasure to see the rapidly growing younger generation, I profoundly mistrust being at the mercy of airline schedules and would prefer to drive my Ford Edge for seven or eight hours north and entertain the illusion of being "in control."

In late October, we embarked on another cruise; this time a "Foliage" round trip from Portland, Maine up the coast to Bar Harbor and across the Bay of Fundy to visit our Canadian neighbors in St John's, New Brunswick. Aside from viewing some of the world's highest tides, the highlight of our voyage was the visit to Campobello, Canada, the summer home of Franklin and Eleanor Roosevelt and where FDR contracted polio in 1921. Weather on the trip was cool but pleasant and the lobster was delicious. Noted with a degree of irony was the ship's daily recap of U.S. news asserting that the best "foliage" in 2018 was to be found in the San Bernardino Mountains; our own backyard!

Travel planning for 2019 commenced when Andrew and Noreen announced their impending relocation from Danville to London, U.K. at the behest of his company, Cisco. Their move stimulated our major overseas trip for 2019 in May. We flew to Heathrow; were met by our daughter, Noreen and enjoyed a brief visit with Annie, Grace, and Andrew prior to our cruise of the North Sea/Baltic littoral on a Princess ship. Ports of call were Bruges, Ghent, Copenhagen, Stockholm, Helsinki, Lithuania, St. Petersburg and Gdansk. The highlight of our tour was the reunion and luncheon we enjoyed with Stella and Niels Friderichsen, our closest friends from our years in Denmark, at the Torvet in Central Copenhagen. We were pleasantly surprised when they arrived together on Niels' motorcycle! When our ship docked in Southampton, Noreen, once again, was there to meet us. We subsequently relaxed with the Ashtons at their home in Surrey, a suburb west of London. We were treated to a play, the experience of a ride on the London Eye and a Chinese Dinner in downtown

London.

Returning to Redlands in late May, we proudly noted our granddaughter, Kiera's 8th Grade graduation and our grandson James Truman's graduation with high honors from Loyola High School. Continuing her program of recognizing each grandchild with a trip of their choice, Evelyn flew to Maui in July with Kiera, Grace, and Noreen. This was immediately followed by a belated 80th Birthday celebration for Evelyn at an upscale condominium in La Jolla. While they were based on the beach below, I was thoroughly content to read and enjoy the spa, pool, patio, and porch facilities. As a most worthy recognition of Evelyn's love, her sister Kathleen McAdam and best friend Jeanne Shevlin were in attendance and were most welcome participants.

As summer turned to fall, Evelyn's travel yen reasserted itself and she devoted her planning skills and finances to a Stanford University trip to Tahiti and French Polynesia. I was actually beginning to look forward to the experience, when on the day prior to departure, Ev had the inconvenience of a scheduled medical appointment. After several repetitions of spiking high blood pressure counts and nausea, she decided, at Urgent Care, to heed the Doctor's advice and forgo travel until her blood pressure was back to normal. This resulted in her decision to cancel the trip itself and receive my personal compliments and relief for her good judgment.

The Christmas week was spent at the Walker's in San Carlos and a reunion there with the Ashtons on their way to Hawaii. We enjoyed the hospitality of the Trumans in "nearby" Redondo Beach prior to our flight north. It's always a great benefit to visit the family and observe, first-hand, the growth of the younger generation and their concurrence with my decision to stay off ladders and not string Christmas Lights below the eaves.

CHAPTER TEN

THE TWENTIES

As the New Year of 2020 dawned, little did any of us realize or imagine what substantial changes lay ahead in our relationships, customs and traditional working or leisure activities. A follow up brain scan generated by the TMI activity experienced at Walker's in December, revealed no abnormalities or problem areas. Substitute teaching, Bridge, golf, and club attendance remained our normal activities. In early February we enjoyed a visit from Kathleen McAdam and were privileged to have her join us at the annual Lincoln Dinner at the University of Redlands. On February 16, we enjoyed a well-attended brunch with our fellow members of MOAA at the Redlands Country Club. Little did any of us realize that social gatherings like these would be indefinitely postponed, rescheduled or canceled.

Our good neighbors, Dick and Rosemary Conway hosted their annual St Patrick's Day feast of corned beef and cabbage (Irish Caviar) on Saturday, March 14, I walked up the block and attended alone as Evelyn had a slight cold. Medical appointments, Masses, dinners, and social gatherings were prohibited in the interest of stopping the spread of Coronavirus 19. Due to our advanced ages, Evelyn and I are practicing home "isolation." Not as drastic as it sounds; in effect we go out together to shop for groceries. Evelyn shops and I drive. Under pressure from each of our three daughters, and with their cheerful assistance, we replaced our family room's couch, chair, rug, and furniture as well as bedroom lamps and desk top computers. It's amazing what can be accomplished when travel and summer vacations are removed from the "normal" summer planning equations! Aside from ennui, it was not a hardship to enjoy the sunshine and coolness of our backyard.

Settling down for an uneventful summer and practicing hoe "isolation" due to age and COVID-19, our domestic idyll was severely threatened on the early evening of Wednesday, June 3. Evelyn tripped on our garden hose and, landing on her right hip, broke her hip bone. The Redlands EMT was commendably responsive. Surgery followed at Redlands Community Hospital, and she was back home with me by Saturday, June 6. She was subsequently administered physical therapy at home and later at the therapy facility for recuperation.

Never to be left out of the action, I experienced a dehydration episode on the evening of July 30. Evelyn's rapid decision to call the EMT took matters out of our hands, and I spent two evenings in the Redlands Community Hospital. After IV's and

EKG's etc., I was told my heart was in good shape and I had possibly experienced a TIA. I feel fine, but 40 years of smoking have substantially slowed my lungs down. As a consequence, I am now equipped with an INOGEN ONE, an oxygen generator, which converts 95 % of ambient air into oxygen. It's somewhat awkward, but I manage to walk a half mile with it in my neighborhood, accompanied by Evelyn on most days.

Just a few short days ago, our family helped me celebrate my 83rd birthday via zoom, a technological device that consolidated the family from "Back East" to Rome and across the U.S. I sit at my desk in April 2021 marveling at the procrastination that has kept me from resuming this narrative for the past six months. The major and saddest event of this period was the passing of Evelyn's sister, Kathleen McAdam on January 29, 2021, after a long struggle with pelvic area cancer Kathleen attended in her final days at her daughter, Mary Jo Fuller's home in Little Silver, New Jersey. Her immediate family was present with her and certainly a source of great spiritual comfort to her and to each other. Kathleen's closeness and love were inseparable from that of our immediate family members.

Not wishing to risk complications from COVID 19 or my COPD lung problem, I remained in Redlands, gratefully attended by Meaghan and Jack Truman. While back in New Jersey for nearly a month, Evelyn and our daughter, Kathleen Truman experienced mild cases of COVID 19 from which they both recovered.

By any conceivable criteria, 2020 was a devastating year from both the COVID pandemic and the loss of close friends. On November 20, 2020, Monsignor Dennis Sheehan died suddenly in Boston. Dennis had officiated at the marriage of all of our younger generation family members. In February 2021 we were saddened to learn of the passing of Sister Maureen Therese McGroddy, RSHM, a close friend of my sister-in-law in Rome, Michaeline O'Dwyer, RSHM. The loss of these devout Catholics serves as a spiritual reminder that we too are now of a generation soon to meet our Maker.

Kathleen McAdam went to her most deserved heavenly reward on Friday, January 29,2021. Her home and hospitality were annual events for us and our daughters. We enjoyed her delightful company at our Lincoln Dinner on February 12, 2020. Kathleen was loving, caring and generous, whose beauty and contagious smile could light up an entire room. "Sic transit gloria mundi" and for her family whose memory of her will never fade.

From my bedtime roost on Sunday morning, August 30, the sound of Evelyn's voice signaled tragedy. In a conversation with our sobbing daughter, Liz, Evelyn was being informed of our grandson, Colin Walker's death by fentanyl poisoning some 10 to 12 hours earlier in his own bedroom in San Carlos. Liz asked that we fly up immediately. While packing our bags, conversation with the airlines revealed no more flights were operating out of Ontario on that day. Ev booked an 8:00 AM departure for Monday, August 30. Evelyn's close friend and bridesmaid, Jeanne Shevlin picked us up at 4:30 AM and delivered us in timely fashion to the United Terminal at LAX.

Arriving in San Francisco, we were grateful to be picked up by Michael McAdam, our nephew, who took us directly to the Walker home in San Carlos. By the time we arrived, the coroner had removed Colin's body for the required autopsy. In unspeakable grief and sadness, a sobbing Liz, Rob, and Aidan informed us of the following details: Colin had gone to his room about 11 PM on Saturday evening. His body was discovered by Rob at 11:50 AM on Sunday. Colin had fallen from his desk, the time of death estimated 10 to 12 hours earlier. He had experimented with drugs that, unknown to him, were laced with a lethal amount of fentanyl. Due to the presence of fentanyl the case was ruled a homicide.

Our oldest daughter, Kathleen Truman flew up immediately and took charge of household and funeral planning. Michael provided an invaluable taxi service to the airport, arriving with our daughter, Noreen on Tuesday, August 31. Their presence was of inestimable value as was Evelyn's in trying to console Liz in her grief. In her own way, heartbroken and shattered, Liz related the tragic details to arriving guests, mutual friends, and Colin's bereaved classmates.

A partial viewing was attended at the mortuary on Wednesday, September 1. Liz, Rob, Kathy, Mary Jo, Joan, Evelyn, and I were present for the last enduring memory of Colin whose body was subsequently cremated. I pray that no future generation of mine will ever have to endure such a tragedy of a young, promising, and beloved young person taken away from our family forever.

By any conceivable measure, 2022 was a "mixed bag". We had a major flood in our kitchen and living room in January, which necessitated a complete kitchen remodel and new floors throughout the house. We suffered through ten months of construction, much of it without the use of a functioning kitchen. The contractors finally completed the remodel at the end of October.

The positive highlight of the year came on June 30th, when our daughters hosted a celebration of our 60th wedding anniversary. This included dressing Evelyn in her wedding dress and me in my Air Force uniform for a gala Duffy boat cruise around Newport Harbor and a lavish dinner with Evelyn, myself, our daughters, our sons -in-law, our grandchildren, and Joan Slachman, reprising her role as flower girl from 1962. We could not have asked for a more loving family!

Our annual Thanksgiving Dinner at the Slachman home in Sacramento was a predictable success with delicious food and three generations represented, including the most recent addition, Brock

Montalvo.

Aware that my brother Richie, and Evelyn's sister, Mary, reside, respectively on the west and east sides of the Hudson River, our daughters planned a family reunion in New York for early December. However, the emergence of COVID-19 and my bout with pneumonia obliged Evelyn and our daughters to cancel the visit and seek a more favorable date in the future.

We are indeed fortunate to have our daughters, Kathleen and Noreen living close enough to visit often to help with illnesses, remodels and other household issues. Steve is our constant computer and technical guru. Liz and Rob flew down for a visit in late October, and, of course, we put Rob to work on fixing closets after the remodel. We remain most grateful for the support and love of our three sons-in-law.

CONCLUSION

It occurs to me, that having reached the age of 85 and encouraged by my brother Richie, whose imagination and literary skills far exceed my own, it is time to bring the narrative of *Decades* to a timely conclusion. I am also encouraged by my daughter, Elizabeth, whose recent love and hospitality made for a holy and memorable Christmas.

I have no profound advice to offer future progeny. I pray for the grace of a happy death and union with Jesus Christ, who sacrificed all for us. I define a happy death as being in the state of grace and one without an excess of physical pain. Join me in this prayer and God Bless you for doing so.

MY FATHER'S JOURNAL

Richard "Dick" O'Prey

I lived in Glasgow until about May 1, 1912, when my mother and I went to live in Ireland and father sailed for the United States on May 12, 1912, on the White Star Liner "Baltic" and landed in New York or Boston on or about May 22, 1912 from where he immediately proceeded to Park City Utah and immediately joined my uncles, John, Richard, and Peter O'Prey who were out there already. My father apparently left Europe with all the best of intentions but he never was fortunate in the United States and he travelled around the Western part of the U.S.A. working in copper and ore mines and no doubt drinking heavily as he went along as drinking was his only vice and when left to his own resources, he was weak in his will power and quite too much of a "good fellow" with his hard earned money but my mother and I heard from him sometimes frequently and other times infrequently until 1921 when he returned to Ireland.

In the meantime, 1912, I lived for some few short months

in the town of Crossgar, Co Down, Ireland where my mother found employment in the Police Barrack as a cook then apparently mother and I moved to live at Mayodds, Killcoo, Co Down, Ireland, where my mother worked at any kind of employment she was able to find there. It was here that the earliest recollections of my life began to form and I can dimly remember the World War No 1 breaking out and seeing the British Soldiers marching past the door where I lived one wet day. Then I can clearly remember my first days at Ballymoney National School sometime in 1915.

Then in about September 1915 my mother obtained employment in the Police Barrack at Newcastle, Co Down where we then went to live. Newcastle is a lovely place at the foot of the Mourne Mountains and on the Irish sea and is a great beach for swimming in. I went to school there and can clearly remember almost every incident that took place there including watching the soldiers train for war and I became fast friends with many of them.

We lived in several locations in Newcastle and I liked it very much and I used to see and spend a lot of time with my grandmother and my Uncle Henry, Aunt Lizzie, and Catherine who lived in Tullaree, about 5 miles from Newcastle. And my grandmother Ellen O'Prey (née McEvoy) adored me and she is one of my fondest memories because I was in constant contact with her until March 1928 when I left Ireland, never to see her again as she died in April 1929 and is buried in Kilcoo graveyard with my Grandfather Richard

O'Prey who died on May 8, 1915. And I can remember being in the room when he was dying and his wake and funeral. But my other recollections previous to his death are very dim although I can still remember walking along the road with him a few times.

APRIL 6, 1917

I remember going to school at Newcastle, Co Down and seeing a large American 'Flag flying from the roof and all the other boys were saying America had entered the War against Germany on our side. And Mr. Traynor our schoolteacher told us that England was sure to win now with the help of America.

But there were also other things that happened when I lived in Newcastle which at that time, I was too young to understand the meaning of but I remember the grown-up people in my mother's circle of acquaintances talking about them in whispers. Things such as the Irish Republican Rebellion of Easter Week, 1916 in Dublin, Ireland, And I clearly remember the execution of Sir Roger Casement in the summer of 1916 but it was not until 3 or 4 years later that I began to realize and understand the cause for which he and many other brave men died for which then became my cause also-that was the fight my native country Ireland had been waging for nearly 700 years to free herself of English Rule, and something that was to be always to the forefront as long as I lived in Ireland. For as it developed, I later lived through the period of Irish history which will always be remembered and while I did not know it, Brave

Irish men were carving a name for themselves in the History of Ireland.

I also remember several ships wrecked on the rugged Co Down coast during this period of war and once in particular an Austrian sailing ship ran aground and all her crew (Enemy) brought ashore in Newcastle. August 1917 We made another move as my mother had entered upon a seaside resort room renting business which evidently failed on account of a very wet and wartime summer (1917) so she decided to seek a better living for her and I elsewhere so we sailed for Scotland and I can remember my first sight of the City of Belfast where we sailed from it was just about the greatest thing my young eyes had ever gazed upon with rows and rows of houses, large buildings, ships and shipbuilding yards, trains, tram-cars, etc. And when we went aboard ship I had the idea we were sailing to America to see my father and I asked my mother where we were going and she told me she did not know which I found out in later years was the truth as she was deeply troubled at that time and was more or less alone in the world except for me as my father's family never really gave her much of a break and she was always a very independent woman who insisted on making her own way and living for her and I.

We arrived in Glasgow, Scotland the land of my birth and as far as I can remember spent about 10 days or two weeks there in which time my mother evidently searched for work and apparently she did not find any there suitable or to her liking because we sailed back to Belfast, Ireland and after spending a couple of days there with some woman whom my mother knew, we proceeded to Lisburn, Co Antrim where my mother and father had lived for a year or so after their marriage in 1908, 1909. My mother had folks she knew there named Coughlan and I remember they gave us a great welcome and we lived with them for several weeks in the meantime my mother had found work in a spinning mill there and we were soon settled down in our own home again and I went to "Catholic School" as I was 7 1/2 years old.

I can remember everything that happened quite clearly and some high points in my memory are crying for my little white dog which we had left behind in Newcastle and which I never seen again. I also remember Christmas, 1917 and about that time my first sight of airplanes which flew over town one Sunday and someone told me they were American planes. At about this time also it was brought home to me on the streets that all people did not think the same way and that there were two different religions, Protestant and Catholic as the school I went to at this time was known as Hilden National School and was non- sectarian and I remember well a boy who sat in the desk next to me and had heretofore been very chummy with me suddenly told me one day that I was a "Papist." I asked my mother what he meant and she explained to me and cautioned me not to get in fights with anyone over religion that my religion was the true one and all others were damned to the flame of hell. Anyhow I did not continue long at this school as my mother wished me to get a Catholic Education and I was sent to Longstone. Hill School in Lisburn and it was the parish Catholic School which I attended until terminated by the Anti-Catholic pogrom of 1920.

In late 1917 my mother having become more or less established and earning money, we had a room rented from people named Mc Kearns at 76 Grand Street Lisburn and I remember spending a very nice Christmas there with lots of toys and everything that make Christmas a gala affair for children. But in the meantime, my mother was on constant lookout for a house of our own and finally got one under very strange and tragic circumstances.

1918

One night in the winter of this year we were in the house of a woman acquaintance of my mother which was situated in a small street and was little more than a slum with an entryway from a larger street and the entry was covered up and about 6feet wide and the houses must have been at least 100 years old. Well on this particular Saturday night, while we were sitting there a man who lived next door came in and asked the women folks to go in and see his wife as she had fainted. I went along and I saw this woman her name was McMullen, lying on the floor beside a tub full of clothes she was washing. My mother went over and examined her and I heard her announce that she was dead. And she told the other woman to go and get a priest from the Church which was only a few 100 feet across the street and he came and administered the last rites of the Catholic Church.

The sequel to this story is that my mother went a couple of days later and rented the house in which the dead woman lived, and a short time later we purchased furniture and moved in there. At this time, my mother was working every day and I would find myself alone in the house quite a lot and my young mind used to think of ghosts and of the dead woman I had seen there. But anyway, I was never frightened during my time there because at night a child's worst fear I always had my mother home with me. The name of this street was Stewarts Court. My mother in later years always said that this house was haunted and that she was often frightened herself which may or may not have been her own imagination, but anyhow our stay there was short lived about 1month I think because we found a house a short distance outside the town in a place called Lisnatrunk-Hillhall and this necessitated a walk of about 1 1/2 miles to school for me but the surroundings were much more desirable than the other place.

But in the whole section there was only one other Catholic family named Hanna with whom we became fast friends. All the other neighbors were Irish Protestants and strict Orangemen who never really interfered with us in anyway, and actually were kind to me particularly during my later illness. But as it is hard to explain to an American who does not understand the age-old enmities of Ireland and the wide difference between the two religions these people always appeared to resent us in their midst and no doubt if my father had been there at that time, we would probably have encountered difficulty and would likely have had to change our abode. But there were 5 children in the Hanna family and they became my playmates exclusively and went to school with me and all together life was pleasant. I can remember several of our neighbors used to like me and some of them told me that I was such a nice little boy that it was a terrible pity I was a Papist or a Roman.

I remember one specific instance when my Uncle Peter came to visit us from Belfast and after he left an older boy beat me and told me he did not care about my old "Sinn Fein" uncle who came to see us. Sinn Feiners were at this time, an Irish Republican Society and certainly my Uncle Peter was not even interested in them and I did not even know what they were. As anyway at this time like all children I was strictly Pro-British in my sentiments as all the toys, books, posters and even in school was British propaganda and naturally all us children had a big hatred and also fear of the Germans who were at this time shaping up like they were going to win the war and we were all in mortal terror of being killed by them when they invaded Ireland.

Even in those days there was danger of "air raids" from air ships. We had a large garden and my mother and I used to work there in summer evenings. When she came from work in the linen mills and I spent a pleasant summer. I remember visiting my grandmother in Tullaree and the whole talk was of the expected conscription by England of all the young men which incidentally never came to pass as when the fall rolled around with the help of the U.S. Army the Germans were pushed back and an Armistice was signed on Nov 11, 1918 which is a day I remember quite clearly when all we children celebrated and all the mills were closed and so to Christmas, 1918 which we enjoyed.

1919

This year opened with a terrible epidemic of Flu and nearly everyone was sick at some time and many died in the town, and tens of thousands all over the world. I was not to escape either, because on the 8th of February 1919 I went to a concert held by my school and had a grand time and next day felt sick all day and getting worse. That night I remember my mother carrying me home from Hanna's and next morning my mother called a doctor, Dr. Clark, the only Catholic doctor in town. She would trust no other one and he diagnosed my illness a double pneumonia. I don't remember the next few days very well except the doctor coming every day and my mother at my bedside at all times, and the neighbors who were Protestants were very kind to me. And I was pretty near death, being anointed and given the last rites of the Church by Father Mc Loughlin of Lisburn. That I can clearly remember. However, I got well again and after a considerable time was able to go back to school.

And in April or May of this year we again moved to a new house, this time in the town of Lisburn at 70 Grand Street, Low Road, and here was a heavily populated section and also more Catholic people and boys to play with and during our stay here until August 20, 1920, I enjoyed life and outside of a few squabbles with other boys everything was pleasant.

On July 19, 1919, I was confirmed at St. Patrick's Church, Lisburn by Bishop McCrory of Down and Conner, later (20 years) Cardinal McCrory of all Ireland. I took the name of Benedict for the Pope of that time, Benedict 15th and my sponsor was a man named Joseph Courtney, who lived next door to us.

At Christmas time of this year, we again visited my grandmother and I met my Uncle Richard who had just returned from America and I used to listen with wide-eyed wonder to his stories about far Western Montana, Utah, etc. and I thought that America must be the greatest place in the world.

About this time one of my teachers in school, Mr. Beckett, used to teach us history and he specially emphasized the history of Ireland. And I began to get a new understanding of Ireland's struggle for independence as by this time there was almost open warfare between the Irish Republicans and the British Soldiers and Police, all over the country and we Catholic boys were all out and out Irish rebels. I remember the summer of 1919 we had a Peace Day celebration after the World War and all the school children paraded except my school, as our Parish Priest, Father Cashin, refused to permit us to salute the Union Jack. (The English Flag). Of course, our parents were all in favor of his actions.

1920

This was a year that changed a lot of things in my life as it meant our moving out of Lisburn and was an all-round upset year in Irish History as everywhere there was trouble and murders. In the first part of the year my mother worked in Belfast, which was only 7 miles away from us and I used to go there with her often on Saturday's shopping. And on the 12th of July (Orangeman's Day) Anti Catholic riots broke out which lasted for about 3 years during which time thousands of Catholics were burned and chased from their homes and employment, and hundreds murdered. However, they fought back as best they could and while many moved to more safer parts of Ireland, the greater number remained there.

These riots spread to Lisburn about July 20th, 1920, on a Saturday night. All the Catholic business houses were looted and plundered and many Catholic homes were attacked by Orange mobs. However, this ended in one night as bigger things were to come month later. During this period, I was an altar boy in our church and we used to suffer severe abuse on our way past Protestant sections and Lisburn was 10-1 Protestant. On August 20,

1920, a police inspector was assassinated in Lisburn. His name was Swanzly and he was shot by the IRA for political reasons, the murder of a prominent Irishman, Mayor Mc Curtin of Cork City. And this was the signal for the Orange Mob to start an all-out pogrom of burning and looting against their outnumbered Catholic townspeople, and this time they did a good job for they did not leave a Catholic business house in town and very few Catholics of any kind. No Catholic escaped the consequences. Even the priests house was burned to the ground and the cemetery violated, tombstones knocked down and ornaments broken, and 4 priests chased for their very lives from their home. Only the Church and the school escaped. The Irish police force was powerless in the face of the mob, and the British soldiers just did not prevent the mob from operating until at the end of one week the mob spent itself for want of victims. In the meantime, the first day of the outbreak my mother sent me to Tullaree to my grandmother's and she remained in Lisburn for about 6 weeks more, when conditions became so intolerable, she finally joined me and I was never again to see my school chums and as a matter of fact I was never in Lisburn afterwards.

In the meantime, I spent the fall of 1920 with my grandmother, Uncles and Aunts, and while I was apparently welcome, my mother was not as money is a big factor and my mother did not have much although she did all she could and worked hard to help them. Still, she and they were dissatisfied and we were practically homeless. And I can appreciate her feelings now. One day in October she dressed me up and we left there and walked about 6 miles to Annsboro, Co. Down where after spending 2 nights with some people she knew she rented a house there and we salvaged what furniture remained from Lisburn so we were set up again. But from then until after the New Year, we were very short of money.

And I remember going to work gathering potatoes for neighboring families for 3 shillings a day with her. And she also made some money sewing. I started going to Annsboro School and got to know new friends some of whom were to become lifelong and as Catholics were more numerous here and we were in Rebel territory so we had no more Anti-Catholic trouble, at least we were not chased from our home.

But the Irish-English War was at its height and I will never forget many instances particularly the death of Terrence Mc Sweeny of Cork on hunger strike and Kevin Barry, 18 years old, hanged at Dublin for Ireland, and men and boys were dying every day for this cause. England had sent her Black and Tans to Ireland, and not so much in the North where we lived, but in other parts they were waging a campaign of murder, shooting and terror against men, women and even children. But the IRA was fighting back bravely and many an English grave was filled. But also, many Irish ones so the year ended and about Christmas time, my father wrote and said he was preparing to come home to Ireland from Salt Lake City Utah.

APPENDIX II

IF I COULD SPEAK ONCE MORE

Richard Joseph O'Prey

The pain started like a sharp stab, but it continued to constrict, tightening my chest until I lost consciousness. I think the car crashed after that. What I remember next was lying on my back straddled by a Black paramedic rhythmically compressing my chest as he counted almost inaudibly. The ambulance careening to the hospital and the frantic efforts to restart my heart evidently were futile, for I recall a clean white sheet being pulled over my face. A pervading sense of peace was disrupted by my panic as I, albeit clinically dead, desperately prayed, "Let me speak only once more!"

If my prayer were answered and I had been given one last chance to speak, I would not call my wife to my bedside to reassure her of my love. Our marriage has been a union of bodies and souls. She needs no dying protestations of devotion or pleas for forgiveness. With one more chance to speak, I would not summon a priest to hear my last confession and assure me of eternal salvation. My life is replete with the foibles of human weakness, but my conscience is clear. My faith in God's mercy and justice is strong. I need no last-minute guarantee of salvation.

Granted a chance to speak, I would not beg to see a crony who could destroy any vestiges of a scandalous or duplicitous life. My life is precisely what it appears to be- that of a man who took joy in his family and in the simple pleasures of nature. If my wish were granted, I would not demand to see a financial consultant who might project a comfortable future for my family. If I have not left my wife Mary with the conviction of her inherent value and natural talent, I have been remiss. If my children lack the self- confidence and ambition to develop their personal interests, then I, too, have failed. I do not believe that financial security or material accumulation will bring them happiness. Rather, let whatever I have managed to provide during my lifetime suffice. It represents my honest effort to do all I could prudently do.

If I could speak one last time, I would call my children, Brendan, Katherine, and Maureen to my side. I would beg them to examine who they are. I would implore them to acknowledge their roots, nourish their heritage, and never sever the links that unite them with their ancestors. My last message to them would be simple, but profoundly important. Unless their lives are rooted deeply in their ancestral strength, they will be vacillating, superficial hypocrites lacking in substance, character, and conviction. Perhaps they shall achieve the American dream without reckoning its cost.

I would ask Brendan, Katherine, and Maureen to pray with me that they might always cherish the twin sources of their identity. They must never forget they are Irish and they are Catholic. These two attributes, neglected by some and derided by others, are in truth what have made our people what we are. It is the pride, even the arrogance, in our cultural heritage that enables us to thrive. Overlook one taproot, I'd argue, and they'd become a sterile hybrid. Neglect both roots and they'd create a homogenized, spineless character, attracted to the fad and fashion of the moment. Brendan, Katherine, and Maureen, with my dying breath, I'd exhort you always to remember you are Irish and Catholic. I'd also like to try to explain that you are Irish and Catholic in peculiar ways.

"Brendan," I'd say, "you have inherited the good looks and genial disposition of the tall, hardworking Burkes from Mallow in County Cork. You have inherited a legacy of charitable thought and kindness epitomized in the gentle giant that is your grandfather Tom." "Katherine, with your gorgeous red hair and intelligent sensitivity," I'd describe, "how you have been tempered by the sectarian strife of Belfast and the nomadic life of the economically oppressed. There was no room for talent or intelligence in the bigoted slums of Northern Ireland. Your ancestors, the Lennons and the O'Preys, never compromised their principles to sup from the trough of the oppressor. Perhaps that may be the price you'll have to pay too!" "And Maureen, of the dark-eyed beauty of the

West," I'd remark, "how you have inherited the poetic soul of the Durkins and the Duggans. The wild, unforgiving grandeur of Mayo has bred in you a love of nature and an appreciation of its simple joys!"

My children, I'd inform you that the Irish culture you received is not that of green beer and frivolous songs on St. Patrick's Day. It is not that of horse racing, golf, and castles. Look for no kings, famed warriors, or poets in the stout branches of your family tree. Rather, I'd remind you that you represent a darker segment of the Irish who possess a perversity, obstinacy, a persistence that, come what may, they shall endure and they shall prevail.

Our heritage is the boast that in time of famine we would not "take the soup." Our ancestors preferred to starve or eke out a meager living on boulder strewn lands around Killala Bay. As a child, I'd tell you how I spent three months on that rocky, inhospitable soil. I'd reminisce how I loved the land and the soil and subconsciously adopted the ways of the poor, although I was then too young to comprehend the sociological and economic facts. For the three months on this tiny, barren farm in Connaught, I'd recollect how we, surrounded by meat sources, never ate what must be sold for money. Duck eggs were for consumption; chicken eggs were for sale. Protein was provided through poaching salmon in the river Moy, or illegally hunting rabbits with greyhounds on the Protestants' lands. On a farm without electricity evenings were surrendered to stirring conversation and tales of Cromwellian atrocities.

When your grandmother, Kitty Duggan, turned eighteen, she had to leave the land and the family that could not support her. Transplanted to America, Kitty did domestic work, married, raised my brothers and me, and died too young when there was no more to give. She preached no Irish history or delivered any harangues. She offered no lectures or uttered any platitudes. Romantic notions were for the idle; not those involved in the industry of survival. Yet her message was transmitted eloquently and inerrantly. Endure, persist, prevail-but don't sacrifice your principles and ideals for fame, fortune or following. Toward those who do, bear witness with silent, but contemptuous pride. Let your satisfaction reside in this perverse sense of integrity. Your grandmother whom you never knew sought no social recognition, nor undue wealth, nor peer approval. Her family was her bailiwick. Their endurance and integrity were paramount.

If your pride rests on noble ancestors, you'll be disappointed in your grandfather too. Dick O'Prey was born the child of an economic vagabond who could find no work in the Protestant North of Ireland. With his four brothers, Paddy O'Prey, your great-grandfather, worked the mines of Park City, Utah and Butte, Montana. He harbored no pretensions when he joined the Wobblies to escape the clutches of the American mine operators while his wife

Lizzie had to flee to Glasgow in search of subsistent income. That same oppression and prejudice set the stage for a harsh, early life where your grandfather as a young Irish Catholic newly returned to the North, was firebombed, machine gunned, and ultimately traumatized for life by the Specials and Orange Lodges of Belfast. They carried few family heirlooms and undoubtedly no peerage papers as they skulked about County Down seeking safety.

While bigotry could brutalize your grandfather's body, it could not contain his spirit. Dick O'Prey developed a passion for reading and wrote with an eloquent pen that unfortunately was stifled by the perfidious effects of the prejudice he so acutely sensed. In this context, Brendan, Katherine, and Maureen, you share a common heritage with the Black and Hispanic in America more so than with The Friendly Sons of St. Patrick, the New York Athletic Club, or the Ancient Order of Hibernians. Don't live in the past; but don't forget it. Don't romanticize your roots. Recognize them for what they truly are. Seek no coat of arms but savor the knowledge you spring from solid peasant stock. Your glory, your beauty, your very strength lies in the ability to endure, not in creating imaginary kings and titles, pretensions, and illusions.

If I could speak one last time, Brendan, Katherine, and Maureen, I'd tell how American soil enabled your family to escape poverty and deprivation. I'd review how your predecessors worked, encouraged education, but sanctioned the freedom to choose whatever career you wanted. Each of you too has the complete license to follow wherever your wishes, dreams, and aspirations may lead you. There is no family business, no professional legacy, no impelling tradition to constrain or inhibit you.

There is one precaution, however, my children. I'd warn you that your wealth, your position, your fame will be transitory if it is not rooted in the inherent convictions of your Irish ancestors. Don't sell out your heritage or trade your birthright for the "bowl of soup." Don't be seduced by the materialism and superficiality of our American dream. Preserve that perverse, obstinate righteousness that will permit you to hold your head high and speak with a clear conscience. It won't make you wealthy or powerful, but it will preserve your happiness.

If I had one last opportunity to speak, I would warn you that your Irish background is not a total unalloyed blessing. I would remind you of your family's propensity for alcoholism, "a good man's failing," as your grandfather used to say. I would urge you to be particularly vigilant and skeptical when that problem surfaces in your lives. I would advise you to balance the bright, articulate, literary art that seems ubiquitous among the Irish, with the sullen melancholy and maudlin sentimentality that presage depression and moroseness. I would encourage you to employ your glib wit to inject humor in times of trouble and to deflect hostility in times of confrontation. I would inform you that sarcasm and criticism, so quick to the lips of the Irish, are devastating weapons that have separated generations and created chasms among friends.

Aware of the strengths and weaknesses of your Irish heritage, Brendan, Katherine, and Maureen, you are prepared for the challenge of the future if you balance your lives with Catholicism. You simply cannot be the Irish descendant of your ancestors if you stray beyond the Catholic Church. The centuries of persecution, the banishment to "hell or Connaught," the violence of Ulster have refined your Catholicism into a unique expression too.

You are not the Catholic who awaits promulgating Pontiffs, prattling prelates or political priests. The parable of the pastor and the flock is not so impelling as the parable of the mustard seed. Your Catholicism is well aware of the humanity in the Church. It separates the people of God from the persons of God. Your Catholicism has witnessed the weakness of a clergy as well as its heroism. It has learned the value of respecting individuals, not positions. You must not rely on human sanctity or clerical leadership often anesthetized by the very celibacy intended to promote service.

The Catholicism of your ancestors left theological disputations to the French, the Dutch, or the Germans. Irish Catholicism is more simplistic and narrow-minded. It is rooted in a Jansenistic sense of moral athleticism, a suspicion of whatever smacks of Protestantism, a theology that is cut and dry, and a quixotic spirit of social justice for the underdog. Large cathedrals in

Ireland belong to the Protestant. Fundraising is the province of the wealthy. Theology belongs to the intellectual dilettante. But Service is the hallmark of the committed Irish Catholic. The injunction to love one's neighbor, to see Christ in the impoverished or abused, the disinherited or the alienated, and to assist the underprivileged are the missions of the Catholic Church you know.

The same arrogance that marks your Irishness also characterizes your Catholicism. Brendan, Katherine, and Maureen, please don't stray from the Catholic Church for whatever reason. Your ancestors saw in it a source of strength and solace. American soil has nurtured us, but a conversion to Americanized religion will destroy one of your vital taproots. For us, one religion is not as good as another. For us, Catholicism is a matter of cultural identification as well as religion. For those who accept the Puritan ethic or Americanize their name and religion, social success is more attainable. But that is selling your birthright for the bowl of soup. You will lose something vital. Money, psychiatry, therapy, or ephemeral crusades cannot replace that root. Savor your Catholicism. Be skeptical of its wealth and wary of its clergy. Allow room for human frailty, but never remove yourself from its protection.

Brendan, Katherine, and Maureen, I offer no advice about money, investment, marriage, or career. They must all be resolved within the context of your inheritance. Cherish, nurture, and preserve your twin roots of Irish culture and Catholicism. Pass these values on to your children. If I had only one chance to speak, this is what I'd say. 'Tis a pity no one speaks from beyond the grave!

FRATERNAL WITNESS

Richard Joseph O'Prey

Anxiously awaiting the arrival of Bernard and his California family, I was disappointed when it had to be cancelled almost at the last moment. Obviously, the decision was difficult, but his ultimate hospitalization for pneumonia proved wise. Nonetheless, the circumstances led me to ruminate about my relationship with my brother Bernard. Avidly awaiting his printed memoir, *Decades*, I decided to record some of my recollections of his influence upon me. If I contradict anything he says in Decades, I yield to his reflections.

Before my parents even met each other, my Aunt Helen Clancy encountered some difficulties when she arrived in New York at the tender age of seven. Surviving her initial placement in a German teaching Catholic School in Yorkville, her mother immediately transferred her to a predominantly Irish parish on the westside. At Holy Trinity she was immediately rebaptized by a zealous Nun who advised her that there were no Nellies in America and that she thence forward would be called Helen. Now Helen lost her father in August 1931. The onus of caring for the young nine-year-old and her mother fell upon my father. Helen would live with him until the day she married Joe Clancy on September 23, 1945. The extended family responsibility was part of the marriage contract when my parents married in St. Luke's Church in June 1935. Two years later Bernard became an addition to this ready-made family that lived in a small apartment at 521 West 182nd Street in Washington Heights. Three years beyond that my entrance into the family led to the occupation of less cramped space, so we moved to 869 West 180th Street. This was a ground floor, four-bedroom apartment with a secondary bathroom and my home for the next fifteen years.

PERILOUS INFANCY

Clearly his early years are not etched in my mind, but my Aunt Helen used to speak of Bernard in very glowing terms. Since she was only fifteen, the arrival of the newborn was significant. When I visited her during the summers while she and her husband Joe lived in Hudson, Florida, she recalled some particulars that are the basis of my description. Helen mentioned that my mother's delivery of her first-born was long and perilous. She didn't include details, but she claimed that when Bernard did arrive, his health prognosis was very poor. Without specifying any particulars, Helen disclosed that the infant was in poor shape and consequently received baptism immediately from the hospital chaplain. Later when his life was more secure, he was baptized as usual in St. Elizabeth's church. In those days there was a common teaching that unbaptized babies were consigned to limbo. Since Baptism was an introduction to sanctifying grace, the infant's death would lead to instant entrance into heaven. Since that analysis was prevalent, many relatives would surreptitiously baptize the child just in case.

LETHAL BATTLE

While I led the O'Prey triad in stitches and broken bones and Ray was the solitary victim of an automobile, Bernard won the reputation for having the gravest health condition. Along with his conditional Baptism, he was also perhaps given Extreme Unction a few years later when he contracted Scarlet Fever. Again, at that time, such an affliction was life-threatening. When my son Brendan suffered from Scarlet Fever, I was unduly alarmed while the pediatrician wasn't. By the 1970's it was as perilous as a bad cold. In the early '40's it was clearly grave and often mortal. Since Bernard was one of the first civilians to receive penicillin, it saved his life. I don't know whether the war was still on, but the military was the repository of almost all the penicillin, but Bernard was one of the first to receive a series of doses administered by a visiting public health nurse. Ray and I also acquired penicillin shots over several weeks, but we had no severe conditions akin to Bernard's.

NOT QUITE LEPROSY

While we were under treatment, our apartment house had a huge quarantine sign posted to warn the public. There was a similar sign across the street where another family was the victim of whooping cough, a disease we seldom hear about today. Medicine has worked marvels during the interim after the introduction of wonder drugs like antibiotics and such.

AFTERMATH AND CONSEQUENCES

Although Bernard survived, the disease had impious effects for many years. His physical condition was debilitated, and body seriously weakened to the point where I could beat him in our fratricidal wars. After several years of triumph, however, one day with no one at home to rescue me, I discovered that Bernard had recovered his strength and advantage of three years, despite my significant 'robust physique' and literally wiped the floors with me. I was intelligent enough to never undergo combat with him again.

PRECOCIOUS CHILD

As a young teenager, Helen enjoyed the presence of her precocious nephew whose curiosity knew no bounds. On one occasion when Helen was accompanied by three friends, Marie Killgallon, Dorothy Hayden, and Kay Coffee, the radio was playing. The toddler recognized a familiar voice emanating from the massive console that held the magical tubes that glowed yellow orange from the various diodes and triodes that comprised the guts of early radios. Helen maintained that the curious toddler crept behind the huge console in search of Dorothy Hayden whose family conducted a popular Irish music show frequently heard in the home. As a child, according to Helen, Bernard displayed a universal curiosity, a broad verbal vocabulary and a penchant for performing for her friends.

INTRODUCTION TO TECHNOLOGY

The radio in the early forties was a formidable addition to one's home. Despite its size and complexity in dealing with its dials, it was a toddler's gold mine for it provided incentives to use one's imagination. The fecund imagination of Bernard soon absorbed some of the lessons hypnotically taught by the electronic device. Much like the smart phone of today, in the forties the radio carried subliminal, almost hypnotic messages to its audience. Along with caped crusaders and heroic figures like the Lone Ranger and Sky King, or Sergeant Preston, the air waves brought ethnicity into every home.

SEEDS OF CONVICTIONS

At the time when Bernie was exploring people, he could listen to programs depicting other ethnicities. For the Jews, there was *Molly Goldberg*, but he had real life examples surrounding him in Washington Heights. For Scandinavians he heard *I Remember Mama*, but they were only fictional characters to him. For Italians he could hear of the adventures of a recent Italian immigrant, named Luigi Bosco, attending English as a Second Language classes. They presented a spoof of a zaftig Italian maiden named Rosa who was always summoned to meet Luigi by a friend. Her obesity was only surpassed by her inane laugh and stupidity.

Irish Americans could encourage Italians to follow civil service if they eschewed the police and fire department. True to their station in life, they were relegated to the sanitation department. The derided Italians were also deterred from joining Mike Quill's Transportation Workers Union, hallowed jobs to the Irish. As competitors in the labor market, the Italians were viewed as incompetent, dense workers, and intermarriage with them was not only discouraged but scorned. Irish Americans would harbor great resentment to the Italians until the descendants of Petrarch, Dante, Machiavelli, Michelangelo, Da Vinci, and Verdi proved they too were Americans. It did not help that Italy was a foe in World War II. That prejudice would be reflected in the derisive humor that made Italians the butt of abusive humor among New Yorkers.

IRISH IDENTITY & INTRODUCTION TO BLACK CULTURE

The Irish had their own ethnic radio program too. It was called *Duffy's Tavern*, "where the elite meet to eat." That program featured a Gothic character named Digger O'Dell, the friendly undertaker. Fibber Magee and Molly had roles too that elude my memory. How strange that the setting would be a pub! Perhaps the most insidious program of all was also one of the most popular.

Amos and Andy offered a glimpse into Black society. It

featured the Kingfish who was a pseudo-intellectual intent on pursuing every shady scheme. He was henpecked by an intelligent wife who kept him on a short leash. The vision of Black society was quite skewered but in the absence of any evidence to the contrary, the audience drew judgments on their own. I can't claim to estimate its influence upon Bernard, but it had some effect upon me. In my later years when I had considerable exposure to Black culture, I confessed to a young Black about the images produced by the radio show. He was incredulous that I could fall for that image.

ZEITGEIST AND HOLLYWOOD

While radio provided some influence upon the developing psyches of its hearers another influence comes to mind. One should never forget the conditioning factors that swirl around youthful, insatiable minds. In Bernard's case it was the movies. The image of the clever, but amoral savagery of the German competed with the bespectacled, bucktooth image of the cruel, robotic Japanese. They generally were referred to as Nazis and Nips.

Movies also bore the image of another conditioning factor of Bernard's youth. Patriotism, like that captured several millennia before in a Horatian Ode was in evidence in the war movies. "Dulce et decorum est pro patria mori" nicely summarized the theme. "How sweet and proper it is to die for one's country." The ultimate sacrifice was praised in such movies as *The Fighting Sixty-Ninth*, a picture showed multiple times in our grammar school, Incarnation, extolling the contribution of an Irish Immigrant played by James Cagney. Thirty Seconds over Tokyo boosted American morale and immortalized Jimmy Doolittle, but particularly glorified those who died at the hands of the Japanese. The Five Sullivan Brothers told the tale of five Iowan boys who went to their deaths together as crewmen of The USS Juneau in the Pacific. We lived near the church on Fort Washington Avenue ministered by the father of one of the heroic chaplains who surrendered their life jackets to sailors when they too went down to their deaths with the ship. Is it any wonder why Bernard would develop a hyper-patriotism that led him to volunteer for a lifetime of service in the United States Air Force?

EARLY SIGNS OF DESTINY

Bernard apparently always had a military career in mind. Sometimes his body didn't agree. Living a block away from the George Washington Bridge provided a temptation for the peripatetic youth of our neighborhood. During WWII we used to see a soldier stationed by the access stairs to the walkways across to New Jersey, but that ceased after VJ Day. We often hiked across the bridge to the wilds of Coatesville or south to Palisades Amusement Park. On one memorable occasion, Bernard murmured to me as he ascended one of the more challenging rides. He exclaimed, "You gotta have what it takes to be a fighter pilot." Reeling off the ride, he immediately sought a waste basket into which he poured what it takes to be a pilot.

Although clearly wishes to pursue the military and a pilot's career, his was far from a primrose path. He tried to secure a nomination to the newly opened Air Force Academy in Colorado Springs. Part of the process required a physical examination at Floyd Bennett Field on Long Island. Discovering his seating posture exceeded the criteria for pilots, Bernard urged the examiner to remeasure him. The examiner claimed, "You wanna be shorter, you're shorter." A more significant obstacle arose when the examination disclosed an obstruction in his nasal passage that precluded a positive recommendation.

His backup plan incorporated the ROTC at Manhattan. When he was participating in flight training at Westchester AirPort, he was attempting a landing using only instrument controls without vision. As he advised the pilot to land, the instructor remarked. "Look again! We're directly over the control tower."

USAF AND REALITY

Bernard wasn't deterred from pursuing his dream, however. He redirected his plans upon commission as a second Lieutenant in the USAF. At an exit interview upon graduation, he was asked where he would prefer to be assigned. Considering his skills and interests, he mentioned he would like to be assigned to intelligence, overseas, and specifically, Germany because he had studied the language for four years in college. His interrogator inquired what his major was and upon learning he was a history major, he assigned him to a shooting gallery in San Antonio.

The newly minted officer was quite unhappy at the shooting range where his disdain for his immediate superior led him to suggest, "Why don't you go back to high school and finish your education." No doubt that added any bonus points to his career, but he then volunteered for flight school at Randolph Air Base. He soon discovered that he might not have the fine motor skills required of a pilot. After making a few mistakes at 400mph, one does re-evaluate his goals. After washing out of flight school, he was sent to navigator's school. There he planned to fail on purpose and then leave the air force and go to law school. The military had other plans. Bernard learned that it was impossible to fail flight school for the student was sent until he mastered the skills however long it might take. He then passed on his first attempt.

SUCCESS

Securing credentials as a navigator on his first time around, he was assigned to the Strategic Air Command as a navigator on a K–97 to rendezvous with the B-47 nuclear bomber for refueling. I'll leave the rest of his official career to the aficionados who choose to read *Decades*, but I'd like to comment on two occasions specific to myself. In my first year in Washington, D.C., Bernard invited me to dinner at the officer's club at Bolling Air Force Club. Decked out in my clerical suit, I envisioned an evening standing at a bar amid officers drinking to excess in a smoky, dank environment.

Much to my surprise I learned exactly what Bolling AFB was truly like. It harbored much of the military brass of the nation stationed at the Pentagon. As we waited online before getting a table, I noted our fellow dining guests were garbed in full military regalia and the wives wore evening gowns. I heard them addressed as General Such-n-such and Admiral So-n-so. The maître d then announced a table for two for Second Lieutenant Bernard O'Prey. As we worked our way to the table, we dodged tuxedoed waiters bearing burning shish kabob spears. Apparently, there were officials from Turkey dining at the time. I was impressed, maybe dumbfounded, by the formality of what I presumed would be a Ratskeller rather than a classy operation.

Foreign Ingrate

In my last year in Washington in May 1962 Bernard stopped on his motor trip from San Antonio to New York and invited me again to dinner. No officer's club this time, for we went to Domino's near the agricultural labs in Ammendale, Maryland. The visitors to the scholasticate often stayed at the motel and dined there near the experimental agricultural labs that were the setting for Khrushchev and Nixon interviews. When Bernard was proffered the tab, he wrote a check from the Second Bank of San Antonio. The owner refused to honor it. After much hassling over failure to accept the money, he was paid for risking his life for this country, the owner insisted he make the check out for the exact cost of the meal and tax. Bernard had originally made a check for the tip and some extra gas money, so rather than wash dishes, he rewrote the check but berated the owner, who happened to be a Frenchman, for his lack of patriotism.

PUBLIC RELATIONS COUP

One more sortie into my connection with the 2nd Lt. O'Prey. In my first year of teaching at Sacred Heart in High bridge, I had some students compose letters to "Lieutenant X" at Maguire AFB. On Armed Forces Day that spring, we were invited to attend an air show compliments of Lt. X.

Several bus loads journeyed down the turnpike to be guests of the squadron stationed there. Bernard had the boys in awe especially when he introduced them to the newly deployed B-52. A close inspection made me ruminate that we could airlift an apartment house after noting its spectacular size. We were also allowed to visit the war room and note the global displays of current deployments. That was followed by teletype messages from around the world wishing my students well. My students were deeply impressed and pleased also that they could identify Lt. X when they saw both of us standing side by side.

"OBSTIPUO" AS VIRGIL MIGHT SAY

Years later a starlit night outside my house in Florida, it finally dawned on me what a fascinating achievement my brother had made in the Air Force. I was dumbfounded, or as Gomer Pyle might say, 'Gob smacked' when Bernard started to identify the various constellations in the clear sky overhead. As a total ignoramus about astronomy, I listened in awe as he recited the locations of the constellations and their interplay in the scenario above. I finally realized that our government had entrusted my brother with a mufti-million-dollar plane and its occupants to navigate from Travis AFB to Tan Son Nhut in Saigon, or rendezvous with an atomic bomber above the Arctic Circle, or land on a tiny island in the Azores. Since I had little knowledge beyond the Big Dipper, the enormity of his responsibility had finally penetrated my consciousness.

FECUND IMAGINATION

Bernard's near fatal bout with Scarlet Fever had left his body with significant debilities. His muscles were weak, his coordination a disaster, and his stamina questionable. While these characteristics did not indicate a future in sports, they didn't betray the special qualities he harbored in that weakened body. Bernard always had an extraordinary imagination in creating his own style of games. It was said that he occasionally donned costumes, but I remember seeing him offering Mass at the kitchen table using some kind of goblet for the chalice. However, visions of producing a priest were short-lived.

BRIGADOON

In 1948 the O'Prey boys had the opportunity very few of their peers experienced. We were going to undertake an ocean voyage and investigation of rural Ireland. When we boarded the

HMS Mauretania each of us 'harbored' some fears. Ray envisioned the ship rolling over on its side like the Normandie and our drowning before the ship left the pier. He had visual evidence of such a catastrophe every time we rode down the Westside highway. Although more optimistic, I truly sensed that as soon as we left sight of land, we would submerge to a watery grave.

I don't know what was in Bernard's imagination, but he soon fell victim to the rolling seas. On the first night out the Cunard liner featured a free movie. While Ray and I imagined John Wayne or Gene Autry or Roy Rogers coping with outlaws, only Bernard and my mother could stomach the British film. Ray and I were exhausted so we retired early. Both deeply comatose, we couldn't awaken even when the staff simulated early rising with a gong that brought the entire section of Tourist class to our door. The ship's carpenter had to saw the lock off our door finally.

In the morning Ray and I were the only persons perky enough to roam the ship seeking adventure. When Bernard did awaken, he was burden with what appeared to be terminal seasickness. Ray and I had little sympathy for him since we had no clue how debilitating the ailment was. Later we witnessed my mother with the assistance of a priest helping the stricken victim ascend some stairs. I suppose it took a few days for him to recover, but his imagination wasn't suffering when we arrived at Ballygarry in Mayo to stay with our grandparents.

On their small farm Bernard discovered two newborn calves that he identified as rodeo material. Those frightened beasts were terrified of us, for Bernard showed us how to wrestle with them and turn them upside down. Moreover, we discovered a stash of potatoes stored in what was once my mother's birth cabin. Bernard directed us in perpetual 'snowball' fights with the essential food commodity as unlimited supply. He was gifted a tiny kitten that he christened Tiger. a cute beast that took an instant distrust and dislike to our uncle Seamus, the recipient of its hissing and threatening by daylight and incessant crying at night. Poor Seamus was further victimized by Bernard's literary skills. He had chalked comments about a love affair between Seamus and the horse Rose on the sides of the horse cart that our uncle drove into Ballina. I doubt Bernard knew about the reputation of buggery, but Seamus became the butt of local humor from his peers thereafter.

Perhaps the 'feather' that broke the camel's back, however, was the lesson the imaginative Bernard provided the Irish with his version of Americana. My grandfather had shot some marauding crows, the birds, not the Indians, and left their bodies in the yard as a deterrent to fellow thieves to stop stealing the chicken feed. Bernard determined that their feathers might provide the raw material for war bonnets. He plucked the carrion and arrayed it into bonnets and then boldly stepped into the house only to be greeted by gagging and nose holding for the stench was truly unbearable. His efforts to enlighten the Duggans only produced a family confab to rescue the small farm under siege and preserve some chance for survival throughout the coming year.

It was no surprise when the oldest of the gossoons was shipped off for a month to my grandmother's brother's farm in Cartoon. After a month's exile, he returned to Ballygarry and I replaced him at the Lynn's in Cartoon, a small town outside Killala. That proved to be a source of further adventure for me for I learned not to arouse the anger of a sow with piglets nor tempt a horse with oats suspecting I was planning to bridle him for some work.

Our return trip to New York in August had its own unusual characteristics. An early hurricane had roiled the Atlantic and prevented our tender or ferry from bringing passengers to the liner too big to enter Cobh harbor. Despite two futile attempts to board, we were told to find lodging in the town until a bell would toll inviting us to try again. On our third attempt we succeeded and so began a violent cruise to make up for lost time. Almost all on board including the crew suffered from seasickness and Ray and I learned first-hand how sick one could feel from the disease. We belatedly could now sympathize with Bernard's first voyage.

I don't connect Bernard to another feature of the voyage home. A drunk was encouraged by a group of kids to jump off the boat and into the ocean. Fortunately, a crewman noted the scene and suggested an alternative. We followed the drunk down to the indoor pool where he settled for diving into the water fully clothed rather than the ocean.

A Venture in Camping

After our return from Ireland my family tried to escape summer heat by tenting or camping at Lake Tiorati for the months of July and August. I can think of few episodes involving Bernard except for two items, neither of which was his fault My father thought he had made a great deal when he bought a used 1937 Pontiac from someone in the 24th precinct where he was a detective. It looked like a prop from a gangster film, and I was embarrassed to be seen in it. In time it was the tool to teach Bernard how to drive. In his very first lesson, the universal joint fell onto the pavement and the wreck had to be towed for repairs.

Ray and I were initially jealous of the special treatment Bernard got, but that later turned to envy that we didn't witness the histrionics that most likely accompanied the disaster. The untoward collapse of the 'hood mobile,' however, led to the purchase of Joe Taylor's used Buick and the family had reliable wheels thereafter.

As a man, my father was all bluster with no action. His virtuoso invocation to the mother of God and the saints was very far from religious performance if one witnessed the incantation and understood its tone. We generally grew to laugh and enjoy as he muttered his 'prayers.' As the eldest, Bernard was placed in charge of "everything he forgot." In our initial camping expedition, we had set up a tent and then my father wanted to ignite the camp stove that was fueled by white gas. He discovered that he had no matches and then berated Bernard for failing to "remember everything he forgot." My father's imprecations rivaled the time I puked on his steak. His audience was soon enthralled with the verbal display that sounded religious and never included what might be termed dirty language.

MILITARY GAMES

An individual is often affected by the conditioning factors and generative forces of his youth. Two major contributors in that department are World War II and the proximity of the depression. Those conditions fed Bernard's imagination. When the construction of an apartment building on the site of our monastery and lots on Haven Avenue began, experimental footings were excavated and then covered by boards theoretically making the six-foot pits safe. During the height of the Korean War, however, Bernard found the landscape a perfect scene for trench warfare. With dirt filled beer cans for grenades, he led attacks against my side. I jumped into one of the pits to seek protection only to discover as gravity assisted my plans that the bottom contained the six-foot iron spikes that used to surround the monastery. I landed on the point of one that penetrated my right leg beneath my knee.

I felt no pain but then found my sneaker awash in blood. I staggered home where my mother quickly contacted Dr. Mulligan who ordered us to come to his office immediately. In the taxi ride there, I learned about lockjaw from the driver. From that point on, I kept check checking for the symptoms of tetanus until Mulligan let us sneak in the back way to his examining table. There he stitched my wound and sent me on my way. The following day at school, I broke the stitches and to this day I have a souvenir scar looking like a bullet hole thanks to Bernard's penchant for wargames.

Entrepreneur

In his introduction to the concept of a mogul, he employed me as a servant for the significant fee of a penny a week. Through my naiveté, I was delighted to have a job and steady income. When my mother caught me shining my boss's shoes, she had me freed from economic bondage immediately, so Bernard pursued other avenues in his quest for revenue. First, he created a detective agency to solve any mystery that a family member who had income might have. For a modest fee, as the head of his self-created agency, he promised to investigate whatever anyone wished.

With few mysteries to solved, he directed his entrepreneurial talents else. Bernard used a rudimentary printing set comprising stencils and ink pads with lettering to become the first editor in the family. He printed and published a hand newspaper that he sold for a few pennies. Lacking any duplicating materials, he soon learned that his new enterprise was labor intensive and not cost effective.

He then developed an interest in shooting. After cajoling my parents to permit Ray and me to have BB guns, he purchased a wonderful, generous Christmas gift of Red Ryder Daisy BB guns for us. His motive soon became apparent when he argued that our youth permitted us to have guns, so he should have permission to buy a .22. Bernard always seemed a step or two ahead of our thinking. When he bought the rifle, he did not use it wisely. He depleted the songbird population in some nearby woods, cut off their heads and inserted them between two slices of bread and surreptitiously planted his concoction into Jack Whiteside's lunch bag. We have no quotes about Jack's reaction, but we may presume it reflected his bird lover's total revulsion.

WORLD WAR II AND IMAGINATION

Perhaps Bernard's influence upon me is least admirable when I recall the use of guns. He planned an indoor shooting gallery down the hallway leading to my grandmother's bedroom. Next, he set up a basin filled with water as well as a quart container of milk with the same. He then stuck a lit candle in the middle of the basin. The objective was to shoot the container high enough up to pour out and doused the candle. We never succeeded in doing so, but the glass knob on my grandmother's door was a casualty.

In another scenario, with the influences of movies and WWII, he pinned a blanket across the wall in our bedroom. After purchasing a balsa model airplane, we were urged to toss it across the bedroom into the range of the BB guns. I don't remember if we were ever able to bring down any with our makeshift aircraft guns. He then changed his venue and decided to fight the war on the open seas. He got some wooden ship models and set them afloat in our bathtub. Eschewing BB guns, he now employed lighter fluid cans replicating dive bombers. This time he was successful in destroying his enemy fleet.

AMBITION FOR INCOME

With little interest or talent in the traditional street sports, Bernard didn't excel in this department and his imagination was of little value. As a matter of course, I was often chosen before him in the competition for teams. Unlike Bernard, I was enamored of most of the sports played on Haven Avenue. I especially relished stick ball, fast ball, and association football. With example from Kenny Fitzgerald and Dennis O'Leary I reputedly was superior to my older brother. While I began to become adept at sports, Bernard took detours in other directions.

A METAMORPHOSIS: FROM LARVA TO BUTTERFLY

While physical prowess was not an asset for Bernard before his teen years, he displayed an extraordinary interest in working for income. Perhaps this was the antidote that transformed the proverbial ninety-seven-pound weakling into Mr. Clean, the icon with a shaved head and earring with the body of Adonis. Almost overnight, Bernard grew to his full height and developed musculature that made him appear as an ideal beau. Inheriting his father's frugality, another gift to the late depression youth, Bernard assumed the role of wage earner early in life. The job was not physically challenging, but it demanded responsibility and consistency.

INTRODUCTION TO THE MEDIA

For three-hundred and sixty-four days a year, he was tasked with collecting the Daily News from a delivery truck on 181 Street and Fort Washington and bringing the 'bible of the illiterate' to Solomon's Candy store between Pinehurst and Cabrini. Paid a pittance for this responsibility, it nonetheless introduced some characters that offer a glimpse of diversity in the Heights. Dwight was a Black veteran of WWI who offered his collective wisdom to the fellow laborers. Typically, no one knew his last name, but he was a super on Pinehurst who was eking by as best he could. Another character was an elderly Jew who owned a nearby candy store. He didn't invest in the expense of a representative and took a constant teasing as a result His nightly refrain was, "Ver ist der Bastard mit der Shit Paper." He also introduced Yiddish comments for the education of others. We learned "Mashugana, Shneebunzer, goy and goyim" in the course of time. To him we were all "Schnitzel in the eggenth" as I phonetically recall which meant "Crazy in the head."

His co-workers used to serenade him with "Deck the halls with balls of Herman, Fa-La-La-La-La." After a few years in the newspaper business, Bernard learned of a job opportunity nearby and struck immediately.

From Media to Meatpacking

Herb Danzig of Hillside Meat Market was searching for a delivery boy. Bernard surrendered his employment with Solomon to me and pursued nobler things. Until he attended college with his state scholarship, Bernard was a familiar figure on 181st Street delivering meat packages to Herb's customers. His other tasks in the store were emptying out chicken guts from eviscerated birds, sweeping and replacing sawdust on the floor, scraping the blocks, cleaning the display trays, answering the phone, and taking orders, but he was primarily responsible for delivering the packages. His best tippers were generally in our economic class and not the gifted in Castle Village or Hudson View Gardens. Some houses insisted deliveries be made in the basement and hoisted up dumbwaiters. Those tips were scarce since there was little interaction between the principals. Some of the more frugal tipped with empty soda bottles and believed the five cent bottles carried the day.

A Study in Contrast

In the summer of 1954 when I was old enough to get working papers and earn my fifty cents an hour wage, I replaced Bernard when he worked at a sleepaway camp as a counsellor with some of his cronies from Cabrini. As often happened, my employment followed that of my brother. As a temporary replacement for Bernard, I only underscored that he was the MVP.

On one of my first days on the job, I learned an invaluable lesson that established that the boss is always right. When a patron called Herb complaining that every fly in Washington Heights was circling me as a strolled through the streets delivering someone's order, Herb berated me for wearing the bloody apron that he himself had given me. I learned the trade through mistakes rather than instruction. Herb directed me to go into the refrigerator and bring out a side of round steak. When I replied in front of the customers that there was nothing in there but the carcass of a cow hanging on a hook, Herb replied venomously that he didn't sell cow only U.S. Prime beef steers. On another mission to bring out a huge clump of beef liver, I dropped it on the sawdust strewn floor. My next instruction was to clean it off. Unaware that water turns liver black, I began to wipe the forty-pound cut with tap water until Herb yelled out to me. He claimed I had made that fresh liver look like it was months old and thereby unsellable.

For the first time in ten or fifteen years, Herb decided to take a day off. He had complete confidence in Con Lavery, if not me. Con was a personable Irishman who also was an excellent butcher who excelled in charming customers. He also taught me some tricks on how to cheat customers if one were so inclined. Inserting lead weights in chickens was a technique that demanded caution when cleaning the carcass for the customers. One had to make sure that the metallic weight that added to the chicken did not echo off the gut bucket when extracted from the chicken. Later, the weights could be extracted from the offal for repeated use. Con also demonstrated how to add additional weight when the chicken would be priced. He advised that a long piece of wax paper should extend beyond the scale and draped over the counter. When placing the chicken upon the wax paper on the scale, the butcher should make an ostentatious show of demonstrating that he did not affect the weight be putting thumbs on the scale. Instead with arms disarmingly extended for show, the butcher then leaned forward and pressed upon the extended wax paper and dragged it down to increase the weight.

Con was a delightful man to work with, but on the day Herb took off, he sent me to the bank to cash a number of checks. Apparently, as we learned later, he intended to regale a friend from Ireland for a night on the town and then replace the money through a loan from his sister. This time was once too many for his sister and she refused to replace his embezzlement. Con lost his temper and attacked his sister who then had him arrested. When Herb discovered his empty till on Monday morning, he immediately called me to ascertain what had happened.

Of course, I knew nothing. According to the butcher union that Con belonged to, protocol insisted he be fired. Herb did not want to fire him but had no choice but to do so and he inherited an uncouth Spaniard who alienated the customers and had no skills comparable to Con's. If he answered the phone, the customer would ask to speak to the order boy instead. Rudy used to ogle the young mothers from a peep hole in the refrigerator, but I never saw him do something Con did. A suspicious woman insisted she watch Con ground round steak at $.39 a pound. Con taught me that one should never alienate a butcher after he told her the board of health demanded she stay out of the refrigerator where the meat grinder operated. Con went into the refrigerator and selected nondescript pieces of stray meat of mysterious composition, added some bones and then blood for coloring and spittle for taste.

When Bernard returned from his counsel job, the happiest man may have been Herb. Although reliable and honest, my ineptitude was more than Herb could handle. It only proved what an excellent hire Bernard was. I don't recall how long Bernard worked for Herb, but it was a symbiotic relationship that must have rewarded Bernard beyond the pittance he was paid. As for me, I took my summer earnings and gave $150 to my parents to allay my tuition expenses at Manhattan Prep and invested in a Marlin .22 that only indicated my youthful naivete. The previous year I had won a Police Holy Name Scholarship that had assisted in tuition at Manhattan. I had little use for the rifle until a number of years later, I eliminated woodchucks one summer in Barrytown. When I got married and my wife Mary was uneasy about guns, I gave it to my nephew Kevin.

While I was in my novitiate year in Barrytown, a year

dedicated to contemplation, prayer and initiation into the religious life, Bernard and some of his friends motored from the Police Recreation Center in Tannersville to pay me an unexpected visit, a virtual taboo during the year of isolation and discernment. Bernard and his cronies were working as waiters at the resort. Using the newly opened Kingston-Rhinebeck Bridge across the Hudson, he and the Cohalans tested the kindness of my director of novices, Brother Andrew Lennon. They arrived while I was working on the farm crew, but Brother Andrew told me to visit with them for an hour and then send them on their way.

Our hurried visit took us to the barn loft where I had been storing bales of hay in the loft. I showed Bernard how we picked up the forty-pound bales and tossed them onto a shelf, perhaps eight feet off the floor. Bernard insisted on trying it himself. I gave him a wet bale that probably weighed three times mine. Wet bales were set aside rather than stored because they threatened to spontaneous combust if they dried in cramped space. When Bernard tried to hoist the bale as I did, he almost fell on his butt. For once, I had played a trick on my older brother who thought my newfound physique harbored immense strength.

EMBRYONIC ECONOMIC EMPIRE

With his steady income from the Hillside Meat Market, Bernard created a reputation of which legends are made. He was notorious for banking even the tips he acquired from his labor. He also was able to pay his entire high school tuition bill. His economic example was not lost on me either. In later years I would attribute Bernard's interest in financial matters to his exposure to parents deeply affected by the challenges of a depression in an unknown world.

DON JUAN IN DENIM

When Bernard entered the seventh grade, he was probably at his ultimate height and his physique took another year to develop into the impressive state he exhibited. His maturation did not go unnoticed by the young ladies. Soon two used to call our house often. Mary Garraghy and Peggy McPartland were fellow eighth graders at Incarnation and annoyed my mother enough to refer to them as 'floozies.' At the time, it was customary for the male to initiate contact in romance. These 'floozies' in later years proved to be genteel ladies. Mary married Tommy O'Gorman from Haven Avenue and Peggy served a lifetime as a Sparkhill Dominican.

A LESSON FROM THE STUDY OF LATIN

Much like the ancient Romans who suffered from a dearth of female companionship and therefore raided the nearby Sabines for females, Bernard, Jimmy Torrens, Al Diaz, and Jack Whiteside determined that they had to expand territory to satisfy their craving for girlfriends. That they found on Cabrini Boulevard. Two young lasses, Annabel and Muriel provided entrée into a whole new segment of friends who made a permanent impression on my brother. Moe Freedman was a very tall Jewish comedian who provided humor on a constant feed. Bob Ryerson was a Norse who offered an athletic supplement to the group as did Eddie Ryder. The most impactful were Henry and Pasquale (Pat) D'Esposito, sons of an Italian butcher who owned a store on St. Nicholas Avenue and 178th Street.

Henry was a fashion plate for the fifties, decked out in pegged pants and sporting a 'Guinea curl' upon his forehead. He also seemed to be imaginative with a talent for overkill. Many boys in the neighborhood got their first job at a greengrocer named by his employees as Cheap Sam the Gonif. Sam exploited his delivery boys by cutting their wages any way he could and had a mantra about his Jewish customers. He would often mutter, "Mutsis, Mutsis, I love the smell of their money." Clients would be shortchanged, or sold bruised vegetables or dated greens, if they were not circumspect.

Resolved to get vengeance on Sam, Henry had been hired by Sam to paint his panel truck black. Believing that Sam would find some excuse not to pay him, Henry painted the entire truck inside and out. The fresh coat of black paint on the windows, dashboard and seats made the vehicle undrivable for a while.

When the fear of nuclear war permeated the society and governments created bomb shelters stocked with huge water cannisters and canned food, the Cabrini mob enlisted in the Civil Defense. They were issued armbands and WWI surplus helmets.

During a periodic blackout, they were supposed to stop traffic and direct humanity to the nearest shelter. Henry took advantage of his role to harass Sam the Gonif. Insisting that all lights be turned off and the sidewalk cleared of obstructions, Henry kicked over a display case that sent watermelons cascading down 181st Street. Years later he mused, "That was the first time I saw a man cry!"

Not surprisingly Henry enlisted in the marines at seventeen. He became a member of Long-Range Reconnaissance Units that were forerunners to the Green Berets or Special forces. He claimed that he was in and out of countries where they were not supposed to be, gathering information and surveillance of covert activities specific to the cold war.

His brother Pat was more like the intellectual type. My parents liked him very much and I know he stimulated my brother with his philosophical questioning particularly about Catholicism. Years later, Henry sponsored a reunion of sorts and I was invited as an addendum. I enjoyed their company very much.

The Cabrini Club members were frequent guests of the local bar called The Riverview on the corner of 181st Street. They occasionally scheduled athletic events with their chief competitor, the Pinehurst, a block north. I was drafted to fill the ranks in those games. In an encounter with another bar featuring big black football players, my young teen body was submitted to a severe jarring when I tackled a running back on an end around run. I am embarrassed to say that I had previously swallowed a quarter on a mission for Mrs. Trainor who had sent me to buy her a pack of cigarettes. Consequent x-rays noted the location of the errant coin within my intestines. If I did not pass it naturally, they would have to operate. For several days, I had no success until that jarring collision. Playing for the bar had eventually spared me an operation.

In another sport, baseball, Jimmy Torrens asked me to play catcher for him on the bar's team. Each player was teamed with an opponent in a five-dollar bet- winner take all. We won the game, but Wolfie, the captain of the Pinehurst squad didn't pay me since he claimed he only had a twenty. Sonny Beck, the resident muscle for the Riverview, persuaded Wolfie to find change or give me the twenty. That was the beginning and end of my professional baseball career.

Unrequited Love or Incompatibility

A byproduct of the exodus to Cabrini was the discovery of a gorgeous young lady named Sheila Waldron. From the photographs I have seen in the Prep yearbook, she lived up to her description. Bernard was soon smitten. Without any details the romance between the beauty and the masculine specimen faltered and my brother Ray was left to negotiate the return of Bernard's school ring. By this time, I had left home for Barrytown.

More recently, I have mused whether Bernard's success in the realm of romance may have been a subconscious influence on my entrance into Barrytown after my sophomore year. My memory depicts him as the chairman of dance committees, a coveted member of the dating population, an influential member of the student council, and generally a Big Man on Campus. Perhaps realizing that I estimated my aura as a fat frump who couldn't in his wildest dreams name a single female who might be interested in him, I suffered a sense of inadequacy when compared to my older brother.

Ironically, after I left home my peers abandoned Haven Avenue for the same reasons as Bernard's and undertook new interests in 'beer and babes.' Meanwhile I was resolved to persevere in Barrytown at least until Thanksgiving. That resolution lasted fifteen years unlike the prediction of the priest whose recommendation I needed for admission to the Brothers. When I approached the Incarnation rectory for the document I needed, Father Ferarius, OSA was on duty. He was also in charge of the altar boys and chided me for poor service. When I was incapacitated for two months from a sled accident and failed to appear for my assignments in the previous spring. He predicted I'd be home in two weeks. I suppose he underestimated how committed I felt to the Brothers after his two-week experiment had ended.

Bernard continued to be prime goods in the dating market and ultimately met the love of his life, Evelyn O'Dwyer. I understand their courtship had some moments, but their two-score marriage proves the endurance of their love.

THE COMMODORE

Bernard and his close friend Jimmy Torrens were co-owners of a yacht and its subsequent club near Dyckman Street in Inwood. Their vessel was a two-man kayak. On one of their voyages around Manhattan, they tied up next to an ocean liner and were basking in the sun on a raft below when a crewmember tossed a bucket of garbage on them. The teens, both well-built and strong also challenged a tug hauling a barge northward on the Hudson. The inexperienced mariners decided to glide their craft between the tug and its trailing barge. For some dumb reason, Jimmy decided to grasp the connecting cable and swamped their vessel. Somehow, they survived but there are no witnesses to attest how.

Bernard's love for Evelyn and his kayak led to an adventure at Lake Tiorati. After relative peaceful cruising on the calm waters, they headed home on the Palisades Interstate Parkway. At the time, the parkway was being built in sections and wasn't opened entirely in either direction. As driver Bernard decided to head south on the northbound section. They were soon interdicted by a policeman. Intent on citing them for their dangerous decision, Bernard told the officer that his father would be very angry if he got a ticket. The officer's response was something like, "For something this stupid, he'd be angry if I didn't issue a ticket.

UNCHALLENGED INFLUENCE

Without a doubt one area that Bernard's influence was very

strong was in academics. He set a high standard to emulate. Teachers were always pleased to get another O'Prey thanks to his earlier performance. The triumvirate of "O's" in his class dominated the honor roll published in the Blue and White quarterly. Bernard O'Prey, Buddy O'Shea, and Martin O'Sullivan would always be found in the upper echelon of the distinguished listing. Despite his work commitments, Bernard never let his academics lag, even in college. In my assignment to Sacred Heart, I had the opportunity to assess his reputation at Manhattan. When I was introduced to Brother Louis who at the time was Dean of Arts and Sciences, he took an abrupt step backwards when I was further identified as O'Prey. Gathering his spirits from that surprise, he offered, "In your family I must be considered a saint and a sinner. A saint for my interaction with Bernard and a sinner with Ray." He had just expelled Ray for spending more time with his 'Uncle Tim Riordan' in the Greenleaf. He nonetheless was very proud of his role in Bernard's education.

Beyond formal education, Bernard was an avid, voracious reader with a predilection for historical fiction. He borrowed several books at a time from the library between St. Nicholas and Audubon Avenue on 178th Street. As he finished one book and undertook another, I would read his finished title. In essence, I was given a reading list three years beyond my age. His selections usually included a work by Kenneth Roberts featuring Cap Huff or Oliver

Wiswell. Early in life I learned to try to see things from the opposite side of life since Wiswell told the story of a Tory in the American Revolution. Periodically Bernard would make himself several sandwiches, grab a quart of milk and commandeer our main bathroom. Propping his sustenance upon the toilet seat, he would fill the tub with warm water and with book in hand bask in comfort for an hour or two. Fortunately, my family was TTI's or Two Toilet Irish, otherwise his amateur spa wouldn't be feasible.

SUMMARY

The influence of my older brother was an important factor in my life. As he was affected by conditioning factors and generative forces, so too was I. His inspiration to me and his silent example set standards that I wished to emulate. I admired his attraction to the microphone whenever the occasion arose. I admired his persistence and determination once he set a course to complete something. I admired his ability to think creatively and derive pleasure from obscure objects. I respected his choices in life and sometimes yearned for the same. Geography separated our paths but not our spirits. For his example, I thank the Lord and our parents who supplied the groundwork for his achievements. I offer him now this reminiscence in his honor and hope it makes his Christmas warmer as its composition has been a hasty labor of love for me. I wrote it intermittently, sometimes awakening in the wee hours to compose a snippet or two. I regret where my admiration for the elements of

French 'preciosite' or the biting hyperbole of Alexander Pope's satire enter my writing style some have identified as Yerponics. As Luther stated in a much more solemn affair, "Here I stand. I can do no other."

49592359R00227